REDEEMING MEMORIES

To Dorothy,
In remembrance
and hope.
Flora A. Keshgegian

REDEEMING MEMORIES

A THEOLOGY
OF HEALING
AND TRANSFORMATION

FLORA A. KESHGEGIAN

ABINGDON PRESS
NASHVILLE

REDEEMING MEMORIES
A THEOLOGY OF HEALING AND TRANSFORMATION

This book is printed on recycled, acid-free, elemental-chlorine–free paper.

Library of Congress Cataloging-in-Publication Data

Keshgegian, Flora A., 1950-
    Redeeming memories : a theology of healing and transformation/Flora A. Keshgegian.
        p. cm.
    Includes bibliographical references and index.
    ISBN 0-687-12915-X (alk. paper)
    1. Redemption.   2. Memory—Religious aspects—Christianity.   3. Victims.
4. Feminist theology.   5. Political theology.   I. Title.

BT 775 .K43 2000
230'.082—dc21
                                                                00-38579

Scripture quotations are taken from *The New Testament and Psalms: An Inclusive Version,* based on the New Revised Standard Version of the Bible. Copyright 1989 by the Division of Christian Education of the National Council of the Churches of Christ in the U.S.A. All rights reserved. Used by permission.

"Remember?" from HORSES MAKE A LANDSCAPE LOOK MORE BEAUTIFUL, copyright © 1984 by Alice Walker, reprinted by permission of Harcourt, Inc.

Portions of "The Last Witness" are from ANY DAY NOW: POEMS by Diana Der-Hovanessian. Copyright © 1999 by Diana Der-Hovanessian. Used by permission of Sheep Meadow Press.

00 01 02 03 04 05 06 07 08 09 — 10 9 8 7 6 5 4 3 2 1

MANUFACTURED IN THE UNITED STATES OF AMERICA

For all those who have taught me the ways and power of

remembering

And for Hannah, a blessing from the moment she was born,

who reminds me of the power of imagination

Acknowledgments

This book took a long time being born. It was first conceived from my doctoral dissertation, but over the years it developed, changed, and took on a very different shape. Portions of that dissertation, entitled "To Know by Heart: Toward a Theology of Remembering for Salvation," published by University Microfilm, Inc. in 1992, are included in revised and updated form in the preface and chapters 1 and 4 of this work.

Many, many people were there along the way, helping this book's formation and birth by tutoring me in the ways of listening, offering their witness, and supporting my efforts. I cannot name all those whose experiences are woven into what I present here. Neither am I able to account adequately for all they taught me. Through them I have come to understand profoundly what it means to be "surrounded by so great a cloud of witnesses."

Time for writing was made possible by a short writing leave from the chaplaincy of Brown University; one semester as a Resident Scholar at the Institute for Ecumenical and Cultural Research in Collegeville, Minnesota; and another as a Visiting Scholar at the Women's Leadership Institute at Mills College. The programs of the Ecumenical Institute and the Women's Leadership Institute also connected me with new colleagues who encouraged me, gave me feedback, and celebrated my progress. The final stages of editing were completed while I settled into the faculty and community of the Episcopal Theological Seminary of the Southwest. Their gracious support eased these last steps for which Nancy Bose provided particular assistance.

A number of other people require special mention. Donald Compier, Patrick Henry, and Barbara Paige read portions of the manuscript and offered numerous helpful suggestions. Susan Ashbrook Harvey, Kathleen Jenkins, Kristine Rankka, and Sharon Welch read the entire manuscript. Their support of my project and their responses helped me immensely in the process of revision. I am grateful for all these readers' generosity of time and spirit, and for their wisdom.

I have many wonderful friends who saw me through the ups and downs of this process. They have sustained me, nourished me, and shared with me the precious gift of laughter. Janice Okoomian, Kenneth Schneyer, Hannah Schneyer Okoomian, and now Arek Okoomian Schneyer are family for me, offering love and acceptance, many meals, and occasional shelter. Hannah, my special godchild, is an amazing source of delight. Much of my own family is gone, now lost to age and illness as well as genocide. For those who remain—especially my mother, Asdghig; my brother, Albert; his wife, Patrice; and sons, Gregory, Mark, and James—I give thanks.

My life has been blessed by years of participation in several women's groups, in which I learned much about the dynamics of remembering and giving voice to the full range of our experiences: spiritual, ethnic, cultural, political, emotional, and embodied. I am deeply appreciative of those who engaged with me fully in these settings and offered companionship for the journey.

Finally, I want to acknowledge the patience, guidance, and encouragment of Abingdon Press and my editor, Ulrike Guthrie.

Contents

Preface

"I Remember"

I grew up in a first generation ethnic household struggling with concerns of survival and hope, identity and community. The past had a particular hold on my family. As an Armenian American, I was bequeathed a mantle of memory with a distinctive texture and weight. Though my formal study of memory as a theological category began in graduate school, my schooling in memory began many years before, even before I knew to name it as such. My family's and community's lesson was simple: remember our suffering, our victimization, and the deaths of so many. Be our witness.

Most of the members of the family I knew—my parents, maternal grandmother, and several aunts and uncles—were survivors of the Armenian genocide, perpetrated by the Turkish government during World War I. This genocide followed upon centuries of domination. Beginning in the fifteenth century, much of the historical lands of Armenia had been occupied and colonized by the Ottoman Empire. Depending on the sultan and the times, Armenians in that empire fared more or less well under such rule. Various accommodations were made. The Armenian community, a Christian minority in an Islamic state, was granted a certain level of autonomy with authority vested in the clergy as civic leaders. Armenians and Turks lived side by side, and although their interactions were strictly regulated by religious and ethnic differences, relationships of trust and respect often developed in local communities. Armenians occupied professional and commercial positions, and their contributions were important and necessary to life within villages, towns, and cities. In the later years of the nineteenth century, the empire's power seemed to be crumbling, and Sultan Abdul Hamid responded with occasional massacres of Armenians, most notably from 1894 to 1896. More years of unrest followed until 1908 when the government of Sultan Abdul Hamid fell to a group of revolutionaries referred to as the Young Turks. These new leaders promised reform and a better status for the Armenian "minority." But their words proved false. From 1908 to 1910 another series of massacres, blamed on Sultan Abdul Hamid but actually conducted by the Young Turks, solidified this new rule and paved the way for the systematic and widespread genocidal activity carried out during and after World War I.

Beginning in 1914, adult males were drafted into service as laborers who were abused and often killed. In April of 1915, intellectuals, professionals, clergy, and other leaders were rounded up and executed. Then followed large-scale, systematic deportations of women and children and the remaining males, often elderly, from their homes. Forced marches moved the Armenian population to "relocation" in the Syrian desert. Many died or were killed along the way; many others did not survive the starvation, attack, and disease of desert camps. In the end, between one million and two million Armenians died.

After World War I, some survivors attempted to reestablish homes in their native towns and hoped for the best from Armenia's declaration of itself as an independent republic. This republic lasted but two short years and fell before the advancing forces of Mustafa Kemal Ataturk. Further starvation and massacres followed. In the early 1920s most of the Armenians remaining under Turkish rule left their ancestral homeland and joined others who had already taken up life in diaspora, often in Western countries. A large number, including most of the members of my family, eventually came to America. My father arrived early, in 1919. After living for many years in Syria and Lebanon, my maternal grandmother emigrated in 1940 and my mother followed in 1946.

My family told me the stories of what happened to them and what happened to others, of those who survived and lived to tell, and those who did not; that is, those who live now in and through these memories. They passed on to me their feelings of emptiness and deprivation, and tutored me in narratives of deportation and brutality, of loss and abandonment, of displacement and poverty. These stories were the stuff of my childhood and the backdrop of family gatherings, especially those which marked a rite of passage. Inevitably there was some thought, sometimes spoken, sometimes not, of all those not there — among them, my other three grandparents, as well as the aunt for whom I am named, and her husband and children. The absences served as reminders of all that had been lost, of all that had been suffered. A tone of lament seemed always to hang in the air. My grandmother and her children bequeathed to me a peculiar inheritance of suffering and victimization, mixed with a bent pride, that asked me to bear witness to their losses and their lives which were so textured by this trauma. The last defense against annihilation became oddly the stories of annihilation, and the proof of our existence lay in the repetition and the remembering of our victimization.

I was taught to experience the world in which we lived as threatening our existence, either by death or by assimilation. Both were forms of genocide as far as the Armenian American community was concerned. And so my family, the Armenian American community, the Armenian church—all of them—schooled me to remember the suffering of my people and to honor their suffering by "being Armenian," by actively and intentionally living in that ethnic subculture. "Remember you are Armenian," my parents declared in one way or another, time and again, whenever they felt the "American" world was threatening their "Armenian" future, which they saw embodied in my brother and me. The victims of the genocide were presented to us as martyrs who died for their faith and their ethnic identity.[1] Indeed, the day of remembrance for the genocide is called "Armenian Martyrs Day." To forget this inheritance, not to be "Armenian," was to dishonor and dismiss these martyrs' sacrifices.

I grew up feeling that forgetfulness was betrayal. Remembering my identity by practicing it, by "being Armenian," was necessary for the future and the salvation of the Armenian people. Remembering our suffering and victimization was a way to honor the dead and preserve the past. Such preservation holds a particular dynamic for Armenians. The Turkish government has never acknowledged the genocide and continues to deny it actively. Thus this history remains a threatened one; the need to hold on to the memory of loss is shaped by denial.

As I grew to adulthood with these legacies, I found that the demands of survival and preservation became more complex, and layers of weight seemed to be added to the mantle of memory I bore. I began to feel a tension, even a contradiction, between the pull of the past and the yearning for a different future. The need to hold on to the history of victimization, which was passed from generation to generation in nurture and in story, seemed to cloud hope and full commitment to life.

Years later my grandmother told me new stories that led me on a yet more complicated journey of memory. She chose the week before my ordination to the priesthood, now many years ago, to share with me these other dimensions of the past. I had often wondered what my grandmother had thought about my leaving the Armenian Church and seeking ordination in the Episcopal Church, an action which most of my family saw as one of betrayal. My grandmother had never said any-

13

thing. Indeed, I did not know if she realized what was happening. Given that she did not speak English and I could understand Armenian, but was losing my facility to speak it, and given that she was becoming deaf, it was very difficult for us to carry on conversations. Mostly she told stories and I listened. This time she told me that when she was a little girl, some eighty years before, a cousin of hers, who was a nun, had come to their town and had led the recitation of the Creed at church on Sunday. My grandmother said that many years later when she had related this incident to my father, her son-in-law, he had said that it could not be, that women were not allowed on the altar platform and, therefore, could not lead the Creed, which was done before the altar by an ordained deacon. But my grandmother said to me: "I remember, it happened and I tell you because you will understand." She also told me that one day in class her sister was asked to lead the lesson. When she had mentioned this other event to my father, again he had said, that it could not be, because when boys were in the classroom girls were not allowed to address the class. Again, my grandmother insisted: "I remember, it happened and I tell you because you will understand." For so many years she had remembered these things and despite the patriarchal interest embodied in my father not to keep such memories alive, she thought I might hear and understand. And I did understand, not only the stories themselves, but also her need to tell me and to entrust them to me. I felt that day that my ordination was indeed acceptable to her, that she was in her own way affirming my desire for religious leadership.

That is the meaning I attached to her stories then. Later on as I thought about them in relation to this project on memory, I realized that she was giving me, through those tales, memories other than of victimization, stories that spoke of resistance and agency, of the practice of leadership even in settings where these were ostensibly denied. There was more to my family's past than a history of victimization.

Indeed, the stories she told point to another history, also threatened. Years after my ordination I was to learn that there were nuns in the Armenian church who had been given deacon orders, which meant they could lead the Creed in the church service.[2] For the most part, this practice and the awareness of it had been lost in the rupture of community represented by the massacres and the genocide. My grandmother's passing on of these stories to me meant that such history would not be lost. When years later I found among our family's photo-

14

graphs a picture of a group of such nuns, whose habits included the wearing of deacon stoles, I realized that I might not have noticed or "seen" the stoles in this picture if my grandmother had not alerted me to this history.[3]

This obligation to remember and to be a witness, which my family and the Armenian American community laid upon me, was becoming more complicated. What did it mean to remember on their behalf: was it victimization I was to remember or agency and leadership? And what difference did these memories make in relation to the threats to identity that Armenians still experience? Why were we to remember the past, what past were we to remember, and in what sense was it for the sake of the future? What relationship was "right" between the practice of remembering and my own life choices and practices? What did it mean, as a person of faith, to remember for salvation's sake?

I had early on sought connections between my past and contemporary social concerns. As a teenager, I chided the Armenian American community for its insularity and urged it to be more socially conscious. I argued that those of us who had known oppression, persecution, and suffering ought to make common cause with other struggles for empowerment and liberation, both in America and throughout the world. The racism, sexism, and self-protectiveness of my community of origin made it defensive and deaf in the face of my admittedly adolescent attempts at reform. In turn, its chauvinism left me feeling torn between my own religious and political commitments, and this community that claimed my allegiance. Although Armenian Americans seemed to resist assimilation, they often adopted the values of this host culture in ways that I found problematic. The desire to be successful, almost as proof of survival, led Armenian Americans to conform to dominant ideologies and cultural norms that I saw to be racist, classist, and sexist, as well as conservative and traditionalist.

I began to look elsewhere for compatriots and a meaningful religious community that would recognize both my values and my call to religious leadership. I yearned for the practice of a political faith that was authentic and liberating. I found myself drawn to political movements and social causes that were also struggling with questions of memory and redemption.

Thus my personal journey with the inherited past led me to search for connections and nuances in understanding what it means to remember, and remember for redemption. I discovered that the ques-

15

tions I had about memory and faith, action and redemption, were not mine alone, nor were they solely characteristic of Armenians. Any group of people threatened with annihilation, colonization, abuse, or systematic oppression is led to such queries. Jews ask whether their remembrance should focus on their victimization in history, with its ultimate climax in the Holocaust, or on contributions to civilization and methods of survival. African Americans also question whether slave narratives witness to a history of brutalization and torture or are memoirs of resistance and the resilience of the human spirit or both. People who are displaced and denied their histories seek to retrieve their past and assess what is the "true" story. Abuse survivors, especially those who struggle with the retrieval of memories, find that they need both to claim their memories of past suffering and develop ways to be free of the choking claims of these pasts on the present and future.

Contemporary Calls to Remembrance

In this search for redeeming memories, I understand remembering as both a problem and a resource for those struggling for life. In attending to the problems associated with remembering, I have come to appreciate the resources it provides. In focusing on it as resource, I find myself uncovering new dimensions of it as a problem. This book will be an exploration and explication of this process of learning the terrain of redeeming memories. More specifically, I witness to three movements/contexts of remembering in our present Western, specifically American, culture that are calling attention to what I term an "imperative to remember." They are giving voice to the submerged memories of persons and groups in American society who struggle with threatened existence. I understand this imperative to remember and witness to be a demand for recognition of particular histories and an attempt to make ethical claims in the contemporary context. Three concrete "cases" will be considered: (1) the recovery and claiming of memory by those who have been sexually abused; (2) the remembering of genocide, particularly the Armenian genocide and the Jewish Holocaust; and (3) the retrieval of cultural histories by historically disinherited peoples and groups, especially women and African Americans.

These three cases may help illuminate current social and political negotiations about the status and meanings of truth and power, especially in relation to violence. In each of the cases, there is an internal struggle to determine the status and meaning of victimization and its relationship to identity. In each case, there is also an external struggle. Demands for recognition and remembrance of histories of violence have been met with resistance and outright denial. In these struggles, social definition, position, and meaning, as well as personal, group, and spiritual well-being, are all being negotiated. Memory exists as both problem and resource for identity, witness, and transformation.

Remembering to Re-member

The purpose of this book is to remember, from the perspectives of those who have been victimized, in such a way that we might re-member Christianity and society. My approach may best be defined as Christian feminist political theology. I use both the terms "feminist" and "political" as reflective of my analytical approach to social "realities," including Christianity, as constructions, produced by dynamics and relations of power. "Feminist" and "political" also point to my interests, which include the empowerment of those who have not been the "dominants" in those relations. At the same time, these terms suggest my social location, as a white, privileged, ethnic minority woman, as both dominant and nondominant.

Further, I understand Christianity as being complicit in relations of domination, as well as providing resources for liberation and transformation. Christianity, the Christian memory, is then itself a problem and resource for a liberating memorative practice. A task of a theology of redeeming memories is to analyze the uses of Christianity in order to display the arrangements of power it produces and reproduces in any given context. Such analysis is necessary in order to render the Christian story as effective for liberation. I proceed by examining Christian theological claims in relation to the memorative practices of those who have suffered. I argue that redeeming memories lead to re-membering the truth and practice of Christianity, especially in relation to histories of domination.

Toward that end, I need to be careful not to engage in dominating discourse myself. I am not seeking to impose theological meaning on the social movements I consider nor am I suggesting that Christianity holds a special truth for those who suffer. Rather, I want to propose that the truth of Christianity is itself in jeopardy because of its complicity in regimes of domination that have perpetrated abuse, persecution, and violence. In other words, this work is also about redeeming Christianity. Not to challenge and change Christianity is to continue to allow it to function as ideology for oppressive and exploitative systems.

The introduction sets the stage for this approach and its implications for theological method. I then turn to the histories of suffering and the calls to remembrance with a listening ear. In the first section, I present the "cases" of remembering sexual abuse, remembering genocide, and remembering marginalized and suppressed histories. Out of the listening emerge the multiple strains of redeeming memories. These are set amid tones of struggle for remembrance in relation to social processes of denial and domination. The listening is also a discernment. My family's storytelling was unusual in some ways. Most genocide survivors do not speak of their pain.[4] Many childhood abuse survivors hide their memories deep in their minds, souls, and bodies. Often marginalized and dispossessed groups do not know enough of their histories to give voice to story because their pasts have been subsumed under "master narratives" written by the historical winners and dominants. Thus the process of remembering must find its origin in silence and silencing.

The second section begins with a consideration of contemporary theological treatments of memory, in order to set my own theological work in a context. Special attention is given to the work of Johann Baptist Metz, who is to be credited with introducing the term "dangerous memory" into theological discourse and developing memory as a theological category. I indicate both how my work is continuous with that of Metz and selected feminist theologians, and how it is different. I also offer some anthropological and theological affirmations that are foundational to my own theological construction.

I then look at the ways in which Jesus' work of salvation has been remembered and outline what it means to remember the story of Jesus Christ in a way that incorporates a multiple memorative practice. I thus narrate the meanings of the crucifixion, resurrection, life, and incarnation of Jesus Christ in relation to a theology of redemption able to witness, liberate, and transform.

The final chapter suggests a theology of church as a community of remembrance that engages in an ongoing multiple memorative practice. I conclude by reviewing my hope both to empower those who have been victimized and to transform Christianity.

I seek in my work to be responsive and responsible in history, for what has been done to me and for what I have done to others, either by commission or omission, directly or by imputation. Only through humility and honesty, through a critical and committed approach to saving knowledge, might the hearing be true and the resonance right. I invite the reader to enter into this process with me, with an ear attuned to remembrance and hope.

A Note About Language

A dimension of coming to a more inclusive view of the world is realizing the limitations and biases of the language and images we use to refer to human beings and God. God has traditionally been used as a male term. Feminist theologians have adopted alternatives such as "God/ess" (Rosemary Ruether) and "G*d" (Elisabeth Schüssler Fiorenza). I prefer to continue to use the term "God," but intend it always in an inclusive way. I avoid gender specific pronouns and any gender specific forms of addressing God, such as "Father."

Introduction

"In the Beginning"

"In the beginning was the Word, and the Word was with God, and the Word was God" (John 1:1).[1] These words, long familiar to Christians, introduce the Gospel of John. The evangelist writes of Jesus Christ as the Word, the *logos*. *Logos* is the Greek principle of divine presence and activity, that speaks God's word. As Jesus the proclaimer became Christ the proclaimed, as the early church community came to give word to its own experience of divine presence and redemption, Jesus Christ was declared the Word itself and the speaking. The Gospel of John proclaims that in the beginning is the speaking, is the word. And this word makes God present to us. Christianity's history may be read as spreading that word to the ends of the earth, to every people, that all might know the Word, Jesus Christ.

This book and the process of remembering begins, however, not with word, but with silence. In the beginning is silence. This silence is not empty, but pregnant with meaning; it is filled with yearning. Indeed, this silence screams words of pain, of ignorance, of evil unacknowledged, and of desire unfulfilled. These words have been denied or rejected; they have been rendered mute. The silencing is of those who have been victimized in history. Their silence contains thousands of words, a host of memories, that we have yet to hear and receive. We are called to enter this silence as witnesses. We are bade to listen attentively to the words of those who have not yet been fully heard.

Theologians of oppression and liberation have taught us about the contours of such silence. They have shown us what happens to those who are continually silenced. Dorothee Soelle writes of mute suffering: "forms of suffering that reduce one to a silence in which no discourse is possible any longer, in which a person ceases reacting as a human agent."[2] Paolo Freire instructs us in the silence that precedes *conscientization,* when the oppressed have no word to name their condition. Such silence inhibits their claiming of their own personhood.[3] For those lost in such seas of silence, floating beneath a deadening and numbing pain, redemption remains a distant echoing word. Yet we know, as Soelle's and Freire's works testify, that even such silence contains a yearning to come to the surface.

Nelle Morton, grandmother of American feminist theology, showed us a way out of the silence and the silencing. She bequeathed to us the insight and the experience of "hearing one another to speech." "In the beginning is the hearing," she taught us. She helped us to enter the silence in order to hear. Nelle Morton describes the moment when with a group of women, amid tears and trembling, one of the participants uttered forth a cry of pain and then declared, "You heard me. *You have heard me to my own speech.*"[4]

And so this book begins with the silence and the listening and the invitation to speech. It begins by attending to those who have not always named their word, whose word has not been heard or has been suppressed and ignored. Those words issue forth as memories, submerged and unclaimed, which now come to the surface and call for recognition. As we hear and remember anew, redemption will take on new form.

The silence that enshrouds the memories of those abused, persecuted, and oppressed is not accidental or chosen; it is a silencing by a world with designs to exclude. These threatened memories and peoples are, in actuality, themselves threats to sociopolitical narratives, which reflect and produce particular arrangements of power, serving certain interests. "Truth" is politically produced through the shaping of meaning. The "word" that we know begins as an empty sign, malleable to the play of power in the world. Attending to the silence includes being attuned to silencing that results from oppression or denial. It requires a critical consciousness of such dynamics and forces, a sharpening of the ear to hear those sounds not found in the scales we have practiced. These sounds will lead to more complex understandings of word and world.

"The Word was in the beginning with God. All things came into being through the Word, and without the Word not one thing came into being. What has come into being in the Word was life, and the life was the light of all people. The light shines in the deepest night, and the night did not overcome it" (John 1:1-5). Christianity claims redemptive power and effectiveness for its word: Jesus Christ, the Word of God, is Savior, the promise of life. The Gospel of John is a celebration of this savior as life-giving Word. The Gospel's intent is to present signs and wonders, testimony and proclamation, that we may believe, and by believing, be saved. At the heart of this proclamation is the declaration that it is through Jesus Christ, the Word of God, that salvation is realized.

The silent and silenced ones stand, however, as a challenge to Christianity's claim to effective redemptive power. Their suffering testifies to the unrealized promise. If the promise of Christianity's redemptive Word is to be kept for those who suffer, then that Word must include their words and their memories in a way that actively shapes redeeming truth. Indeed, we must begin with listening to and receiving these memories. New words will constantly come forth in this process of hearing and speaking, of witnessing and proclaiming.

Such words will reveal the ways in which Christianity itself has engaged in silencing and its word has not been true to its redemptive promise. Feminist and other biblical and historical scholars have demonstrated that we must remember Christianity anew in terms of its deployment of excluding and hegemonic practices. The goal is to discern the practice of its word as liberating amid the uses of its word for repression and colonization. Such discernment requires a clearer understanding of the relationship of Christianity and the world.

"The Word was in the world . . . yet the world did not know the Word" (John 1:10). The Gospel of John plays with the tension between the Word and the world in order to underscore Jesus Christ's redeeming work. The world is both the place where "the Word became flesh and dwelt among us" and where the Word is rejected and killed. The world is the arena of our encounter with and reception of the redeeming presence of God, and of our turning away from it. For the evangelist, the world is an ambiguous space, a construct positioned as foil for displaying Jesus Christ as triumphant in the face of defeat, as hidden and revealed. Christian truth is placed in the world, but remains not fully of it. The world is the arena where the power of that which is false and evil, personified as those who question and attack Jesus' truth and power of good, is manifest.

In contrast, the truth of the memories of those who suffer and are defeated in this world are fully in the world. Redemption is in history even though there is much pain and loss in history. The world and history remain ambiguous spaces, constructed by processes of power welded into foundations held firm, except for those historical earthquakes that cause cracks and occasional splintering. There is no true certainty among those who remember suffering, only a learning to dance amid the tremors, to move with grace and hope and "with no extraordinary power, reconstitute the world" (Adrienne Rich). Though the world is dangerous, it is only by remembering in the face of the danger that new life can be fully claimed.

23

In that process of faithful remembrance, Christians will find the silences and the silenced amid their own history. Indeed, as contemporary biblical scholars and feminist theologians have been revealing, in the beginning was not the Word, but Wisdom, Hokmah, Sophia. Wisdom for both Hebrews and Greeks was a female figure who personified God's presence and activity, but not only in word. Elizabeth Johnson describes the biblical figure of Wisdom pervading "the world, both nature and human beings, interacting with them all to lure them along the right path to life."[5] As Christianity developed, the female, saving figure of Wisdom was replaced by the male principle of *Logos*, Word, Son, that eventually became the final word of christological orthodoxy. Johnson and others argue that retrieving the "forgotten" figure of Wisdom and subjecting the christological tradition to new interpretation might lead to a more open and inclusive Christology.[6]

My hope in writing this book is to enable Christians to listen to the memories hidden and silenced in our history in such a way that the redemptive potential of Christianity may be realized anew in this ever-changing, ever-challenging world. To that end, in the beginning is the hearing out of silence that leads to remembering and witness. This practice of remembering results in new theological formulations of Christ's redeeming work. I understand theology to be a discursive practice that seeks to realize and embody in wisdom and word the transforming and liberating practice of Christianity. The truth of theology is manifest in its effectiveness; the word is true if it redeems. That word is Wisdom, the agent of redemptive action. In the beginning is not word, but the silence and the hearing. In the beginning is the remembering, which leads to re-membering.

"Remember, You Were Slaves in Egypt"

When Jews gather annually for the celebration of the Passover, they recite the story of their liberation from slavery in Egypt. In the midst of the retelling, they are to imagine that they themselves are being liberated from slavery. They are bid to "remember, you were slaves in Egypt." That command is repeated often in the Hebrew Scriptures as one that is integral to Israel's awareness of itself in relation to God. Being a faithful Jew involves remembering a past of slavery and oppression.

This remembrance is for a particular purpose. Jews are to remember their oppression in order to conduct their present practice, their current lives, in specific ways. Because Israel knows what it is to be poor and an outcast, it should attend to those who suffer in its midst. Because Israel has known the experience of seeming abandonment by God and then rescue, Israel should remain faithful and hopeful.

In other words, the remembering of past suffering is for the sake of a present ethical intent. Remembering is not meant to enshrine a memorial but to point to and affect present action. So too with this book. Its practice of remembering is not simply a historical recital, but a theological and ethical practice meant to effect change and make a difference. Remembering lays claim to the continuing redemptive activity of God into which we are called as partners.

Further, that activity is partisan. It is from a particular point of view. The Passover story is told from the perspective of the Israelites, not the Egyptians. The God of Moses and Miriam sides with the Israelites. The God whom Jews and Christians worship is one who hears the cries of those who suffer and are afflicted. This book also takes sides and is written from a specific perspective. I write as witness to those who have been traumatized, abused, oppressed, enslaved, and killed—"hated unto death."[7] It is their stories and their memories I seek to bring to voice and hold up to all of us as having the potential to reveal dimensions of the divine.

In thus locating myself and my work, I am not making any absolute or ultimate claims about the locus of truth. Rather, I am being clear about my interests: to attend to those who have suffered and who struggle for life, who are reminding us of the importance of remembering, and whose experiences point to the unfulfilled promises of redemption.

Warrant for this work is found in the command: "remember, you were slaves in Egypt." No matter what status Israel achieved, no matter how powerful a nation and a people Israel became, this command to remember might have held in check its tendency to forget its origins and obligations. In other words, this command served to remind Israel of the dynamics of power and social location. Status was a historical reality, not a birthright. The abuse of power remained an ever-present possibility. When I read the Hebrew Scripture, it seems to me that Israel "got in trouble" whenever it forgot that, when it took for granted its power and position. Christian faithfulness necessitates attending to such dynamics of power. It requires that we be honest and responsible about our power and status, our social and political location, *and* that we remember and bear witness from the perspective of the disinherited and disempowered. To forget either our own status or our obligation is to act unfaithfully.

Remembering, then, is both a practice of self and community formation, and potentially of self and community correction. It is necessary that we always be clear about what we are remembering, on whose behalf, and to what end. If we intend our remembering to be transformative and liberating for all, then we need to engage in a continual and faithful recalling of such questions. For Christians, this means exploring the connections between our remembering and God's redeeming work.

"Do This in Remembrance of Me"

Christianity has long claimed the practice of remembering to be important and related to redemption. The Christian story recalls and rehearses God's saving action and presence in and through Jesus Christ. The church embodies that memory in its practice. Indeed, the central action of Christian worship is one of remembrance. In the Eucharist, whether understood as memorial or as real presence or as transubstantiated essence, Christians remember Jesus Christ and Christ's saving actions. In this act of remembrance, the command to remember is rehearsed: "Whenever you eat this bread or drink this cup, do this in remembrance of me."

Remembering, then, is a Christian obligation that holds redemptive potential. It is through the practice of remembering that Christians constitute their identity as a faithful people and a community, embodied as Christ's own. The Eucharist makes that real in worship, but the whole of Christian life involves rehearsal of the saving actions of God in Jesus Christ. To be a Christian is to practice in one's life and in the world those saving actions, to be a follower of Christ. The act of remembering both forms identity and contributes to redemption. Christians come to be in right relationship with God through remembering and so become reformed, transformed, re-membered.

This book focuses attention on the centrality of remembering for Christian witness, practice, and identity, *and* seeks to reformulate what is meant by remembering. When Jesus bid his followers, "Do this in remembrance of me," what did he mean by the command, "do this?" What is it Christians are bid to do? Historically, there are several answers to that question. The most obvious one is the act of worship in the Eucharist itself. Christians gather and share bread and wine in response to Jesus' command. But that communal practice has always pointed to more. The "do this" command has often bid Christians to follow Jesus' action of giving up his life. The bread and wine, as body and blood, sign Jesus' suffering and sacrifice. Too often Christians have interpreted the obligation to remember Jesus as necessitating their own suffering and sacrifice, in thanksgiving, imitation, and/or penitence.

As Christianity turned to orthodox doctrine for its self-definition, the "do this" command of Christian discipleship tended to be interpreted as conformity of belief. Jesus Christ was to be remembered in a particular way, the right way, and faithfulness was judged by whether the proper content was given to one's affirmation of faith. Christian identity and communal formation were shaped less by practice and more by ideology. The inability to achieve unity in this central action of worship witnesses to the splintering effect of stress on right belief over practice.

But there were more harmful effects. The lack of specificity of the command to "do this" allowed for an empty space that might then be filled by whatever and whomever was in power. Jesus' life and actions of solidarity with humanity were transformed into conformity to Jesus as Lord. As Elisabeth Schüssler Fiorenza has argued, Christianity as kyriarchy (which means the multiple and complex systemic grading of dominations, subordinations, and power arrangements) shadowed and forgot the active work of Jesus in healing and transformation. In its stead, this kyriarchal form of Christianity inscribed particular social patterns of hierarchy and control.[8] Jesus as Lord fit well with the purposes of imperial Christianity, which set out to conquer the world in "His" name.

Liberation movements and theologies of our own day are recalling us to alternative readings and to reconsiderations of the centrality of Jesus' mission and saving actions. "Do this in memory of me" is seen as a command to participate in Jesus' *praxis*, in God's transforming and liberating activity. To remember Jesus is to become partners in making right relation and realizing redemption. Christian memory functions both as a problem and a resource in this partnership. The work of a critical political theology is to expose and attend to the problematical dimensions of Christian memory, and to develop this memory as a resource for liberation. The goal is to be faithful to the command to participate in God's work of redemption.

Such partnership in redemption calls us to remember Jesus and ourselves anew. Indeed, remembering becomes a complex and ongoing narrative process. The remembrance of Jesus is in dialogue, in interrelation, and in witness with memories of those who struggle for life. As Christians, we read the narratives of social and cultural remembrance through the story of Jesus. But we must also read the story of Jesus in the light of social imperatives to remember. The connecting goal is the desire for redemption, healing, liberation, and transformation. Value and criteria for evaluation are drawn from the ability to realize redemption.[9]

A theology of redeeming memories is a form of narrative theology. Narrative theology suggests that God's revelation is communicated through remembrance and story, rather than through propositions and abstract truth claims. Remembrance and narration of God's presence and actions in history are redeeming. As George Stroup suggests: "To remember [what God has done] is to 'actualize' the past and 'actualization' is one form of interpretation. To actualize the past is to bring its redemptive power and significance to bear on the present situation."[10] For Stroup and other narrative theologians, the redeeming story of Jesus Christ establishes the framework by which other narratives are to be assessed. Revelation and faith begin in the collision of a personal narrative identity with "the narrative identity of the Christian community."[11] If it is to be redemptive, the collision leads Christians to look to the narrative history of Jesus to define their identity.[12] I agree to the extent that Christians tell their redeeming story using the narrative framework of the story of Jesus Christ, but I see the process of "collision" as more dialectical. Indeed, the method implied here is to begin by witnessing to those who have been silenced by violence and suffering, and suggest that their processes of remembering might be revelatory in a way that changes how Christians tell the story of Jesus Christ.

What emerges from these processes of remembering is a practice of remembering as multiple, complex, and inclusive. This memorative practice includes three foci of remembering that serve different purposes. First, it is important to recall and remember the suffering and losses that are threatened by forgetfulness or erasure. They stand forever as a challenge to notions of historical progress, complacency, or vindication. We witness to the suffering by preservation and by honoring all who died and all that was lost. Such remembrance expresses the desire that nothing be lost: that everything, literally, be saved.

Second, we need to recall and lay claim to moments of resistance and resilience within the victimization. These memories offer a counternarrative to the dominance of suffering and loss, and suggest that the victimization was not total. They challenge the *status quo* and reveal the interests of the dominant powers that would have us believe there is no freedom, no escape, no alternative. Their content includes those ways, large or small, through which the victimized acted on their own behalf to survive and escape. Such remembrance also includes the retrieval of alternative narratives and the practice of cultural traditions as ways to defy erasure. These bear witness to the resilience and persistence of the human spirit.

Third, it is vital to remember life experiences beyond or alongside those of victimization and resistance, and to incorporate them into a more encompassing narrative. Because memories of suffering and of resistance function in relation to threats and dynamics of domination, they are often oppositional or marginal to prevailing cultural discourses. A liberating practice of memory needs to move beyond opposition and marginality to a more integrative process in order to "incarnate" new narratives of personal and social histories. Remembering for life connection, affirmation, and wholeness results in an ongoing and multiple witness to the power of life. The goal is to integrate new and emerging voices through remembering that is inclusive and reflective of diversity. Such memories of life affirmation and connection help create integrated and pluralistic meanings.

All three types of remembering are necessary for a memorative practice of transformation and redemption to take place. Together they form a multiple and complex memorative practice. Memories of life connection both give place to memories of suffering and resistance, and put them in their place. The memories of suffering point to the precariousness of any integrative social narrative by recalling the dangers of domination. Memories of resistance and agency continue to provide an internal critique of tendencies to complacency or loss of historical rootedness. "Redeeming memories" refers to the process of both memory retrieval and redemption through remembering.

For Christians, this multiple memorative practice takes on shape and further definition through remembering Jesus Christ. The person and redeeming work of Christ bears witness to each type of memory. The remembrance of Jesus Christ's incarnation, life, death, and resurrection produces a redemptive narrative that re-members us as God's people, as friends of Jesus, as followers of Christ. When we gather as church, it is as a community of remembrance, engaging in a multiple practice of remembering for the sake of redemption.

29

To Remember Suffering

The next three chapters are about paying attention to those who have been victimized, and bearing witness to their contemporary struggles to emerge out of silence and speak of their experiences in a way that encourages transformation. There is a discernible pattern to such a process of remembering, a pattern that informs the structure I use to present each case. This structure includes (1) the experience of suffering, violence, and oppression; (2) a form of captivity, which includes silence and silencing and which is given cultural sanction through institutions and ideologies;[13] (3) the coming to and claiming of memory, both personally and societally; (4a) personal and social challenges to the "truth" of memories for the sake of reinforcing captivity; and (4b) the personal and societal exploration and working through of the memories. In this process, it is hoped that remembering becomes an effective strategy for honoring and healing, resisting and connecting, in a way that nurtures new understandings of self, society, faith, and redemption. Whether the process of remembering results in a reinforcing of captivity (4a) or a process of transformation (4b) will determine the redemptive potential of the practice of remembering. This struggle for cultural meaning is an ongoing one; the threats to remembering are ever present. Memory persists as both problem and resource for those dealing with a history of victimization. There is a continuing dialectical relationship between the claiming of memory and threats to memory, as well as between coming to new understandings of self and society, and the reinforcing of particular societal arrangements.[14] Thus remembering for transformation is an ongoing process and practice.

My presentations and analyses are informed by the works of trauma theorists and those social theorists who are keenly attuned to the effects of violence and the workings of power. Trauma studies, a recently defined field, has helped me understand the contours of personal and societal responses to such life-threatening and life-changing events as I attend to here. Social theory provides tools to comprehend and analyze the dynamics of remembering as political processes. Both trauma and social theorists suggest that what is at stake in the remembering of suffering and survival, of death and life, are particular social arrangements of power. They also turn our attention to the complexities of remembering, as a process of personal and social transformation.[15]

In this process, truth emerges as fragile, contextual, perspectival, and ambiguous. It is neither abstract nor absolute. Truth is relational and political. What is ultimately to be deemed as true is that which both honors suffering and empowers. There is, then, much at stake in these memories, not only for those who seek to remember in witness, but for our social, cultural, communal, and political identities and connections. Our future will in some sense be determined by whether and how we live with these practices of memory, and what difference they make in our life together.

Ultimately, truth is found in the meeting of remembrance and hope. Redemption is the practice of remembrance and hope to effect witness and transformation. Theologically, the redemptive potential of the memory of Jesus Christ will in no small measure be known and realized by the capacity of that memory to hold and carry not only the story of Jesus, but the stories of all those who suffer, struggle, live, and die.

Section One

To Remember Suffering: Contemporary Movements

1

"And Then I Remembered"

Childhood
Sexual Abuse

During my first semester as a chaplain at Brown University, one of my colleagues, a Roman Catholic sister, and I organized an interfaith retreat for women students. The program, which was based on the biblical book of Ruth and drew heavily upon Phyllis Trible's interpretation, included a series of group reflection exercises.[1] In one exercise, the participants were asked to name times when they felt powerless as women. I expected these female students to cite situations in which teachers called on the males in class and ignored the females, or to name their own reticence to speak up. Instead, I heard story after story of sexual harassment and assault. Not all the students contributed to this discussion. One, who had been particularly quiet, came to see me soon after. She then told me her story of childhood sexual abuse, including incestuous abuse by her brother, which she had begun to recall only recently. Over time, as she shared with me more and more of her history of abuse and the uncovering of memories, she would periodically say: "and then I remembered." As we continued to meet, she not only remembered even more details about her traumatic past, but developed new perspectives on her victimization. She asked me to be a witness and to accompany her in this process. We thus began a long journey of remembrance and witness. Along the way, she tutored me in the paths of recovery, even as I tried to support and accompany her. From this young woman's experience, and also from numerous others, I have learned about the difficult and complicated, yet important process of coming to memory—a process that is ongoing and fraught with dangers and distractions. Because this process entails the experiencing of deeply buried pain, the temptation to "forget" is ever present. Yet always at the heart of the process is the call to remember in order to re-member one's life.

A number of months after this retreat, some women students at Brown University planned a "speak out" on sexual harassment and assault, a public gathering with a few initial speakers, followed by an invitation to any and all present to speak. The organizers expected the "speak out" to last an hour or two. It went on for almost four hours as woman after woman stood up and spoke, often about her own experiences. The next day, one of the students, who had been present but silent, told me she had begun to feel ill as she stood listening. It was then that she realized her stepbrother had abused her, years before. She also told me about an instance of date rape by her first boyfriend. Only as she had heard others speak about their experiences was she able to understand her own. Even though she had never "forgotten" these incidents, she was naming and remembering her past in a new way.

These examples are not unusual. Indeed, they have become all too common. In the last thirty or so years, more and more adults, mostly women, have been speaking up about experiences of child abuse — often sexual abuse perpetrated by persons known to the child.[2] As those who have been victimized gain a public hearing, others come to recognize their own pasts. At speak outs and in other settings, those sexually victimized as children have literally claimed to be "breaking the silence." Such silence has sometimes been consciously self-imposed. These victimized children, now adults, never told anyone of the abuse and/or have not spoken about it for a long time. They carried the knowledge of the past inside themselves and rarely, if ever, shared it publicly, either because they were afraid to share it or did not know what name to give their experiences of abuse.[3] In other instances, however, the silence was internal as well: the victimized persons had no access to the knowledge or memory of the abuse. They had hidden away the traumatic realities even from themselves. For such persons, at some time after the abuse, often in adulthood, the memories return as intrusive and frightening reminders of a past long buried in the psyche. In that sense, these persons were silenced by the terrorizing behavior of their abusers and by the self-protective responses of their psyches. "Forgetting," in the form of repression or blocking or dissociation, became a way to adapt to the situation of abuse when they felt no power as children to escape or change the victimization.

In this chapter, I examine the experience of childhood abuse and, in particular, the common experiences of "forgetting" and then later remembering by those who, abused as children, blocked the memory from awareness and/or never disclosed it. I suggest that the current social phenomenon of so many persons remembering childhood abuse is, in part, the result of changing cultural and social contexts that create the safety and setting necessary for such memories to emerge. These changes are eliciting a countermovement that labels the memories as false. What is at stake is not only the authenticity and validity of survivors' memories, but social constructions of gender and family relations, including patriarchal definitions, and of power and knowledge.

The Trauma of Child Sexual Abuse

Child sexual abuse is understood to be sexual and/or sexualized behavior directed toward a child by an older person. It is incestuous if that older person is someone with whom a child has a relationship of some intimacy, trust, and/or dependency. Such persons may be parents, grandparents, siblings, other relatives, caretakers, and family friends. By virtue of age and dependency, the child in such cases is not able to give consent; the sexual behavior is to be considered unwanted and potentially abusive. Currently available statistics indicate that the great majority of those who perpetuate abuse (over 90 percent) are male.[4] Those who are victimized are more often female. Statistics vary and are difficult to verify, especially when dealing with a phenomenon that is blocked from memory. Conservative indications are that 25 percent to 30 percent of women are sexually abused at some point in their lives and somewhere between 10 percent and 20 percent are abused as children, more often than not by someone known to them. The statistics for males are even more unreliable and are generally considered to be lower than that for female victims, but more and more cases are being reported. The age of those victimized can vary: infants as well as teenagers have been the objects of childhood incestuous sexual abuse. Such abuse occurs in all socioeconomic classes, in all racial, ethnic, and religious groups, and across all educational levels.

Childhood sexual abuse is most often experienced as a traumatizing event. Traumatic events, as Judith Herman suggests, "overwhelm the ordinary systems of care that give people a sense of control, connection, and meaning."[5] They not only do physical injury, but inflict psychological harm by causing fragmentation and disintegration. Thus sexual abuse hurts a child in some very fundamental ways, not simply by the potential physical injury caused, but by its psychological impact. To be abused by someone is to be violated; to be abused by someone whom a child cares for, trusts, and may be dependent upon is to disturb, and maybe even destroy, her sense of trust and safety.[6] Because the abuser is most often someone with greater power through age, position, and relationship, and because the child is asked and/or forced to do things she does not choose and often does not understand, the abused child experiences a loss of control and an increased sense of powerlessness. Repeated experiences of abuse reinforce feelings of powerlessness and may render the child as a victim who is not able to protect herself appropriately in new instances or occasions of abuse: "When a person is completely powerless, and any form of resistance is futile, she may go into a state of surrender. The system of self-defense shuts down entirely."[7] Feelings of powerlessness thus may contribute to a common pattern of repeated victimization.

Judith Herman suggests that repeated victimization and trauma can result in what she terms a state of captivity, a relationship of "coercive control" in which children "are rendered captive by their condition of dependency."[8] The ultimate goal for the perpetrator is "the creation of a willing victim" through total control and tyranny.[9] If the trauma and tyranny are not faced, a victimized child may continue to choose situations and behaviors that reproduce her victimization even after she is free of the perpetrator. Trained to be a willing victim, she often does not know the root causes of her destructive patterns of repeated self-defeating behaviors.

The trauma of childhood abuse "forms and deforms the personality."[10] It results in a damaged self, characterized by affective responses such as a sense of self-blame, guilt, and shame; a negative self-image, low self-esteem and self-loathing; an inability to trust and to feel safe and secure; depression and sadness; fear and/or anxiety; and a sense of isolation and withdrawal. There may also be behavioral manifestations and somatic effects, such as eating disorders, self-mutilation, sexual disorders, headaches or other chronic physical symptomology, and sleep disturbances. The abused child will feel hopeless in relation to self, world, and God. Yet, despite a child's helplessness, she "must find a way to preserve hope and meaning" and "will go to any lengths to construct an explanation for her fate that absolves her parents of all blame and responsibility."[11] Often the child will conclude that she is "bad" and use this as an explanation for why bad things are happening to her. In a distorted way, this explanation may allow her to feel some control and power: "If she is bad, then she can try to be good. If, somehow, she has brought this fate upon herself, then somehow she has the power to change it."[12] Thus abused children often have problems with issues of power and responsibility, and their sense of themselves as acceptable to others and to God. Shame affects much of their lives. Any sense of healing or wholeness is subverted by feelings of shame and lack of worth.

Buried Memories of Abuse

In order to protect themselves as best they can, a common adaptive defense strategy, deployed by children in situations of continuing abuse, is to separate their conscious selves from the abuse and hide their awareness of it, even from themselves. When a child is abused, if she is not able to tell someone either because she is preverbal or is too confused or frightened or has no one she feels she can trust, she will often block the trauma from her awareness through denial, repression, or dissociation. If a child does tell someone and is not believed, is dismissed and/or punished, she will experience another level of injury that reinforces the lack of safety and may make blocking the memory seem like the only option. With denial, the child refuses to acknowledge or be aware of the abuse. When employing repression, she buries it deep within her unconscious. With dissociation, she separates and hides the memory. In situations of repeated abuse she may dissociate in the abuse experience itself, thus removing herself mentally from the abuse while it is going on. In that sense, she is not present to what is happening to her. Survivors often talk about themselves as disappearing into a lamp or floating up to the ceiling as ways to separate from the abuse, from what is being done to them. Such dissociation allows a child to cope during the abuse, especially if it is ongoing.[13]

Although these defense mechanisms may help the child survive her abuse, ultimately they silence her. The child does not speak of the abuse; she may not even allow herself to know it. Such reactions may persist for years, decades, or a lifetime. Occasional intrusive reminders or memories, experienced as unwelcome and "terrorizing" flashbacks or unexplainable anxiety reactions, may again be repressed or suppressed if there is no context or environment of safety in which to give voice to them and have them validated. Without a social and cultural context that encourages remembering, it is difficult for survivors to feel that they can speak of their experiences, even if they know what name to give these moments of intrusive terror and even if they can state they were harmed. Remembering and telling require a social context that will support and validate the narrative. Without such social support, especially in the case of traumatic memories, the abused person often opts for silence and burying of the memories. Remembering, then, necessitates some measure of safety and a supportive climate. If the survivor feels no power or freedom, she may well not be able to tolerate the remembering.

Claiming and Working Through Memories of Abuse: "And Then I Remembered"

When a survivor who has recovered memory is able to tell her story, there is sometimes a moment that she points to as a turning point toward remembering. That moment may be the result of intrusive flashbacks, which carry their own terror, or may be found in the response to a new situation or life stage, or to hearing another survivor talk about her experience.[14] Although such a moment is a turning point and may be very dramatic, it is only a moment in a process.

Remembering, as I am using the term here, refers to a complex and ongoing process, with multiple stages that involve not only recalling the event of abuse, but revisiting the abuse cognitively and affectively in order to reclaim the parts of self that were hidden or lost along the way to terror, blocking, and dissociation. It also involves reinterpretation and reintegration. As Judith Herman indicates: "This work of reconstruction actually transforms the traumatic memory, so that it can be integrated into the survivor's life story."[15]

This is an immense project and may literally call on the survivor to rebuild her world. That process is dialectical: a survivor will often doubt her own experiences and/or be frightened to let go of the world, albeit dysfunctional, she constructed in order to survive. She may believe and then return to doubt again. She may even repress again, especially if she is not able to find adequate support. Beyond cognitive recall of the memory of abuse, a survivor must also allow herself to feel the feelings that she blocked at the time of the abuse: "Remembering is the process of getting back both memory and feeling."[16] Such remembering includes not only the feelings associated with the events of abuse, but the betrayal and pain caused by the lack of response and protection from others, which reinforced the initial injury. This is a very difficult part of the process. Survivors who are able to speak of what happened to them are still reluctant to experience the feelings of terror and hurt. Remembering affectively requires much support and safety since it means living through the pain that was blocked. In a seeming contradiction, healing necessitates much pain. Survivors need to be willing to experience frightening pain. This part of the process may take a long time and may need to be revisited again and again as survivors discover more layers of betrayal and injury.

Recalling the abuse and the painful feelings attendant to it lead eventually into a process of mourning and of reinterpreting and working through the past. Mourning is for all the losses experienced: psychological, physical, relational.[17] This is another difficult part of the process of remembering. Judith Herman refers to it as "at once the most necessary and the most dreaded task of this stage of recovery."[18] It plunges the survivor into profound grief; so mourning may be resisted. But mourning, itself, is a strategy of resistance to the totalizing effects of the abuse. Mourning entails facing the truth of what happened and accepting the injury fully, at the core of one's being. It involves suffering the reality of the losses. As a survivor mourns, she comes finally to a letting go of the pain and the loss, even though scars of injury will remain forever. Those scars are reminders of the past suffering, but they will not have the capacity for reinjuring her.

Reinterpretation of the past involves a reassessment of the dynamics of power and responsibility, and an appropriate assigning of blame. In this process, a survivor turns from blaming herself to being able to recognize and affirm what she did to enable her survival, as well as face ways she may have injured herself. She lays claim to what she was able to do to exercise power and agency in the situation of abuse, even by means of adaptive defense mechanisms. I see such reinterpretation of the narrative of injury as crucial to the healing process. In a way, reinterpretation means the survivor is retelling the story of abuse from a new perspective. The narrative interest shifts from maintaining a sense of shame and self-blame, and/or an idealized image of the perpetrator and/or her family, to a focus on her own healing and empowerment. These new lenses suggest different readings of her behaviors. For example, in a situation of powerlessness and "captivity," dissociation may be claimed as an assertion of the will to survive rather than a dysfunctional behavior. Only when it becomes habitual beyond the abuse is it to be deemed dysfunctional.

Mourning and reinterpretation are key to transformation. Indeed, they are the points at which survivors "turn the corner," so to speak, in leaving fragmentation and victimhood behind, and reclaiming a hopeful and integrated self. Because the original trauma was, in a sense, arbitrary and clearly undeserved, the survivor must also deal with questions of meaning, action, and moral behavior.[19] Not only does she need to develop a different narrative, but her understanding of self, truth, and even goodness may change. A goal of the process of remembering is integration, which enables transformation. Such integration comes only through this long, complex, and dialectical process of remembering.

According to Herman, the next stage of recovery is reconnection, which is focused on the future. The process of remembering at this stage is about further development of a narrative in which the abuse has place, but not dominance. As Elizabeth Waites writes: "Learning that the past will always be there and that the self is safe from getting lost makes it possible to explore new territory."[20] This new territory includes integration toward transformation. The goals are: forming a new sense of self and relationships, claiming a sustaining faith, and reclaiming the world.[21] These goals require that the survivor be able to celebrate her resilience and her capacity for risk and transformation. This stage may entail finding what Herman calls a "survivor mission," a way to take action and make a difference. It also involves reconnecting with others and nurturing relationships. Evidence of reconnection is a renewed and fuller sense of commitment to life.

To Witness and Accompany

The process of remembering described above, the claiming and transforming of one's memories of abuse, requires a supportive and safe relationship and/or setting. It is difficult to remember for oneself without such a connection and context, either with individual persons or in a group setting. Remembering proceeds as a dialectical process: validation of the experience of survivors helps them feel safe and, as they feel safe, they are able to engage more fully in the process of remembering. A trustworthy relationship or a good therapeutic alliance or a support group is vitally important to remembering. It begins to break down the isolation the survivor may well be experiencing and helps her feel that she is no longer alone in dealing with the trauma.

Such relationships—whether with a single person or in a group setting—serve not only to support and encourage the survivor, but function to bear witness. It is vitally important that the survivor be believed and her testimony be received. The role of witness entails such a validation, as well as a receiving and holding of the testimony. This role includes being trustworthy and able to handle the memories of abuse. It requires the creation of an environment and a relationship that is safe, supportive, and empowering. The witnessing relationship stands in for a larger social context that recognizes and hears the survivor's testimony. This need for witnessing and support operates both interpersonally and societally. Indeed, the personal and social reinforce one another.

For a long time, the silence of survivors was reinforced by active silencing in a social context that did not recognize abuse. Abuse was a hidden and secret occurrence and, for many persons, it did not exist. Such a climate did not allow those who were victimized as children to feel that they could speak about their experiences; indeed, they often did not know even what to name those experiences.

Neither did therapists and support persons know how to respond. When abused persons sought help in counseling or therapy, they often presented symptoms of depression, anxiety, or more extreme manifestations such as multiple personality disorders or dissociative identity disorders. Because therapists were not trained to look for histories of abuse, unless the abused persons were willing and able to name and claim their histories, the abuse would not be dealt with in the therapy. Given that the role of a therapist or support person is to provide safety and to take in the testimony of the abused person, this lack of connection often made remembering more difficult for survivors.

Change came as a result of social movements that began to alter consciousness about the experiences of women, children, and other traumatized persons in our society, and so nurtured an accepting and believing climate. The first contributions to such a change of consciousness came from the child welfare movement. In 1962, C. Henry Kempe and associates published an article entitled "The Battered Child Syndrome" that served to focus attention on all forms of mistreatment of children, including child sexual abuse.[22] Another important historical factor was the greater attention being paid to trauma and its effects. The experience of returning Vietnam War veterans has done much to raise our social consciousness about the enduring effects of traumatic events. The recognition of "post-traumatic stress disorder" as a diagnostic category has influenced treatment greatly.[23] Since trauma is regarded as injury rather than illness, the treatment of it is significantly different.[24]

Although awareness of child abuse and awareness of the impact of trauma on people's lives have helped change ideas and treatment, the women's movement is to be credited with making the greatest impact on changing consciousness. Beginning with a focus on rape as violence against women, rape crisis centers, speak outs, consciousness-raising groups, support groups, and other settings have encouraged women to claim and name their experiences of emotional, physical, and sexual violence. These contexts have provided validation and support, and altered awareness not only about violence against women, but about social and ideological structures that support and encourage such violence.

The women's movement also indicted the patriarchal family and society as loci of violence. It held these structures responsible for the suffering inflicted upon women and children. From these initial critiques, an ever-increasing body of literature has developed that examines and analyzes the nature of patriarchal systems and how they subtly and not so subtly harm and abuse women. Such examinations have challenged traditional notions of family and gender roles, as well as the economic, political, social, and religious structures that reinforce male dominance.

Feminist theologians and pastors have pointed out the ways in which Christianity provides legitimating ideologies for patriarchal structures that breed and hide violence. They have also pointed to the effects of Christian teaching on those who are abused. Often Christian teaching has contributed to silencing through generating feelings of shame and guilt. The silence of churches, themselves, on abuse has further reinforced such feelings and revealed the lack of a religious community of support for survivors. Although individual survivors witness to the saving and restorative power of God and/or Jesus in their lives, many feel they are unworthy in God's eyes.[25]

Abuse does not occur on a blank canvas, but in a social context that allows for and encourages it. Remembering is not only a personal and interpersonal process of retrieval and transformation, but a social and political one. Remembering toward healing and recovery is enabled by a culture of belief and validation. It is disabled by societal denial. Such remembering also influences society and its narratives of identity. Remembering by abuse survivors may well lead to remembering ourselves differently as a society and a culture. It will require redefinition of relationships, family, and social and religious self-understandings. Such changes have and will continue to elicit resistance.

The "Truth" of Memories of Abuse: The Legacy of Sigmund Freud

In the last decade, as a response to the emergence and retrieval of repressed memories by adult survivors of child incestuous sexual abuse, a countermovement has arisen that has received much media attention. This movement, under the title of "False Memory Syndrome," claims that the vast majority of memories of early childhood abuse are false fabrications and are often "planted" by therapists. Some proponents of False Memory Syndrome cite scientific evidence about memory to support their contentions. Often they argue for family and social "stability" over against "attacks" by therapists and lawyers.

Before turning to a more detailed look at the False Memory Syndrome and its proponents, I will offer a historical example of the social and political stakes present in the struggle over the authenticity of memories of abuse. This example centers upon Sigmund Freud, the father of modern psychology. Recent studies have drawn attention to the fact that the young Freud, in attempting to understand the cause of hysterical symptoms in his patients, believed that most of them had experienced early childhood sexual trauma. Hysteria, then, was a reaction related to and rooted in real traumas and events. In Freud's view, which was labeled the "seduction theory," it was not the traumatic events themselves that created hysterical symptoms, but the repressed memories of the trauma. In his work with patients, Freud would enable them to uncover these memories, which then pointed to an experience of early childhood trauma. Freud believed such traumas to be inevitably sexual in nature.[26] What caused the hysteria, Freud suggested, was not the traumatic events themselves, but the unconscious nature of memories of them. Treatment of patients was to consist of "transforming their unconscious memories of the infantile scenes into conscious ones."[27]

Later, Freud began to change his mind about the causation of hysteria and eventually came to believe that adults did not sexually abuse children; rather young children fantasized sexual relations with adults.[28] Reports of patients' memories were thus to be treated as fantasies. If anything overt did happen, it was to be understood as a wish fulfillment of these fantasies. In 1905, in "Three Essays on the Theory of Sexuality," Freud publicly stated that he had exaggerated and misrepresented the role of sexual trauma in the causation of hysteria. He repeated this conviction in "My Views on the Part Played by Sexuality in the Aetiology of the Neuroses."[29] Although Freud did not go so far as to say that childhood sexual abuse never occurs, he minimized both its occurrence and its impact. Whereas initially Freud had been arguing for childhood sexual abuse as *the* cause of hysteria, he later substituted and developed his ideas about infantile sexuality and the Oedipus complex.

Critics today agree that Freud's change of mind resulted in a denial of patients' experiences. Those patients were then, in a sense, revictimized by analysts who did not uncover or believe their early experiences of trauma. An interpretation was imposed that did not allow those patients to deal with the reality of what had happened. The theory of infant sexuality sexualizes children in such a way that traumatic childhood sexual experiences are interpreted as being about sex rather than about power. Such an interpretation ignores the real dynamics of the situation and tends to minimize the harm done to the child. Further, in Freudian tradition, the male and his experiences are normative.

Women are defined as naturally lacking and envious of the male penis, role, and status. If the patient was female, which was very often the case, her sexual drives were interpreted as being rooted in a basic sense of lack of a penis. Not only was her experience discounted, but she was told that she could only be cured if she became reconciled to her lack. Thus Freud made women's best option a state of resignation.[30]

No one disputes that Freud changed his mind about the roots of hysteria. Rather, the debate revolves around whether the changes resulted in a more or less accurate theory. The traditional psychoanalytic posture and Freud's own, as indicated, is that Freud came to realize he had been wrong and had overestimated the frequency and severity of early childhood sexual trauma. Thus as Freud continued his investigations and proceeded to refine his theories, he developed what he deemed the more adequate theories of infantile sexuality and the Oedipus complex.

Such explanations have been challenged recently, especially by feminist critics who indict Freud for his need to uphold the patriarchal, adult order and thus discount the experience of children. Florence Rush, in *The Best Kept Secret,* which contains the first fully argued delineation of what she calls "a Freudian cover-up," states that Freud "could not reconcile the implications of that [sexual] abuse with either his self-image or his identification with other men of his class, and thus he altered his telling of reality."[31] Judith Herman concludes that Freud's repudiation of the seduction theory was based "not on any new evidence from patients, but rather on Freud's own growing unwillingness to believe that licentious behavior on the part of fathers could be so widespread."[32] Alice Miller does not attribute Freud's shift so much to the influence of patriarchal ideology, understood as a gendered worldview, but as one upholding the rights and privileges of adults over those of children.[33]

Whatever the motivation, in seeking to hold on to a world that he could live in, Freud discounted the real experience of many of his patients. In fact, he seems to have stopped listening to them. His theories seem to take precedence and define the experience of those patients.

Neither did the problem end with Freud. Because the theories of infantile sexuality and the Oedipus complex were enshrined as the very foundations of psychoanalysis, psychoanalysts and other therapists and counselors were trained not to believe the experience of their clients, and to interpret their reports of trauma and memories as fantasies.

Children have been dismissed as credible witnesses to their own lives. Memories have been lost, discounted, manipulated, and distorted because of psychoanalytic orthodoxy; other interpretations have been imposed. The Freudian legacy can thus be read as one of institutionalized distortion and even erasure of the memory of those who suffered abuse in childhood.

This legacy has not encouraged remembering in a way that can heal and transform. It has made it difficult for survivors to find help and reliable witnesses. It has discouraged theoretical approaches or ideological stances that recognize women's experience. As indicated, such approaches have emerged only in the last thirty or so years from the women's movement and from those dealing with other forms of abuse, and with responses to trauma. These approaches not only assist the survivors in a process of recalling the abuse, but in remembering and reconstituting themselves in such a way that they claim power and begin to redefine societal definitions and roles.

False Memory Syndrome

Freud was not the only one, however, to come to the conclusion that reports of childhood incestuous sexual abuse were not accurate representations of past events. More recently, the False Memory Syndrome Foundation has been promoting the idea that many adults who say that they are retrieving repressed childhood memories of abuse are actually manifesting False Memory Syndrome.[34] The False Memory Syndrome Foundation was established in 1992 by parents claiming that they were falsely accused of abuse by their children. A number of researchers, clinicians, and writers have also emerged as key voices in this movement to discredit the memories of survivors. Many of these serve on the "professional advisory board" of the Foundation. The most notable one is Dr. Elizabeth Loftus, an experimental scientist working on memory at the University of Washington. She argues that, based on her experiments, memory is malleable and highly susceptible to suggestion. The implication is that memories of abuse are being "planted" by therapists and by social suggestion via media reports and popular therapeutic and self-help books.

Elizabeth Loftus points to her own research to argue that subjects can be persuaded to "remember" certain events that never took place. Once these subjects are convinced of the "truth" of these false events, they will even develop narrative elaboration.[35] Based on this research,

Loftus rejects the idea of repressed memories that can later be reliably recalled. Although she does concede that there are instances of corroborated repressed memories and that lack of corroboration does not mean that the memories are false, she yet questions the concept of repression, what it means, and whether it is prevalent.[36] Her overall argument is that abuse does happen frequently, but repression does not.

In *The Myth of Repressed Memory,* a popularly written book coauthored with Katherine Ketcham, Loftus's biases are more apparent. The dedication to that book reads: "Dedicated to the principles of science, which demand that any claim to 'truth' be accompanied by proof." The authors also write: "We seek *terra firma* under our feet, and we send thick roots downward into the soft soil of our history, seeking to embed them in something called the truth. Ambiguity makes our hair stand up on end."[37] This book, however, is not a scientific study, but a series of personal stories. Chapters begin with quotations from Arthur Miller's play *The Crucible,* which is about the Salem witch trials. The clear implication is that those claiming to remember abuse by family members are like the young girls pointing the finger at witches in Salem. For Loftus, accusations against family members based on the recovery of memories are similar to a witch hunt. She claims to be arguing only against "repressed" memory recall, which she defines as "memories that did not exist until someone went looking for them."[38]

Michael Yapko makes a similar claim in his book *True and False Memories of Childhood Sexual Trauma.* He notes that there are four possible cases of remembered abuse: (1) someone was abused and has known all along; (2) someone independently remembers; (3) a therapist facilitates remembering; and (4) a therapist suggests memories of abuse to a client. Yapko argues that he is dealing only with the fourth type or case.[39] Others writing to indict repressed memory make similar disclaimers. Yet in their zeal, they slip toward including the other "cases." Most of these authors also focus on a small group of notorious cases that have received a great deal of media attention, such as that of Paul Ingram who is in prison for incest and ritual abuse.[40] Whereas they say they are dealing with specific incidents and particular definitions, their rhetoric suggests broader claims.

Many of these writers, such as Loftus and Yapko, question the whole notion of repression and whether it exists. They criticize Freud for introducing the concept into psychological thinking. In pursuing their criticism, they define repression in a way that suits their argument.

There is thus a certain lack of clarity about what is meant by repression.[41]

Charles Whitfield tries to address such challenges by distinguishing between repression, dissociation, and denial as three adaptive mechanisms. He suggests that all three of them affect memory. Lack of recall of the abuse is thus not only a function of repression, but of trauma-related "forgetting." He points out that "most trauma survivors with delayed memories are experiencing not a simple repression, but dissociative phenomena and often some degree of denial."[42] Whitfield also notes that the initial trauma of the abuse is compounded by dissociation and blocking of ability to feel and to grieve.[43] All of these reactions affect memory: not only the ability to recall the event of what happened, but to feel appropriately in relation to it and to experience the impact of the trauma. Other psychologists have offered related arguments. Elizabeth Waites describes the lack of memory as a function of dissociation, rather than repression; as previously noted, Jennifer Freyd argues that what leads the victimized to "forget" is the betrayal of trust experienced in the trauma.[44]

Those who write about memories of abuse as false are often critical of psychologists, who are accused of inducing memories in their patients. Loftus's scientific experiment on the suggestibility of memory is used to argue that therapists can convince their clients that they were abused as children and then turn those clients against their families. Such writers are also critical of the legal system and the ways in which it has investigated allegations of childhood sexual abuse, especially how children have been questioned. Such critical nets are cast widely, leaving the impression that these phenomena are the norm, rather than the exception. What is not given sufficient voice is the way in which for years abuse was never dealt with in therapy because therapists did not know to look for it, or that children were long discounted as reliable witnesses.

The Social Context of Remembering

Whereas psychologists try to keep the focus on the battlefield of repression and memory, I understand the false memory debate to be primarily a sociopolitical phenomenon. Two things seem to be at stake in this countermovement. One is the social standing of traditional institutions that claim authority, such as the scientific establishment, the patriarchal family, and the priesthood—particularly the Roman

Catholic priesthood—as more and more cases of abuse are revealed. A second is the nature of knowledge, including traditional notions of empirical scientific knowledge. Authoritarian institutions and models of scientific knowledge participate in mechanisms of social control, including definitions of what is right, natural, real, and true. They tend to oppose ambiguity.

The higher incidence of reports of abuse and changes in social awareness challenge traditional notions of family, especially patriarchal families. In the last thirty to forty years, American society's knowledge of trauma and of the existence and dynamics of abuse has altered dramatically. By 1962, the "battered child syndrome" had been named; by 1974, the "rape trauma syndrome" and by the late 1970s, the "battered woman syndrome" were also introduced into social awareness. In 1983, Roland Summit named the "child sexual abuse accommodation syndrome."[45] As noted, returning Vietnam War veterans helped us to recognize and understand the dynamics of trauma, including post-traumatic stress disorder. It is not surprising that there would be a defensive response to such challenges to traditional social patterns of family and even of war and heroism. Neither is it surprising that the False Memory Syndrome Foundation was established by families of those alleging abuse. Judith Herman and Mary Harvey point out: "It has taken 20 years for women's organizations to bring the enormity of sexual assault to public attention and establish minimal standards of fairness for victims. As more victims try to hold their abusers accountable, it is natural to expect a backlash."[46] In this process, therapists are labeled as those who challenge these institutions and turn children away from their parents.

What is evident in Loftus's book and others, such as Yapko's, is that although the authors express sympathy for those who have been abused, they identify with those accused of abuse. Their allegiance is toward those whose authority is being challenged in some way. Why is this so? Perhaps because their own authority as clinicians and scientists is also being challenged. The recovery movement began outside the traditional clinical community. It began in the women's movement and through self-help groups. *The Courage to Heal,* which has served as a critically important book for those recovering from abuse and which has been singled out for special attack by the proponents of false memory, is not written by traditionally trained clinicians.[47] This book and others in the "self-help" category provide important resources easily available to survivors. It may be the case that the rhetorical interest of such books—to support and validate the experience of survivors—occasionally results in tendencies to overstate their point of view and to identify too strongly with "victims." Such interest is most often due to the authors' awareness of how difficult it is for survivors to believe their own experiences.[48]

My own perspective, gleaned through my pastoral and personal experience with survivors and through my reading of survivor literature, is that survivors are often reluctant to accept their own experiences of recall. They are hesitant to face the abuse until they can no longer ignore the intrusions of memory or the haunting sense of disease. As Charles Whitfield points out: "Most people with painful memories of having been mistreated or abused would rather not have them, and if they blame anyone they tend to repeatedly blame themselves."[49] Most survivors struggle to know the truth of their own lives and only reluctantly accept the reality of abuse in their past.

That struggle sometimes brings about a tendency in survivor literature, especially popular texts and self-help books, to overemphasize the absoluteness of experience and to read any ambiguity or doubt as sign of weakness or lack of support. I see this as another pole of the quest for certainty shared by those who want scientific and evidentiary proof. It is a stage that has to be left behind if abuse is to be fully faced.

The reality for most survivors who remember toward healing and transformation is that, in the process of working through the memories, they come to an understanding of truth, not as certainty, but as complex and ambiguous knowledge. They also realize that there are few absolutes about good and evil. Survivors often live with the reality that those who nurtured them are the same people who betrayed and harmed them. They find themselves needing to maintain relationships with family members and others who continue to deny or minimize the abuse. In relation to their own behavior, survivors may have to face things that they may find difficult to accept or believe about themselves and about what they did. They may never have proof or validation of the past and yet their lives depend on coming to terms with it. These survivors choose to live "as if" the abuse were true and trust their emerging perceptions. Such a stance, however, does not provide the *terra firma* that Loftus desires. It offers neither the certainty and absoluteness of scientific truth claims nor that of personal experience.[50]

Instead, what emerges from survivors' accounts and the process of witnessing is remembering as a complex, multidimensional, and ongoing process of reappropriating and coming to terms with the past. Witnesses serve to receive and validate the survivors' memories and provide a context, relational and social, political and theological, in which those memories can be spoken and heard as true. This context serves as a community of remembrance. Remembering does enable healing, but only, as I have indicated, through a long, arduous, and painful process of revisiting, feeling, and reinterpreting the past.

This process is made more difficult by those who would deny the validity of memories and seek to reassert cultural messages of control. Although there may be those who fabricate memories or exaggerate instances of abuse, these instances are rare. It is important to ask why these incidents receive so much attention. It is also important to consider the implications of such challenges for survivors who always remembered but never spoke, as well as for those who are remembering perhaps for the first time. The attention would no doubt make these persons question their experiences and the reception they might get if they speak up.

The James Porter case offers a remarkable example of recovered memory leading to connections, validation, and vindication. Frank Fitzpatrick, a private detective in his early forties, with a wife and children, could not understand a persistent sense of depression in his life. In his seeking to find its cause, he began to remember abuse by a Roman Catholic priest when he was a young child. He placed an advertisement in a local paper, simply asking for those who remembered "Father James Porter" to contact him. Over the course of the next weeks, he heard from a number of others and the case began to receive some media attention. Eventually, more than seventy adults came forward, male and female, who had been abused by James Porter. Some had remembered all along. Others had their memory triggered when they heard the news reports. Meanwhile, Fitzpatrick tracked down James Porter, who had left the priesthood, married, had children of his own, and was living in another state. In a telephone conversation, Porter admitted to molesting more than one hundred children. After a lengthy process, Porter was convicted and sent to jail. Fitzpatrick has since devoted himself to investigating abuse and supporting those who come forward, through an organization called "Survivor Connections."[51]

Remembering Toward Healing

A person who is abused as a child, especially if that abuse is hidden and not dealt with at the time, never fully heals in the sense that the abuse is dealt with and put aside forever. Scars always remain, which serve to remind the person of her traumatic past. Yet if the memories are brought to the surface and the abuse relived affectively, reinterpreted cognitively, and mourned in a supportive context, the survivor can go on to claim the rest of her life in a way that keeps the effects of the abuse in place.

In that process, remembering shifts from being a problem to serving as a resource. Indeed, remembering comes to be understood as a complex and ongoing process of retrieval, reinterpretation, and reintegration. A survivor not only is able to recall the past abuse, but to remember it differently. She will face into the ways in which she was irreparably harmed and thus victimized. Yet she will know herself as more than a victim; she will recognize what she did to enable her survival, including the use of defense mechanisms such as dissociation and denial. As I have indicated, by claiming these as survival techniques, once useful but no longer effective, the survivor begins to see and know her own agency and power, in the past as well as the present. She begins to know herself as resilient and not only victimized; as someone who resisted as best she could and who was able to exert a kind of power in a situation of powerlessness. She did what it was possible to do to survive in a context that was, in some sense, meant to destroy her. Another step of healing comes when the survivor is able to move from blaming herself—for the abuse and idealizing the perpetrator and/or the family—to a different perspective on what happened. In order to claim her agency, she may well adopt a new understanding of family and society, beyond denial and toward a critical, political analysis. She may also develop insight into the ideological structures that supported the denial and self-blame, including religious systems.

After the survivor has moved through the process of dealing with the abuse and it begins to "shrink to size," so to speak, so that it no longer dominates her life, her energy shifts toward integrating this past into the rest of life. This process requires yet another act of remembering that seeks to reincorporate the rest of her history and make new connections with the past and in the present. This act of integration is a sign that the survivor is ready to move on. Along the way, she has not only recalled the abuse but remembered it through this complex and multidimensional process of reworking the suffering, and re-membering herself. Re-membering involves developing a different narrative of life; it entails a type of reconstitution of self, including self in relation with family and society. The survivor thus enters into a new set of relationships with different norms and expectations. It is crucial that she be helped in this process by the support of others: counselors, friends, family (one hopes), groups, and communities, including religious ones. These form, with the survivor, a community of remembrance that shares in the wider community of those who recognize abuse and seek change.

It is easy to see how this whole process can be undermined and thwarted by those who challenge these memories. Often such challenge reinforces mechanisms of denial, especially since there is already personal and societal resistance to recognizing the extent of abuse. The prevalence and reality of abuse is very difficult to believe, for society as a whole and for individual survivors and their families. The false memory movement feeds into this desire not to believe; it allows many people not to face into the reality of abuse. It also reinforces the dynamics of victimization by either blaming the victim for making up the abuse or seeing her as someone easily manipulated by a therapist.

In facing the abuse, we attend not only to the healing of those who have been abused, but to our awareness and understandings of family and community, society and power. Remembering and witnessing to abuse require that we move beyond denial about misuses of power to recognizing the realities of abuse among us and the need for social transformation. This will result in social change through a similar process of healing: facing into the pain of abuse, mourning the losses, recognizing and claiming arenas of resistance, and seeking transformation. Just as a survivor has to move to a new self-understanding and integration, so do we as a society. What is at stake in that, as it is for the survivor, is our future, our health, and our wholeness. As the women's movement has so importantly reminded us, these new understandings need also to be institutionalized in order for change and transformation to be realized.

Even under the best of circumstances, the process of remembering and transformation continues to be one of struggle for the survivor and for society. Even without outside challengers, there is still the impetus to slip into denial or seek return to an idealized past and hide the pain. The process of redeeming memories is an ongoing dialectical process and struggle between past and present, self and society. It is characterized by a particular type of knowing, a critical and committed knowing, that retreats neither into the certainty of scientific objectivity nor the absoluteness of personal experience. Rather, it is a practical knowledge that is assessed by its ability to make a difference and enable witness and care, healing and wholeness. If we attend to those on the healing journey, we will begin to know in these ways. Such knowing may re-member us personally and socially.

The survivor I wrote about at the beginning of this chapter, who shared her memories with me long ago, is still on a journey of recovery. The years and experiences of adulthood have uncovered for her deeper and even more hidden levels of injury and victimization, so her process of remembering is ongoing. As I continue to accompany her, bear witness, and offer support, she teaches me still about the struggle for healing and for life itself. There is yet to be resolution and integration. Rather, she is finding a type of wholeness as integrity in the way she remains true to the process. As frightening as that process is, and as much as she yearns to embrace denial, she keeps coming back to a hope born in connection and in her own creative will to survive. Along the way, she is able to offer validation and support to others with a wisdom hard won. Her practice of re-membering extends to the community, as well as herself, and plants seeds of transforming possibility.

2

"Never Forget"

The Armenian Genocide and the Jewish Holocaust

As I moved through the United States Holocaust Museum in Washington, D.C., I tried to take in as much as I could of this monument and memorial. Because the need to remember is always, it seems, accompanied by fears of forgetting and of oblivion, the museum is meant to be a permanent witness, strong armor against the threat of forgetfulness. Even as I felt the immensity of horror and loss, I sensed that the imperative to remember suffering and death had been realized here in concrete and steel. Because the dead can no longer remember for themselves, and the survivor generation, the direct witnesses, are dying out, we need other forms of witness.

This obligation to bear witness, to hear and respond to the command—"never forget"—is no easy yoke. It is laid on us by those who died in the Holocaust and those who survived. Their cry for remembrance echoes throughout the universe forever because it cannot be satisfied. For Christians, that yoke bears a particular weight. Theologians such as Johann Baptist Metz believe that Christian theology cannot be done without attending to Auschwitz. Metz bases his claim on the massive evil of the Holocaust and the reality of Christian complicity in that evil.

Although the cry of those who suffered and died in the Holocaust has a particular hold on Christians, it is not the only voice that rises from the grave. Many scholars and writers have portrayed the twentieth century as the bloodiest in history. They cite the multiple examples of mass slaughter and attempts to exterminate whole peoples, including the Armenian genocide, the Jewish Holocaust, Stalin's purges, the reign of the Khmer Rouge in Cambodia, tribal warfare in various parts of Africa, and "ethnic cleansing" in Bosnia. I could add to this list yet other examples from this century, as well as from former times, such as the United States's extermination of Native American populations or the British campaign against Ireland or the Spanish invasion of the Southern-Western Hemisphere.

The term genocide was coined in 1944 by Raphael Lemkin in his book *Axis Rule in Europe*. The United Nations used the term in its 1948 Convention on the Prevention and Punishment of the Crime of Genocide.[1] Genocide is defined as the deliberate and systematic attempt to eliminate a whole people. The Turkish campaign to eliminate the Armenian population is often referred to as the first genocide of the twentieth century. The Holocaust tends to dominate the century's landscape, especially for us in the West. Hitler himself linked the two.

Ironically, as Hitler planned the annihilation of European Jewry, he is quoted as having said: "Who today remembers the destruction of the Armenians?"[2]

The need to bear witness to these two genocides is the focus of this chapter. The call to remember leads to more complicated questions of what is to be remembered, how, and why. Such questions are shaped not only by the demands of those who suffered and died, but by challenges to history and remembrance. I choose these two genocides not only because of the reasons stated, but also because of the role of Christianity and of America. In the Holocaust, the perpetrators were Christian, and Christian anti-Semitism is understood to have played a role in Hitler's ability to implement the Final Solution. In the Armenian genocide, the victims were Christian, and religious differences with Moslem Turkey contributed to its intolerance of the Armenian minority. Many of the survivors of these genocides emigrated to America, which continues to play a key political role in redress and remembrance. I begin my exploration with the Armenian genocide and then examine the Jewish Holocaust.[3]

Before proceeding, it is necessary to remind ourselves of the inadequacy of any witness. We, who seek to remember, find ourselves in the eternal dilemma of having to witness to what is incomprehensible and reprehensible, that which defies our attentiveness and witness. As Leonardo Alishan writes: "though this witness tells the truth and nothing but the truth, it fails to tell the whole truth."[4]

The Armenian Genocide

As narrated in the preface, in the early part of the twentieth century, during World War I, the Turkish government carried out a plan of extermination of the Armenian population within its borders. Whereas the term "ethnic cleansing" was coined to refer to the more recent activity in Bosnia, it is an apt term for Turkey's crusade against the Armenians. Under the banner of "Turkification," the government sought to eliminate the Armenian minority. Estimates of lives lost during the genocide range from one to two million Armenians killed. Few Armenians remain in Turkey presently; most of these live in the city of Istanbul.

A good number of the survivors of the genocide emigrated to the United States and continued their lives in diaspora. As refugees and immigrants, they concentrated on building lives in this new land. They found work in factories, established businesses, married, and had children. They were intent on survival. Success, evidenced through the establishment of families and making a living, was a sign of such survival.

Because of the presence of American and European missionaries in Turkey, as well as the activity of statesmen such as the American ambassador Henry Morgenthau and the British viscount James Bryce, the Armenian "massacres" received public attention. Near East Relief, which directed most of the relief services during and after the war, mounted a major propaganda campaign in the United States to raise money. The popular designation, "starving Armenian," can be traced to these efforts, which depicted Armenians as good Christians who were being brutalized by savage Turks and who deserved to be helped by the civilized Christian West. In this way, the genocide received much philanthropic and political attention in the West, especially in America.[5]

Yet by the mid-1920s silence fell over this past and awareness was lost. The survivors, themselves, contributed to the silence. Sometimes they spoke of the horrors of the past; more often they did not. Even when they did speak, it was most often within the context of their families and communities. Although survivors sometimes wrote and published memoirs, they did so sporadically. There has been a somewhat stunning silence about the experiences of those who died and those who survived. Indeed, oral history projects were only begun in the 1960s when remaining survivors were quite elderly.[6] Donald Miller and Lorna Touryan Miller suggest that survivors became more preoccupied with the genocide as they aged.[7]

Those writing about the genocide today point out that it was only in 1965, the fiftieth anniversary of the genocide, that communal attention began to focus on this past.[8] It was at that time that "Armenian memorials were erected, studies and memoirs relating to the genocide appeared in various languages, and a rising generation took to the streets with placards and chants to remind the Turkish government and the world that the Armenian Question still existed."[9] Even more public attention was drawn by a series of terrorist attacks by Armenians against Turkish officials during the 1970s and 1980s.[10]

In various ways, during the last third of the twentieth century, renewed attention has been focused on remembering this genocide of the first quarter of the century. This genocide is arguably the historical event that most defines the Armenian past for the second and third generations in America. Yet, though these generations may well be able to list those in their families who were killed and who survived, they do not often know details of these narratives. The Armenian American community can best be characterized by preoccupation with the memory of the reality of the genocide, but silence regarding personal narratives and the impact of it on people's lives. That odd juxtaposition has shaped Armenian American awareness and identity. This traumatic past, which has directly influenced the majority of Armenian American families in some way and which holds a certain dominance, has not been faced or worked through.

These issues also greatly affect the nature of remembering and witnessing. What is it the community seeks to remember? Do memories emphasize suffering, loss, and victimization; or survival and even heroism, resilience and new life, or some combination of these emphases? What does it mean to bear witness when Armenians today are removed from the experience and when the vast majority of the survivor generation have died? In other words, how is this memory of genocide to be held and passed on to the future? How does it relate to other memories of the Armenian past and life in diaspora?

Turkish Denial and Allied Betrayal

The texture of Armenian memory of the genocide has also been shaped by a number of historical factors. The Turkish government, through its policies, official pronouncements, and its agents, including scholars, has maintained an ongoing denial of any genocidal activity. No apology or reparations have been offered to the Armenian people. The official Turkish position on this history is that, given the exigencies of wartime, alleged insurrections by Armenians in Turkey, and Armenian alliance with enemy Russian forces, the government found it necessary to put down such uprisings and to relocate most of the Armenian populace. The Turkish government has persisted in this argument despite contemporaneous eyewitness accounts by Western missionaries and diplomats, government documents, and its own "war trials" of government officials during the early 1920s. Eyewitness accounts are dismissed as propaganda; documents and trials are explained away as having been forced by Western pressure.

Turkish denial is an active and ongoing political stance. Edward T. Linenthal, in his chronicle of the history of the United States Holocaust Museum, narrates the discussions about inclusion of the Armenian genocide. Whereas some of that debate centers on the issue of the uniqueness of the Holocaust and the nature and purpose of the museum's witness, Linenthal weaves in and through such debate a chronicle of the Turkish government's "persistent campaign to keep any reference to Armenians from entering the boundaries of Holocaust memory."[11] Pressure was put on both the United States and Israel. In the end, the only mention included in the museum was the quotation by Hitler: "Who today remembers the destruction of the Armenians?"[12]

Dealing with ongoing Turkish denial has occupied a great deal of the energy and attention of Armenians. It has affected Armenian experience and memory on many levels. The Armenian community worldwide continues to react, lobby, and protest against the Turkish stance; historians and other scholars focus much of their work on proving the "Armenian case"; survivor communities continue to struggle to have their experience validated.

This denial has enacted a psychic and political price. Whereas survivors' testimonies function literally as evidence and witness against Turkish denial, that denial may shape the character of the testimonies. Because survivors do not want to give any credence to Turkey's claim of Armenian rebellion, they may tend to emphasize their innocence and victimization, and gloss over acts of resistance. On the other hand, lest Turkey feel victorious, they may emphasize heroism and endurance as signs that Turkey has not achieved its goals, including portrayals of the occasional armed encounters, such as the siege at Van.[13]

These dynamics of denial by Turkey are further intensified by betrayal and abandonment by Western allies, including the United States. Immediately after World War I, British and French troops occupied parts of Turkey and promised protection for the remaining and returning Armenians. These troops withdrew before the vengeful onslaught of Turks and left the Armenian inhabitants defenseless. In 1918, when Armenia declared itself an independent republic and asked the United States for protection, Congress refused the request. This young Armenian republic only lasted until 1920. These acts of betrayal and nonsupport were solidified in the Lausanne Treaty of 1923, which recognized the Turkish republic of Mustafa Kemal Ataturk and its claims to historical Armenian lands. The treaty made no reference "to Armenians or to past promises of a free Armenia."[14] The United States did not ratify the treaty but did establish diplomatic relations with Turkey in 1927. The American government, missionary groups, and the press endorsed the economic and political benefits. As Richard Hovannisian concludes: "The Lausanne treaties in 1923 marked the international abandonment of the Armenian cause."[15]

Such experiences of betrayal continue today as America and other countries equivocate on their position regarding the genocide and continue to court Turkey as an ally. For example, in the case of the United States, Linenthal points out that one or other house of Congress has in 1985, 1987, and 1990 failed to pass resolutions recognizing April 24 as the commemoration day for the Armenian genocide. He concludes: "The geopolitical importance of Turkey as a NATO ally, and the fear of angering such an ally, was judged as more important than official recognition of the Armenian genocide."[16] Although the American government does not deny the genocide, it has not consistently recognized it.

Denial and equivocation influence the shape and texture of memories of the genocide. Such factors keep Armenian American awareness focused on the genocide because the threat of loss is still present. In other words, Armenian Americans continue to feel threatened by annihilation. The dynamics of living in diaspora adds yet another dimension to this threat. Diasporic existence threatens identity by the prospect of assimilation. The memories of the genocide, any Armenian memories, stand as resistance to assimilation. They help to preserve Armenian identity as distinct.

Gérard Chaliand, a French Armenian political scientist, defines diaspora as "collective memory." He observes that "diasporas draw from a disaster as the matrix of their collective memory."[17] If this is true, then letting go of the disaster or reinterpreting it would threaten memory. For Armenians in diaspora, forgetfulness of suffering and betrayal of identity are linked. Chaliand's remedy: "Now, how do you deal with that disaster? The worst thing you can do is to keep it inside and groan and moan like we've been doing for seven decades. Or you can go public, you give it back, cure it, transform it into a work of art, of history."[18] Such suggestive recommendations remain unelaborated and Armenian attempts to deal with the genocide most often continue to follow established patterns.[19]

Martyrdom and Rebirth

On the occasion of the fiftieth anniversary of the massacres of 1915, the Diocese of the Armenian Church of America published a book entitled, *Martyrdom and Rebirth: Fateful Events in the Recent History of the*

Armenian People.[20] The poles of martyrdom and rebirth are apt names for the ways in which the Armenian community and the church in America have tried, and continue to try, to deal with the genocide. These poles define the nature of the community's witness. On the one hand, emphasis is put on all that has been suffered and lost. On the other hand, attention is drawn to the need for vindication through continued existence and even through a triumphalist endurance. Such rebirth, however, continues to be shadowed by the loss and is often viewed primarily as compensatory, as evidence that the Turkish government did not achieve its aims.

The commemoration day for the genocide, April 24, is referred to as Armenian Martyrs Day. The rhetoric that accompanies this designation portrays Armenians, who suffered and died in the genocide, as having been willing to die for their faith rather than convert to Islam as a means of saving their lives.[21] In recent years there has even been a call for the church to confer sainthood on all those who died: that is, to declare them martyrs and witnesses to their faith.[22] Martyrdom does give value and meaning to suffering, persecution, and death. The word, itself, means "witness" and so the designation underscores the importance of witness and remembrance as a witness. But the declaration of martyrdom and sainthood is a particularly problematic strategy for the living who struggled to survive, rather than die. Martyrdom also presumes some measure of choice in dying, which was not available to most Armenians in the genocide.

Another approach to remembering the genocide, related to martyrdom, is lamentation. Lamentation focuses on the loss and the suffering, which is understood to be undeserved and innocent. As Leonardo Alishan notes: "Lamentation can console but can't conceive."[23] Writing of Armenian literature, Alishan suggests: "lamentation, though at times indispensable, is at all times sentimental and often repetitious. . . . It is always a bowl of tears, tears that always overflow the bowl. . . . *It is an infertile and barren genre.*"[24]

Such lamenting of loss is often juxtaposed with emphasis on "rebirth." This emphasis is sometimes triumphal in tone: despite Turkey's best efforts, Armenians continue to survive and to thrive. Success in the present becomes a way to vindicate the losses of the past. The point of remembering the past is to contrast it with the present. Economic and social success in the host culture are taken as evidence that the genocide has failed. Chauvinism about things Armenian is seen as a witness to the past, a boasting and a holding on to culture and tradition, pride and value.

There is a way in which these categories of interpretation have been imposed upon the experiences of individual survivors. These categories became the primary modes of remembrance: Armenians were either innocent and helpless victims or strong, defiant, and even heroic survivors. Both approaches seek a type of meaning for this past suffering. Yet what seems more evident from survivor narratives and oral histories is a lack of resolution regarding the experiences of suffering and loss. The wounding trauma often remains in place; ongoing life is layered on top of the wounds.

In their work with collecting survivor stories, Donald E. Miller and Lorna Touryan Miller have identified a typology of responses by survivors, which also suggest a schema for remembrance. The typology they present includes (1) avoidance and repression; (2) outrage and anger; (3) revenge and restitution; (4) reconciliation and forgiveness; (5) resignation and despair, and (6) explanation and rationalization.[25] Survivor responses may move from one type to another and are influenced by a number of mediating factors, which the Millers cite, including the Turkish government's ongoing denial, the severity of trauma experienced and the presence or absence of mitigating circumstances, future success and life status, and religion. The Millers also found that "survivors often have extremely ambivalent and conflicting feelings that preclude classification."[26] They suggest that the typology indicates the range of responses, rather than a chart for easy or simple categorization.[27]

The Millers propose three constructive responses under the rubric of "moral reflections on the genocide." One is recognition of the presence and role of what they term "the good Turk," those Turks who helped Armenians; another is attention to those instances of "moral heroism" and sacrifice by Armenians when they manifested agency and enabled survival; and the third is "resurrection" through commitment to the recently established independent Republic of Armenia.[28] For the Millers, these three responses function to ease the sense of monolithic evil that genocide breeds, as well as to mitigate the totalizing nature of the victimization. In other words, Turks were not only evil perpetrators and Armenians were not in all cases totally helpless victims, but were capable, even in the midst of victimization, of agency and altruistic behavior. The commitment to the Republic of Armenia and claiming it as a resurrection symbol allows for hope that is about more than survival. In all cases, there seems to be an interest in pointing to the endurance of goodness. That interest is about allowing life to go on, with commitment and hope. It is a form of rebirth that is still shaped by the event of genocide. Continuing to live is the most fundamental revenge for those who feel their existence is threatened.

Further Patterns of Remembrance

The terrain that those who seek to remember the Armenian genocide travel is a very complex one that knows no easy resolution. The Millers' ending on a note of hope stands in contrast to Rubina Peroomian's final words. She concludes her book on Armenian literary responses to the genocide: "After seventy years, Armenian diasporan literature is still unable to confront the Genocide of 1915; artistic expressions of that event still bear the imprint of an enigma, an unencountered terminus."[29] Armenians continue to struggle over the nature of remembering. Those struggles reveal deeper layers of preoccupation: what survivors did or did not do, could or could not do. They lead to questions of power and powerlessness, identity and being, history and hope.

There is no suggestion of resolution in Peroomian's study and though the Millers strain to find an ending, it is the strain, rather than the resolution, that impresses itself upon this reader. The horror of the past stands unresolved, contested, and often unrecognized. In order to bear witness to the suffering and the violence, especially in relation to internal and external denial, there is a tendency to underscore the victimization. Yet the horror obscures the landscape of the past. It is difficult for Armenian remembrance to see beyond the genocide to claim the rest of its history. The horror also functions to drive survivors and witnesses away toward a different future. They seek a type of normalcy as proof that they are alive.

Remembering continues to reverberate between these poles of martyrdom followed by rebirth, a traumatic past, and a desire for normalcy. Does honoring the memories of those who suffered mean reiterating the losses and clinging to the traumas of the past, reinforced by layers of denial? Or is honor to be found in claiming courage and heroism, and celebrating rebirth, as a way to move beyond the past? Remembering the past remains problematic.

Vigen Guroian, an Armenian American ethicist and theologian, argues that Armenian theology offers few resources for this work of remembering. Guroian faults the Armenian Church for its commitment to nationalism and nation building, which has tended to conflate faith and ethnicity, and which has supported political movements seeking justice and even revenge. He sees this as an easy theology of redemption, which is triumphal and which overlooks the cross.[30] Guroian's own proposal is for a theology of the cross, for which he draws upon the work of Jürgen Moltmann and Hans Urs von Balthasar, but most especially upon the liturgy and traditions of the Armenian Church. Guroian points to the form of the Trisagion found in the liturgy from 471 C.E.: "Holy God, holy and mighty, holy immortal/Who was crucified for us/Have mercy upon us" as a key.[31] He argues that the suffering God, who is present in the suffering of the people, is the true source of healing and redemption. Faithful Armenians and the church ought to embrace the suffering God as the one who has already and is still doing the work of redemption. Redemptive remembrance is to be found in recalling the suffering of the people through the suffering of God: "Such remembrance and struggle must be done in the spirit of love and sacrifice as an offering of self in solidarity with all suffering people in this strife torn and agonized planet."[32] Thus Guroian seeks to substitute a theology of the cross and suffering love for the triumphal strains of a nationalist resurrection. Hope is through suffering and not, as the Millers suggest, through the establishment of the Armenian nation.

The struggle for how to remember this past is by no means resolved by these suggestions. They remain cast within the poles of martyrdom and rebirth. More complex and creative hints about ways to proceed can be found in narratives, essays, and other literary responses, such as Arlene Avakian's autobiographical work, *Lion Woman's Legacy: An Armenian-American Memoir.*[33] In this work, Avakian, a third generation Armenian American, describes her family and her grandmother, who survived the genocide and earned the name "lion woman": "I did not think very much about what my grandmother had told me, but unconsciously the knowledge that I belonged to a people who were despised contributed to my drive to get as far away from being Armenian as possible. The family, with its adherence to old world traditions, *was* Armenia. . . . I vowed [to] be like my friends. . . . I would get away from family as soon as I could."[34] She then chronicles a personal and political journey of assimilation, discovery, and activism. Years later she goes to hear a talk by Andrea Dworkin that focuses on the oppression and powerlessness of women, and Avakian's surprised response is:

"Not my grandmother."[35] Avakian writes: "[Dworkin] wasn't talking about me. I was not a total victim. I could act. I could change my life. I did have responsibility for my actions."[36] This experience was a turning point in her relationship with her Armenian past and heritage: "Over the next few months I began to feel that my grandmother's story had had a powerful effect on my life, though I was not at all clear about it. . . . Now I realized that twenty years earlier, when she'd said, 'Tell it to the world,' she had charged me with ensuring that her story did not die with her."[37] But what was that story about? Avakian returns home to record her grandmother's narrative and through the process of hearing and then retelling the story she learns: "There was more to the story, however, than pain and rage. . . . Now I understood her story was about survival. Not only had she overcome her circumstances, but she had resisted victimization as well. The high point of her story was when the Turks came for Ashot and she said no—that they had no right to her son."[38] They took him off anyway and she went in pursuit. After an arduous journey on foot for a couple of days, she got to the town where he had been taken. She used whatever resources she had—friends and connections, as well as her own will and wit—to find a way to retrieve her son and keep the family from deportation. A kind Turkish police commissioner, known to the family, helped by arranging for her and her family to renounce their being Armenian and become Turkish.[39] Her son was eventually returned to her. This renunciation of ancestry was only a public act to enable their survival.

Avakian concludes her recounting of her grandmother's actions: "It had been the knowledge of my grandmother's resistance and survival that had made it impossible for me to accept a feminist politics that focused only on women's victimization. Unwittingly, she'd taught me that, even within a strict patriarchy, women were not rendered helpless."[40] Thus Avakian comes to understand the power in herself and her grandmother, and she begins to tell the story on which she was nursed in a way that does not negate the victimization, but does not focus only on it. Avakian lays claim to the power her grandmother managed to exert even in a situation of seeming powerlessness. Such a process of reinterpretation and reappropriation moves to a memorative narration that remembers the violence of the past, but does not reinforce the victimization. It is not triumphalist; nor does it seek vindication. It seeks to communicate the complexities of suffering and survival, and strives for integration.

Avakian is a witness to her grandmother's story. Indeed, her narrative makes that story available to a wider audience. She remembers it not only through preservation and dissemination, but through interpretation. She attaches to the story a particular set of meanings that grow out of the relationship she has with her grandmother and with her own struggles in life. As Avakian and others from the succeeding generations examine their role as witness, the complex terrain of memory is beginning to be explored in ways that attend to the issues of generational transmission and purpose. How does one remember the suffering and the agency, the being "hated unto death" and the claim to life, the defeat and the resiliency, the irreducibility of the losses and the desire for integration, and even a kind of reconciliation? How does one shift from the problems of remembering to the potential of remembering as a resource for transformation? Avakian is able both to honor her grandmother's experience of suffering and survival, and to transform it into a resource for her own life.

The Jewish Holocaust

Similar questions attend the memories of the Jewish Holocaust. The straightforward command—"never forget"—becomes anything but a simple task once we begin to explore its obligations. The more mysterious admonition, attributed to the Baal Shem Tov—"the mystery of salvation means remembrance"—leads us into yet more winding paths.[41] How do we witness to this event that defies categorization and comprehension? Much has been written and argued about the uniqueness of the Holocaust and whether it must stand alone as an event without compare in history. The motivations for uniqueness and incompatibility seem rooted in a need to witness unqualifiedly to the horror and its incommensurability: there never was or can be anything like this evil. A Christian memorative witness to the Holocaust, because of Christianity's own heritage and memory of anti-Semitism, of which it must continually repent, ought to honor this demand of uniqueness. Christians owe this as obligation to those they have persecuted over the centuries. But uniqueness may be plural. I would suggest that each genocide, each event of mass persecution and murder, has a certain uniqueness and specificity that ought to be recognized.[42] My task here is to attend to the Holocaust in this way.[43]

Hitler's adoption of the Final Solution meant death for six million Jews.[44] Those who survived carry within their bodies, psyches, and souls the deep wounding of loss and of persecution. The horror and trauma persists, for the most part, unresolved and unanswered. Comfort, if not explanation, is sought in remembrance. A type of duty is expressed through remembrance as well: a determination to preserve the memory of those who died and of all that was suffered.

Much has been done to effect such remembrance: museums, memorials, oral history projects, studies, educational projects, university courses, school curricula, many books, films, and much more. In comparison to the relative dearth of scholarship and reflection on the Armenian genocide, the amount available on the Jewish Holocaust is astounding and impressive. Yet more stunning is that all these words do not and cannot seem to resolve the questions of remembrance, not to mention explanation. It is as if the words pour into a vast bottomless container that cannot finally hold this event, let alone any description and/or interpretation of it. The human obligation, however, remains to keep speaking and writing and remembering, lest oblivion overtake us.

During World War II, Hitler's government systematically rounded up Jews and transported them to labor and concentration camps. Throughout much of Europe, Poland, and other eastern European countries, wherever Hitler had established his rule, Jews were vulnerable. This "Final Solution" was preceded by various measures of discrimination and persecution throughout the 1930s, during which Jews were stripped of their rights and forced to wear yellow stars, carry identification papers, and live in poverty and hunger in ghettos. These actions were accompanied by an ideology of Jewish inferiority and Aryan superiority. Jews were seen to be less than human; indeed, they were compared to vermin. Physically, psychologically, politically, economically, and culturally, Hitler tried to destroy the whole Jewish people in Europe. He came shockingly close to succeeding. Many Jews died before reaching labor and concentrations camps; others perished in those camps from disease or from the brutality of guards and/or from subhuman conditions—including cold, hunger, and other forms of physical duress; many, many others died in gas chambers. When the camps were liberated at the end of the war, the survivors emerged as skeletons. More Jews died in the refugee camps set up to tend to them.

A great deal has been written and argued about how much was

known, both inside and outside of Germany, about the concentration camps before the end of the war and liberation. A somewhat mottled picture emerges. The refusal of port to the SS *St. Louis,* which in 1939 carried Jews trying to find refuge, is one bit of evidence indicating that many Western countries, including the United States, turned away and would not face, let alone take responsibility for, what was happening. The ship was forced to return to Europe and discharge its passengers, many of whom were killed. The Allies did know that Jews were being persecuted and killed and gassed, as did the Jewish American community. They did very little to intervene. Yet the horrified reactions of servicemen, as they discovered the death camps, reveal that even if they had known of the existence of mass persecution and execution, they had not realized its extent or its character.

The shock waves of those revelations were felt strongly, but briefly. Although there was general acknowledgment of the Holocaust and offers of aid to survivors, there was not much interest in dwelling on it. Acknowledgment was accompanied by a certain silencing. For the most part, survivors concurred with the silence. Many kept their traumas to themselves. Elie Wiesel, now a major spokesperson for survivors, made a promise to himself to remain silent for ten years. As he puts it, he wanted "to be sure that what I would say would be true."[45] Aharon Appelfeld, another survivor, describes such initial silence: "there was more in that stillness than merely the inability to translate traumatic sights into normal speech. There was a desire to forget, to bury the bitter memories deep in the bedrock of the soul."[46] If survivors talked about their experiences, if they shared their memories, it was among themselves. This reticence seemed tinged with shame: how does one talk about such human debasement among those leading "normal" lives?

Survivors set out to build new lives in new places. Those who emigrated to Israel found little interest in their past among the Jews there. The goal was to build Israel, a new, free homeland for Jews. Those who came to the United States encountered a similar lack of inquiry from the established Jewish communities. Commemorations and memorial services were held for the dead, but there was little discussion, scholarship, and/or education focused on the Holocaust. As Judith Miller sums it up: "The 1950s were years of public assimilation and private pain."[47] She goes on to write: "So most survivors buried their memories by keeping busy. They learned English, built businesses, created new identities, raised families. They were preoccupied not just with survival but with succeeding in this new land."[48] The resilience of these survivors was remarkable, but their trauma and loss remained unattended to, as did the accompanying feelings of grief and shame. The horrors of the past remained with them as shadow lives. Though the task of remembrance was understood to be an obligation, the content of memories lay unexplored.

More public disclosure came with legislation passed by the West German government in 1954 to make reparations to Jews who had suffered during the Holocaust. This arena proved, however, to be a distorted setting for the memories of survivors. These survivors had to demonstrate the harm they had endured to German evaluators whose interest was in minimizing damage. Emphasis was put on what had been suffered and lost; physical trauma and injury were privileged over the psychological and personal. How was the loss to be measured after all? How could one give an account for the loss of the years of one's youth or the loss of one's family?

For many years there was no setting provided in which survivors might name and explore their memories. Their witness and those of others was to the event of the Holocaust, but not to an exploration of it. Scholars of the Holocaust suggest that historically this situation began to change in the 1960s, as was true for the Armenian genocide. Raul Hilberg's monumental history, *The Destruction of the European Jews*, the first comprehensive work on the Holocaust, was published in 1961.[49]

The year 1961 was also the year of Adolf Eichmann's trial. This trial seems to be a turning point in public awareness of the Holocaust. It focused world attention on the Holocaust and what happened in the death camps. It broke open the silence. The location of the trial in Israel linked the present state of Israel with the Holocaust in a new way. As Aaron Hass argues: "During the Eichmann proceedings, the witnesses whose Holocaust experiences had been silenced for the preceding fifteen years were now asked to render precise accounts and encouraged to disclose even the most horrifying details. Suddenly, the country's leaders realized that this newly acquired consciousness of a common destiny was an invaluable asset in consolidating a national identity and promoting Israel's case abroad."[50] Hass goes on to suggest that David Ben-Gurion's motivation for this attention was to show that only the state of Israel could guarantee security to Jews.[51] Thus remembering the Holocaust served Zionist purposes. Such a message was reinforced by the Six Days War in 1967, which both incited fears for the future of Jews worldwide and underscored the necessity of a powerful state of Israel in order to preserve Jewry.

Thereafter, remembering the Holocaust became an important aspect of Jewish identity and history. Since the late-1960s, there has been more and more attention focused on awareness and education, including the development of curricula for schools, the publication of innumerable books and articles, the building of memorials and museums, and the creation of films and television shows. These cultural productions intend remembrance, but they also raise a variety of questions about the nature and purposes of such remembrance. With each production, questions need to be asked and answered about what is to be remembered, how, and to what end?[52]

Listening to Survivors

Since the 1960s more attention has been paid to listening to survivors by eliciting their testimonies. As indicated, some broke their silence and were able to speak of their experiences publicly for the first time with the Eichmann trial. Recognition that the survivor population was aging added impetus to the establishment of oral history projects. Archives were established to house these testimonies. These testimonies, in part, were intended to bear literal and direct witness to the reality and horror of the Holocaust.

Survivors began also to write of their experiences. A few, such as Elie Wiesel and Primo Levi, achieved international recognition and have become, in a way, icons of the Holocaust.[53] Others found recognition in smaller circles. Everywhere, the voice of survivors bore a moral authority that could not be ignored or dismissed. The experience of having lived through the Holocaust became an emblem of Jewishness that carried great weight in certain discussions of Jewish identity and history.

Questions remain, however, about the witness of these survivor testimonies. What do they reveal about the nature of the experience of the Holocaust? Lawrence Langer, in his work with oral histories of survivors and through his insistence that these survivors be heard on their own terms as much as possible, stresses the lack of resolution in survivors' testimonies. In *Holocaust Testimonies: The Ruins of Memory,* Langer portrays the character of the oral and written remembrance, and witness of survivors, as antiheroic and antiredemptive.[54] These testimonies reveal disruption and a type of double existence. The Holocaust experience stands alongside or underneath the rest of survivors' lives, unintegrated and potentially intrusive.[55] For Langer, this is evidence of the irreducibility of the experience and the persistence of fissure. He refers to survivors' use of language as a "lexicon of disruption, absence, and irreversible loss."[56]

Through his study of these testimonies, mostly from taped interviews, Langer identifies a typology of memory that includes common memory, deep memory, anguished memory, humiliated memory, tainted memory, and unheroic memory. Common memory tries to make common sense of the survivor's life and establish connection, whereas deep memory reveals the lack of coherence: "Deep memory tries to recall the Auschwitz self as it was then; common memory has a dual function: it restores the self to its normal pre- and postcamp routines but also offers detached portraits, from the vantage point of today, of what it must have been like then. Deep memory thus suspects *and* depends on common memory, knowing what common memory cannot know but tries nonetheless to express."[57] Anguished memory recalls "the past that may be evoked but not restored" and is wary of the ability to fully image that past.[58] It divides "the self between conflicting claims—the need and the inability to recover from the loss."[59] Anguished memory thus witnesses to discontinuity. Humiliated memory deepens the sense of discontinuity and foils attempts by survivors to construct a unified self. Humiliated memory reveals the past as festering wounds and as "uncompensated and uncompensatable loss."[60] It witnesses to the simultaneity rather than the sequence of past and present; the past is always already present, but not acknowledged in ordinary, common time.[61] Tainted memory reveals the behaviors adopted by survivors functioning as "impromptu selves," as Langer names them, and the inapplicability of common moral standards to their behavior.[62] As a result, he sees survivors living with "the disequilibrium between the impromptu self, which followed impulse in order to stay alive, and memories of the morally dignified life that was the goal of their prewar existence and continues as their aim today."[63] These two cannot be reconciled and so a certain discomfort persists for which the label of guilt is "inadequate and indeed misleading."[64] And finally, unheroic memory enters to salvage "what it can, often transferring to itself unwarranted personal responsibility in order to forestall the unhappy (but accurate) denouement that the drama of the victims was played out on a stage where guilt and innocence had no meaning."[65] Langer warns: "As heroic memory honors the connection between agency and fate, unheroic memory records its absence."[66] He concludes: "For the former victims, the Holocaust is a communal wound that cannot heal"; it is suffered in unheroic memory by "diminished selves."[67]

Langer's important work on the memory of survivors challenges the reader to think differently about memory. Instead of the memories of survivors helping them to establish meaning, purpose, and connection, to integrate the sequence of the events of their lives, most memories function in the opposite way: remembering witnesses to the persistence of disruption and injury and loss. Indeed, for survivors, Langer suggests, memory is "the reverse of redemptive."[68] Langer's motivation is to have us not gloss over the horror, not seek an easy resolution or any resolution of the victimization and suffering. That is an important reminder, as is his warning: "Holocaust memory cannot be used to certify belief, establish closure, or achieve certainty."[69] Rather, the process of remembering puts the survivor back into the experience, undigested and disconnected. For Langer, attending to the witness of survivors requires those of us who listen to these testimonies and bear witness to them, to hear them on their own terms. To do so, we must be prepared to forsake our understandings of order and meaning, morality and purpose, in order to see the unhealed wounds and lack of unified selves that are revealed in the oral and written testimonies of survivors. Langer's work thus bears witness to the inarticulate groans that remain in the souls of those who endured, and which stand, and will do so forever, unanswered.

Yet these survivors are not to be viewed only as victims. Indeed, Langer also points to the present lives and "normalcy" that they have built alongside these memories. Whereas the unhealed wounds have not prevented these survivors from continuing their lives, Langer's point is that the ongoing living has not healed the wounds. For Langer, the wounding is irredeemable pain and loss. The victimization remains intact. In that sense, survivors inhabit two worlds simultaneously.[70]

Langer's witness, grounded in careful attention to the testimonies of survivors, makes us mindful of the persistence of loss and suffering, and the complexities of memory for survivors. His contribution underscores the impossibility of finding a unified or singular memorative narrative into which the Holocaust experience might fit. Langer also points to the extent of brutalization that deprived victims of the Holocaust of agency and choice, and left them with a sense of self as "permanently provisional."[71] This is an apt description for the practice of self that seems to be the condition of those whose existence has been, and remains, threatened in the world. Existence as a self is a creative practice in the moment, for the sake of survival, and a continuing to live with hope for redemption.

Yet Langer, himself, does not seem to fully embrace a definition of self as provisional. His understanding of human agency still tends to assume an autonomous, unified self capable of free choice and even heroic action. Given such a definition of self, there are few examples of autonomous agency to be found in the memories of survivors. Their choices were almost always circumscribed and practical; moral agency was limited. For Langer, memory is categorized as heroic or unheroic. The hero is the fully responsible and free agent who chooses his or her actions and path. Instead, Langer refers to the "choiceless choices" of victims of the Holocaust: "where the situation that consumed so many millions imposed *impossible* decisions on victims not free to embrace the luxury of the heroic life."[72] Such "choices" are choiceless because they are made in a context of powerlessness and lack of freedom—the prerequisites for moral action. I agree that there were few heroes in the ghettos and camps and there was immensely limited freedom, but there were numerous human beings who did make many, many choices: choices which were extremely limited, choices among undesirable options, choices that no human being would ever choose to face. But they did face them, and they did act. When they could, these victims of the Holocaust chose for life: they tried to figure out how to live, how to keep going, how to survive. These were actions of resistance and hope, even if they caused death.

Survivor memoirs describe many moments and instances of such behavior.[73] For example, in *Seed of Sarah: Memoirs of a Survivor,* Judith Magyar Isaacson narrates an event, during a selection, when she was ordered to go in a different direction from her mother—a direction that she assumed would have sent her off to be raped, as well as separated from her mother. She ignored the order and walked in the same direction as her mother. Though she expected to be shot in the back, she was not; she and her mother were able to remain together.[74] Other examples of choice and resistance include stealing food, extending support and care, and hiding away. Frieda W. Aaron writes of wanting to live, for herself and for her mother and sister, and "to survive not only physically but spiritually as well."[75] Harold Kaplan suggests that "even the barest continuance of breath was a form of that resistance."[76]

There were at times horrible choices people had to make, choices that caused difficult and problematic feelings such as guilt and shame. Survivors have often kept silent about these moments because of their shame and because the moral standards they had known did not fit their experiences. They had trouble integrating their Holocaust selves with their "normal" selves or "normal" life before and after the Shoah. Survivors also did not believe that others would understand or accept their lives and choices during the Holocaust. They were, in a sense, correct in this belief—their actions did not fit traditional frameworks of meaning and interpretation.

To be sure, not everyone had choice of any kind. Many were subject to selections and other forced behaviors. They could do nothing other than walk into their deaths. Some did not know where they were heading. There were also those too old or too young or too ill to be able to act in any way. There were others who did give up, the so-called "musselmen." To say that there were those inside and outside the camps who practiced a type of resistance and made choices for life is not to judge those who did not or could not. Such judgment ought not to be applied to those in such situations of deprivation and terror.

Rather, to speak of resistance is to suggest that one needs to use a different lens to see and remember the choices for life that people made. Much emphasis has been put on the passivity of Jews. Emanuel Taney, in "On Being a Survivor," goes so far as to suggest: "Throughout the war there were many episodes when my own efforts saved me from certain death and yet I chose to believe that I was a passive recipient of rescue by others. This is typical for nearly all survivors."[77] It was easier to see oneself as victim than face all that one did or experienced. Emphasis has also been put on a few instances of dramatic heroism, as if to imply that these acts might "redeem" the people. However, if one only looks at the poles of victimization and heroism, powerlessness and freedom of choice, as Langer and others seem to do, then actions of resistance and hope may receive little notice. If resistance is defined only as armed resistance or organized group opposition, then the minuscule daily acts of maintaining physical survival, self-respect, and human and spiritual bonds—in other words, of maintaining humanity—will be overlooked. If there is a fear that the victimization, pain, suffering, and loss will somehow be dismissed if resistance and agency are claimed, then there will be little motivation to look for these actions. If one only uses the measures of morality that are associated with "civilization," survivors will continue to feel the need to hide what they did and experienced.[78] These poles and measures are themselves an inheritance of Jewish memory that need to be examined in order to continue to struggle with what it means to remember the Holocaust.

Catastrophe and Redemption/Martyrdom and Heroism

The history of the people of Israel and of Israel's relationship with God, as recorded in the Hebrew Scripture, may be read as a story of catastrophe and redemption, of disaster and heroism, of martyrdom and rebirth. As Saul Friedlander points out, these are the frameworks of meaning, and I would add memory, that Jews have used for centuries to make sense of their historical experiences. Although the inadequacy of these frameworks for representing the Holocaust is apparent, no other frameworks have emerged.[79] Because they continue in place, these frameworks shape the character of Holocaust memory and testimony, both individually and communally. Questions regarding the behavior and response of victims, concerns about innocence and responsibility, claims of vindication and redemption, are then posed and addressed within the field allowed by the frameworks.

There are, to be sure, problematic concerns if the emphasis is put on one or other side of these perspectives. Herbert Hirsch describes some of these contrasting points of view through revisiting the controversy between Bruno Bettelheim and Terrence Des Pres over the meaning of survival. Hirsch argues that Bettelheim, using psychoanalytic theory: "has little positive to say about survivors. . . . According to his views, the 'best' died; those who survived did so because they were selfish or because they controlled the 'cruder demands' of the body; survivors identified with the aggressor or cooperated with the SS; and survivors regressed to childlike behavior and were passive."[80] Des Pres is critical of Bettelheim for subjecting concrete, historical circumstances to psychoanalytic interpretation that "reads" behaviors through too narrow a lens. For example, a preoccupation with eating is evidence for Bettelheim of regression to infancy; for Des Pres, it is an understandable and appropriate response to conditions of starvation. Des Pres's own emphasis is on how people managed to survive in the camps. A vast variety of behaviors are to be found under the banner of surviving.

Bettelheim, in turn, criticizes Des Pres for making too much of surviving, as well as attributing too much to the "prisoners" agency and behavior. Bettelheim "argues that whatever the prisoners did was of no consequence because survival depended on chance or outside forces over which the inmates had no control."[81]

Hirsch indicates that Bettelheim is not consistent in this perspective and does suggest that prisoners engaged in protective and resistant behavior.[82] Bettelheim's perspective is strained and constrained, however, by his attachment to a heroic model of action, ending in a martyr's death, which occludes more mundane survival behaviors.[83] It is these that Des Pres celebrates, as evidence of resistance and life. Des Pres's survivor fights and chooses in circumstances of great restraint. For Des Pres, the hero is replaced by the survivor, who serves as educator and witness.[84] Bettelheim's approach not only keeps the poles of victim and hero, but finds death at either pole. Des Pres, suggests Hirsch, is reconstructing a memory that is more "life affirming."[85] Such memory seeks a different understanding of human action that is able to recognize resistance and effective action in the midst of victimization, and a different view of morality as rooted in action in context, rather than in the character of the moral actor.

These issues of victimization and survival; powerlessness, agency, and heroism; morality and identity, are present in one form or another in most characterizations of what happened in the death camps and what people did or did not do to survive. I would suggest that how one views the character and behavior of those in the camps will affect how the Holocaust is remembered. Conversely, the motivations of remembrance and/or the need to remember in particular ways will affect how one talks about what happened to people in the Holocaust. If one's memorative narrative wants to underscore the catastrophe, then one will emphasize the powerlessness of the victims. If one wants to point to the failure of the Final Solution and the valor of Jews, one will emphasize acts of heroism and dramatic resilience. As Langer's work reveals, survivor testimonies seek to tell more complex tales of victimization and resistance, defeat and resilience, irretrievable loss and survival, dehumanization and affirmation of life. The threads of such complex tales, however, lose their texture and hue when woven into traditional and limited frameworks.[86]

Such frameworks seek to account for the experience not only in the lives of survivors, but for the people of Israel as a whole. The catastrophe/redemption model of understanding history is the one most often used to "explain" the Holocaust. In the Hebrew Scripture, Israel's "catastrophes" were most often punishment for sin and apostasy. Some Orthodox Jewish responses have offered such explanations of the Holocaust, with accompanying calls for repentance and a turning back to the traditional practice of Judaism. Most Jews, however, recoil from this view in protest: how immense could Israel's sin be to warrant the forfeiture of such life? Many argue that such an explanation tends to "blame the victim." Alternatively, "catastrophe" is followed by lamentation, as expressive of suffering. Such lamentation questions the role of God in the experience of suffering. Lamentation often ends with an affirmation of God's goodness and faithfulness. Others argue that no explanation can account for the immensity of loss in the Holocaust. God has either disappeared or does not care or is a weak monarch, unable to stop evil.[87] There is, then, no redemption possible after the catastrophe of the Holocaust. In a somewhat different vein, Saul Fried-lander argues that redemption language implies a closure on this event that defies any such closure.[88] Instead, he points to the need to balance the seeking of coherent historical narration with resistance to it.[89]

Others, however, insist on coherence in narrative and meaning. For example, the most common use of the catastrophe/redemption model points to the establishment of the state of Israel as evidence of rebirth and even vindication. The Holocaust, in a sense, gave the impetus for Jews and the world to support the Zionist agenda. The Jews who suffered and died are to be regarded as martyrs and heroes. Jews today can honor them by continuing to support Israel. Even Saul Friedlander, who as we have seen, emphasizes the limitations of these explanatory models, ends the memoir recounting his own experiences during the Holocaust with his decision to go to Israel and fight for the establishment of a free, Jewish homeland.[90] For Jews who continue to feel their existence as threatened in the world, the state of Israel represents security. Yet its embattled status also represents the continuance of threat. As long as these feelings of threat persist, there is a reactive quality to Jewish responses, with an emphasis on survival at all costs.

There are those who look for other signs of redemption and vindication outside Israel. Some point to the success of Jews in the diaspora and to the establishment of families, the continuance of generations, and the thriving of Judaism as a religion and/or cultural system. Again, there may be a reactive quality to this striving for success: Jewish survival as proof that Hitler's aim was defeated. The question also remains and haunts: what redemption or vindication could possibly account for, let alone make up for, the evil and losses of the Holocaust?

In the end, existent frameworks cannot hold the immensity of the horror. They cannot provide adequate housing for the complexity of the memories of the past. In other words, no resolution is to be imposed. Paying attention to these complexities and trying to make some sense of the past in order to bear faithful witness, yet honoring the lack of closure and coherence, is a difficult obligation. The frameworks, themselves, need to be examined and challenged. That task is rendered more problematic, however, by those who threaten Holocaust memories, whose interests in revision and denial pose yet more menacing challenges.

Revision and Denial

There are those who would seek to change the meaning and status of Holocaust memories in ways that survivors and all those who seek to bear witness find especially problematic. There are two general categories of such challengers to memory: revisionists and deniers. Revisionists seek to change how we interpret the Holocaust in order to minimize the claim of that past; deniers argue there was no Holocaust. I will examine each movement in turn.

In 1985, when President Reagan went to Bitburg to place a wreath on the graves of German soldiers killed during World War II and it was revealed that the cemetery contained the graves of members of the SS, he set off an immense wave of reaction from those who felt endangered by his gesture. Arguments in favor of the act referred to the need to grieve all the suffering and loss that occurred during World War II. Any hint of comparison between Jewish and German suffering, however, seemed to smack of a reinterpretation of the past that threatened Jewish life in the present, as well as a dishonoring of the memories of those who suffered and died in the Holocaust. This one action by the president of the United States touched the tip of an iceberg of unresolved feelings about the past. Despite apologies that had been offered by Germany and attempts at reparations, there was no confidence that any fundamental change had occurred. The incident at Bitburg supported that lack of confidence. Although Germans desired reconciliation, it was clear that such reconciliation had yet to be achieved in a way that fully recognized their past actions or was satisfactory to the victims. German reunification has created further unease. The more Germany yearns to move forward and leave the past behind, the more those who seek to remember the Holocaust feel threatened.

Yet another example of touching the raw nerve of threatened Holocaust memory can be found in the attention surrounding Kurt Waldheim's election as president in Austria. His successful election in 1986, despite revelations about Waldheim's Nazi past, stirred up many concerns about whether the memory of the Holocaust would be preserved or would be compromised by nationalist agendas and political expediency.

In these cases of historical reconstruction, competing and conflicting visions of what is necessary for reconciliation, healing, and movement toward the future produce tension. Questions of guilt and responsibility add to these dynamics. Who is guilty and responsible, and for what? Are the perpetrators motivated by the desire to duck responsibility by universalizing the victimization—"everyone suffered under Hitler"—or are they struggling to understand what happened and why? What is the responsibility that the present generation in Germany or elsewhere bears for the past? Related questions persist for Jews. How does or should the Holocaust define Jewish identity? Does it keep Jews trapped in a victim mentality rooted in the past or does forgetfulness breed threat and danger? Such questions and concerns are immensely complex, with no easy resolution. As I have suggested, simple—and even simplistic—frameworks of memory have obscured the complexities. Other roadblocks have come from more overt opposition.

Holocaust deniers practice a more extreme form of revisionism. Deniers are those who argue that the Jews were not victimized or that gas chambers never existed. As the Turkish government denies the Armenian genocide, these Holocaust deniers argue that no massive killings took place. Indeed, some deniers argue that the Holocaust "myth" is part of an international Jewish conspiracy. Much of the agenda of deniers seems to be driven by a virulent anti-Semitism. Their goal is to destroy the memories of the Holocaust.

Deniers deploy various strategies to work toward their goal. One strategy is to eliminate teaching about the Holocaust from school curricula or to substitute their own version of history as truer. Another strategy is to place advertisements, often in college and university newspapers, alleging that the Holocaust never happened. Those employing these strategies and tactics invoke the principles of free speech and fairness: if a newspaper or a school is committed to free speech, it ought to let all voices speak. If a school or community wants to practice fairness, then each side should be represented.

Deniers have elicited strong reactions. Deborah Lipstadt's *Denying the Holocaust: The Growing Assault on Truth and Memory* focuses on chronicling and refuting the activities of deniers, especially in America. She begins the book with the story of her refusal to appear on a national television show in a debate with a Holocaust denier. She told the producer that the "existence of the Holocaust was not a matter of debate." To the argument that both sides deserve to be heard, Lipstadt replies that there is no other side when it comes to the existence of the Holocaust, that deniers are not "doing history" but engaging in ideological distortion.[91] Indeed, she uses the term "denial" rather than "revision" because "the movement to disseminate these myths is neither scholarship nor historiography."[92] Deniers seek to rewrite the facts of history, not simply offer new interpretations. They argue the Holocaust, as such, never happened: though Jews died, there was no plan to annihilate them; though Jews were put into camps, these were comfortable settings where the Jews were treated well. Lipstadt suggests that the goal of deniers is to assert that "Jews were not victims but victimizers" who wanted to gain money and sympathy and support for the state of Israel.[93]

Holocaust denial is not only a contemporary phenomenon. It has had its proponents since the late-1940s. Whereas the arguments of deniers seem so extreme that they are hardly credible, they have managed to gain a hearing in the popular press and among champions of "free speech." They have also sought to establish credibility by the use of scholarly apparatus: the creation of the Institute for Historical Review and the use of persons with scholarly credentials to present arguments.[94] In these ways, they nurture the cultural strains of anti-Semitism that persist in the West. Part of Lipstadt's argument is that although the claims being promulgated by deniers are so extreme that many will not accept them, they open the door to forms of revisionism: "Extremists of any kind pull the center of a debate to a more radical position."[95] Deniers create a climate in which other, less inflammatory, arguments will appear acceptable. The result, for Lipstadt, is a dilution of the reality of the Holocaust, by likening it to other instances of genocide or of mass murder, or by mitigating the responsibility of Germany and other countries. Lipstadt fears such "relativism," which "attempts to rehabilitate the perpetrators" and lessen the immensity and atrocity of the Holocaust.[96] She concludes: "If Holocaust denial has demonstrated anything, it is the fragility of memory, truth, reason, and history."[97]

Holocaust denial and revisionism play not only to the spirit of anti-Semitism, but to the desires of those who do not want to face these horrors of the past and the responsibility that attaches to such attention. The reality of the Holocaust is difficult to believe. How is one to imagine the deaths of six million people or the forms of deprivation, brutality, and murder deployed in the camps? The need for balance and a type of normality might cause anyone to "revise" these realities, to lessen their sting somehow. Such normal tendencies of good people add to the vulnerability of truth and memory. Combined with a general disinterest in the past, especially an "unpleasant" past, this is an easy recipe for forgetfulness. The fact that many school children today report they have not heard of the Holocaust, or do not know much about it, adds weight to these threats to the memory and history of the Holocaust.

Memory is vulnerable both to such unintentional forgetting and to intentional alteration. James Young, in *Writing and Rewriting the Holocaust*, provides an extreme example of intentional alteration. He points out that Hitler had plans to build a museum to the extinct Jewish race. Through this museum, Hitler intended to construct and control how the Jewish people would be remembered. Physical extinction was not the end of the road for Hitler; he also wanted ideological control. As Young concludes: "it grows clear that if the first step toward the destruction of a people lay in the blotting out of its memory, then the last step would lie in its calculated resurrection."[98] Unintentional forgetting leaves the door open for those who would exercise such control.

Bearing witness through remembering is an important defense against such forces. For Lipstadt, that witness is to the "truth" of the Holocaust, which retains for her an absolute status, rooted in fact and reason. Yet her distinctions seem at times too absolute for those who seek to witness to the awful reality and the narrated meanings of history. Harold Kaplan similarly argues for truth that is not relative or reduced to power.[99] He roots his perspectives in a fundamental commitment to human rights. Both Lipstadt's and Kaplan's approaches are grounded in liberal commitments to rationalism and ethical humanism. But it is precisely faith in reason and ethical human action that is so shaken by the Holocaust. Friedlander and others grasp for another understanding of truth that remains tentative and critical, but effective. James Young suggests that "none of us coming to the Holocaust afterwards can know these events outside the ways they are passed down to us."[100] In that sense, there is no absolute truth, no history that is not interpreted, no memory that is not shaped by ideology. Bearing witness needs to embrace these uncertainties and complexities, and affirm multiple, even conflicting, truths. In this process, what emerges as authentic memory is that which, as James Young points out, has the "capacity to sustain and enable life itself."[101] Deniers, those who seek to continue to persecute Jews and render their existence vulnerable and threatened, are practicing inauthentic memory, which disables life. Remembering authentically is necessarily a complex process of preserving the memory of all those who died and were victimized, but it is also claiming the ability to go on. It is knowing that, although the event of the Holocaust defines modern Jewish identity, it cannot confine it.

Deniers and revisionists complicate these processes further by requiring those who seek to bear witness to the Holocaust to focus energy on continually asserting its reality and impact. The tendency, when doing so, is to underscore Jewish victimization. Having to attend to denial and revision are complicating factors that detour, stall, and distort the processes of remembering. Even if they never succeed in gaining a widespread hearing for their views, these deniers and revisionists will have established a certain control of Holocaust memory.

The remedy, however, is not to assert the absoluteness of truth over "myth," fact over narrative, but to strengthen witness. Only such witness, expanded in number, complexity, and commitment can authentically carry the memory of the Holocaust. That witness is institutionalized through programs and museums, curricula and books, films and monuments. It is an ethical obligation for all who would argue the truth of Holocaust history.

Christian Witness

Christians cannot claim to witness to the Holocaust without facing Christianity's own history of anti-Semitism. We cannot join in remembering the Holocaust without remembering the ways in which Christianity has helped shape and sustain a climate of persecution of Jews. We are not innocent bystanders, because our religion is complicit with the persecutors. The kinds of ideological arguments that were used to

dehumanize Jews are rooted in centuries of Christian hatred and persecution of Jews, and in mythologies about Jewish character and Jewish evil. Christian inaction during the war did nothing to redeem this
history. Although there were numerous Christians who hid Jews and
were active in resistance, most churches went along with Hitler's policy. Even those churches that protested Hitler's policies did not always
include the Final Solution in their protest. They resisted the war, but
most remained silent about or removed from Hitler's policies of extermination.

For Christians, remembering the Holocaust requires a reformation
of Christianity such that it might never again foster anti-Semitism.
Numerous Christian theologians have been engaged in such endeavors
in the last several decades. For example, Paul Van Buren has sought to
construct Christian theology in humble awareness of its Jewish origins
and its status as an offspring of Judaism.[102] Franklin Littell, Alice
Eckhardt, A. Roy Eckhardt, John Pawlikowski, and Clark
Williamson, and Johann Baptist Metz have explored the history of
Christianity, sought to reform Christian theology, and called on churches to learn and change.[103] Yet others have focused on the peculiar history of Germany, and Luther's contributions to anti-Semitism, as well
as on what the churches did or did not do during the Holocaust.

As these theologians and scholars have argued, Christians cannot
remember the Holocaust responsibly without undergoing repentance
and transformation. Christians, in a sense, have to earn the privilege to
witness. Remembering is not only about recalling the past, but re-membering in the present in a way that pays attention to the implications of
those memories. The theological offerings of this book are meant to
remember in a way that takes responsibility for the evil Christians have
done, knowingly and unknowingly. I return to such considerations of
Christian theology in later chapters.

The Witness of Remembering

In facing the Holocaust, those who seek to bear faithful and authentic witness are caught between the imperative to remember and the difficulties and complexities encountered in any response. As Karl A.
Plank points out: "For the survivor, memory is a form of the wound
itself; testimony, a repetition."[104] Remembering is both necessary and
exceedingly painful. The past stands unresolved and unredeemed. Yet
so much seems to be at stake in the present: the Jewish people

continue to experience identity, history, religion — life itself — as threatened. The threat of forgetfulness and distortion adds yet another dimension to such concerns. Remembering seems more a problem than resource; the questions of what to remember, how, and why are exceedingly complicated. Answers and explanations are quickly rendered inadequate. The yearning remains, however, for remembering as a remedy, or at least an effective deterrent, especially among those who seek to bear witness.

Harold Kaplan writes of such yearning in *Conscience and Memory: Meditations in a Museum of the Holocaust*: "Every memory of the Holocaust begins to strive for replacing what was lost and destroyed. Or to put it this way, we think of the Holocaust in order to deny murder and suicide a complete victory."[105] He also writes: "The true death is the death of memory" and "Resistance is continuous in remembrance, the acknowledgment of guilt, the refusal to repress truth or remain silent."[106] Such instructions are important reminders for those who would struggle, as does Kaplan, to remedy silence through remembering. Anne Roiphe adds further nuance to this process of remembering:

> If we forget we dishonor the past and we dishonor the dead. We have no right to forget or to allow others to forget, but on the other hand redemption is not as simple as mere remembering. Redemption will lie in understanding, in examination, in finding a way to remember that allows the reseeding of the forest, that permits the natural energy of life to take over with its enthusiasms and its partial but inevitable callousness to the past.[107]

Though we may recoil at the suggestion of callousness, Roiphe is struggling to name and maintain the complex realities of Holocaust remembrance: how to remember the loss and still go on — not only as survivors in defiance or desperation, but with a measure of commitment to life and its goodness.

All those dealing with histories of violence and loss, degradation and horror — be they Jews, Armenians, or others — know this struggle. Remembering that focuses only on the loss and horror may continue to render the people only as victims or as perpetual mourners, unable to embrace life and the future. Forgetting, however, tends to submerge, but not deal with, the trauma. How is life to be affirmed without hiding or overlooking the dead and the lost? How are we to acknowledge clearly all the suffering and victimization, yet not totally define those who suffered and died by their pain and loss? How is the trauma, for the survivors, heirs, and bystanders, to be worked through so that it is remembered and not repressed, so that it is not a fixation, or the totality of one's life? How is the historical impact of the Holocaust or any genocide to be maintained without having it become the only defining reality for a people?

In attending to these complex dynamics and the struggle of survivors and their heirs, a multiform process of remembering seems to emerge. This process heeds the imperative to honor the dead and to remember suffering, by recognizing the persistence of an unhealed wound, and yet responds to the yearning for life. It gives due place to the threats to identity and history, and the corresponding challenges and threats to religious faith and spirituality, yet affirms identity, history, and the divine. Such remembering is able to preserve the memories of loss, and claim resistance and power—effective agency—on behalf of the victims. It faces the deaths and losses without avoidance, yet makes possible new and renewed connections in life. Such remembering is practiced by those who seek to witness to the past and embrace the future. Before turning to a further elaboration of the forms of such remembering, we have yet another contemporary call to remembrance to consider.

3

"I Remember;
It Happened"

Retrieving Voices,
Reconstructing Histories

When my grandmother told me the stories of Armenian women leading worship and of girls reading in class, she was giving me my history — a history I had not known existed, a history that validated me in the present and added new dimensions to the bonds we shared as grandmother and granddaughter. The step of ordination, which I was about to take, seemed no longer in opposition to my family and my past. Indeed, my grandmother's gift was of continuity and connection. There were women in the past who had acted in similar roles. I had Armenian foremothers, spiritual as well as biological. My grandmother's revelations changed my understanding of the past and allowed me to view the present, and the choices I was making, differently.

I remember being deeply moved when I began to read Elisabeth Schüssler Fiorenza's book, *In Memory of Her: A Feminist Theological Reconstruction of Christian Origins*, a scholarly tome that few would find emotionally evocative.[1] Schüssler Fiorenza dedicates the book to her daughter, with words taken from Alice Walker: "We are together, my child and I. Mother and child, yes, but *sisters* really, against whatever denies us all that we are."[2] I resonated with the claiming of connection and power against all that would oppose self. Because I had experienced both such opposition and such bonding, I could relate to her sentiments. Soon after reading the book, I preached a sermon in which I told the story of my grandmother passing on her memories to me, and spoke of the work of Elisabeth Schüssler Fiorenza and other feminist scholars who were claiming a past for women. The point of the sermon was that Christianity was not authentic for women until our experiences and our voices were included. Christian history, the Christian story, needed to be retold, as Elisabeth Schüssler Fiorenza had so diligently demonstrated, in memory of all the silent and silenced women who had not been remembered.

The retrieval of women's history and the claiming of their own histories by numerous groups of people, struggling against oppression and toward liberation, constitute a contemporary movement. They are emblematic of a critical project that has the potential, through remembering anew, to re-member us as persons, as a society, and as a religion. Peoples who have been marginalized in society and whose voices have been suppressed are seeking to uncover their pasts in order to claim the present in a different way, and to change the future. They are, in a sense, on a quest for identity and recognition, to know themselves and place themselves differently in the world. At the heart of these quests is a desire for empowerment, to claim and exercise power in their own lives and in the world.

Historical Context

A melting pot society in which differences are homogenized and distinct cultures blended together into a shared identity and unified culture has been the dominant ideological model in America. In recent years, this version of American society has increasingly been criticized by those who point out that there has never been any blending of differences; there was only assimilation that required a forgetting of one's past and one's culture. Assimilation meant conforming to the dominant culture and its narratives that served the interests, not of those marginalized and disenfranchised, but of those who were already in power and intended to stay there. The "melting pot" ideology pretended that differences did not exist, even as those differences were institutionalized as oppressions, in systems of race, class, and sex hierarchies that further disempowered and marginalized those with less power in the culture. An effective strategy of the dominant culture was to encourage "forgetting" of distinctive pasts and identities that might provide alternative narratives or sources of empowerment. A related strategy was to shape those memories through controlling their cultural production. For example, Native Americans—American Indians—were most often portrayed as villains and savages in film and other media. These portrayals then provided much of the "knowledge" the culture had of this history. The emphasis was on the brutality of Indians; Americans seeking to "civilize" the west were the ones depicted as victims, vulnerable to attack by savage Indians. Despite some current attempts to change these images, many of them persist in popular culture.

In the last thirty or so years, different groups of people in American society have set out on their own journeys of discovery, to find their "authentic" pasts, to find their roots. Through uncovering their stories, they hope to define and nurture identities and meanings that seem more their own and from which they might draw power to change their lives and change society. This search for one's own story, for one's own identity, is an attempt by those who feel constricted by the weight of oppression to remember from the present to the past, to discover or reconstruct a historical narrative that can explain and give meaning to present circumstances.

Different ethnic and racial groups are claiming their own histories, as are other identity groups such as women, gay and lesbian persons, and working-class persons. As a result, we are witnessing the pluralization of history. Multiculturalism, as descriptive of American society, assumes recognition of distinct and different narratives and cultures that do and ought to exist and persist together. It celebrates differences and encourages toleration and the acceptance of variety.

Beyond the recognition of pluralism, however, is an awareness of power. It is not enough to uncover and celebrate one's past. An analysis of power needs to be applied to it. An oppressed group retrieving its history is a different exercise from that of a dominant group writing memoirs or tracing genealogies. Reconstructing the past is always also about the present and the deployment of power in the present. When groups such as women, African Americans, or Native Americans, seek to find and name their histories, they are claiming power in a different way. They are claiming voice and recognition in a sociopolitical context that is constructed to silence and submerge them. If conquest is completed when people's memory has been replaced, when they no longer know any other reality than the one being imposed by the dominant power, then the act of finding an alternative tradition is potentially revolutionary and threatening to the powers that be—to the status quo.

Michel Foucault named such processes as the "insurrection of subjugated knowledges." For Foucault, the mechanisms of power are displayed and strengthened through the control of knowledge. Indeed, he sees them as one operation: power/knowledge. The emergence of subjugated knowledges is evidence of shifts in the social arrangements of power. Such knowledges challenge "the way things are" and offer alternative approaches and arrangements. Foucault's project is to offer an analytics of power that explains such shifts and mechanisms. His interest is not in normative claims; he offers no "oughts."

Groups who are retrieving their histories are interested in making such claims. They argue for inclusion of their narratives in a way that would alter the "master narrative" of the dominant culture. Such inclusion leads ultimately to transformation of social relations and cultural identity. Thus the claiming of their own memories by silenced and submerged peoples is a political and potentially transforming act. It not only changes them, but has the ability to affect our cultural self-understanding. For example, during the recent sesquicentennial commemoration of Columbus's voyage to the "new world," there was much rethinking of the way that historical action is narrated. In some circles, that voyage was no longer a celebration of discovery, but a commemoration of conquest and the beginning of the colonization of the Americas by European powers. Such conquest and colonization resulted in the slaughter of numerous populations of indigenous peoples, the destruction of their cultures, and the submerging of their religious and cultural practices. When we in America begin to tell the story of Columbus in this new way, we can no longer claim innocence and/or the childlike adulation of Columbus that my generation learned in school. When we as Christians begin to tell the story in this way, we must take responsibility for the complicity of Christianity in colonization. The Americas were dominated under the banner of the cross; such conquest received ideological justification from Christian theological understandings of salvation and the sovereignty of God.

Those who have identified with and benefited from the prevailing culture need to take responsibility for their compliance with such distorted and oppressive historical narratives. The task is different for those in groups who were conquered and slaughtered. Retelling leads them to reclaim and revalue their own histories and cultural practices. Native Americans are finding rich resources in the past and laying claim to their value in new ways. Yet that past is also one of much suffering, destruction, oppression, and subjugation. The past offers a complicated history of victimization and loss, as well as creation and community. What is to be remembered, how, and why?

As in the cases of remembering childhood sexual abuse and remembering genocide, the task of remembering their own histories by marginalized and oppressed groups is neither easy nor straightforward. The initial imperative to remember, with its promise of the gift of identity and the transformation of culture, leads into a more complicated journey of discovery and evaluation. Along the way, these groups need to mourn the pain and losses of the past: to recognize that the oppression, victimization, and silencing were real and resulted in irretrievable losses, of persons and culture. They need also to sort through their inheritances in order to discern and decide what to claim in the present: what of their histories is of importance and value, and ought to be retrieved and nurtured.

These tasks are complex and ongoing processes. Remembering the past in new ways reconstitutes groups in the present and shapes identity and sociopolitical positioning, but these altered identities and power relations change how the past is viewed and approached. In such dialectical fashion, the cultural narratives are formed and reformed. There are other dynamics to consider, however, which also affect how the past is viewed and, indeed, which past is looked for.

What is one's motivation in searching out one's particular history? Is one trying to indict the dominant culture for the harm it has perpetrated? If so, then one will be searching the past mainly to reveal victimization and oppression. Emphasis will be put, for example, on the stories of European conquest or the brutality of the system of slavery or the persecution of women in order to underscore the suffering. If, however, one wants to transform that suffering or claim a past that is more than victimization, then one may look for modes of resistance within the situation of oppression. In other words, the brutality of slavery did not produce docile, passive slaves, but clever resisters. Another motivation might be to look for resources in the past in order to confirm present directions or bolster present agendas of identity. If so, one will look for past achievements and cultural narratives that witness to creativity, power, and strength, and offer a foundation in ancestral roots. If one wants to emphasize empowerment in the present, then that will lead to a quest for stories of agency, if not a certain dominance in the past: the golden age of African culture or a gynocentric society. In other words, one's particular political agenda will guide the kind of history one seeks to uncover. For example, looking for past evidence of women's liturgical leadership in Christianity or of the blessing of gay unions, is a way to normalize and render less revolutionary the changes one seeks in the present.

The quest for a group's or people's "authentic" past is further complicated by how much evidence is available and the points of view that are represented in the available evidence. Most of the history that has been transmitted to us was written by the historical "winners," so to speak, whether they be men or Europeans or other conquerors or those deemed "orthodox." Our historical memory is thus perspectival in a particular way. The retrieval of their own histories by marginalized and excluded groups is intended as a corrective to the dominant—and partial—histories we have.

It is also the case that those who sought to control the historical narrative often destroyed or submerged or silenced the other voices. For example, there are few texts written by women from the early centuries of Christianity. What is said about women is meant to serve androcentric interests. It cannot be considered reliable evidence. If it is used, it must be subject to ideological critiques and "decoded." Elisabeth Schüssler Fiorenza, for example, suggests that proscriptions about women's behavior—such as women should not speak or dress a certain way or engage in certain activities—ought to be read as indications that women were active in those ways and needed to be controlled.

The lack of texts and other cultural indicators has led historians on a quest for different kinds of historical evidence and for different ways to read the available evidence. The search for one's past has also confirmed the realization that all history is a construction. There are those who would argue that when they go looking for their past, they are uncovering the "true" history of their people, which has been hidden and distorted by others, but always there to be discovered. The more political view is that history is construction and reconstruction, from a particular perspective, and is to serve certain interests. Historical memory, then, is not fixed. Whereas it is dependent on and grounded in evidence, it is also always ideology. Some go further and suggest that history may even be invention. Monique Wittig, in a line claimed by many a feminist in search of a past, offers the directive: "But remember. Make an effort to remember. Or, failing that, invent."[3]

There are yet further complications in this claim to memory, and witnessing to the past. A different dynamic is operative, for example, in the case of childhood sexual abuse where survivors are recovering their own memories of what happened to them. What are the dynamics of historical connection and identity, however, when someone is retrieving history centuries old and continents removed? How am I connected with a woman in the early church or a Chinese woman in the third century B.C.E.? In what sense are their stories my history? Or what history does an African American today share with an ancient Ethiopian?

Such questions and considerations point to yet another complicating dynamic. To what do the identifiers of these particular histories refer? What does the category "women" mean? Who is included and who is not? Or in the case of Native American history, do "Indians" identify as Native Americans or as members of their particular tribes? Is African American history the story of life in slavery and postslavery or does it include a search for African roots and an African past?

All these issues and questions suggest that the task of remembering and bearing witness is not only complex, but politically charged. A choice in one direction means aligning in a particular way. The claim of the past for present political purposes, the directive to remember, carries a liberatory and transforming intent. It is meant to confer identity and change society. Memory is a resource for the present; the lack of historical memory is a problem for those who seek to claim "cultural space." In all these ways, remembering is seen as a political action that empowers.

Implicit in my arguments is the claim that history is memory. This assertion is in itself controversial. Traditional historians contend that their academic pursuit of knowledge of the past is neither a political nor a subjective process. History and remembrance are two separate activities. Those who pursue historical knowledge with a political agenda are not engaged in scholarship but in advocacy. Questions of evidence and verification also arise. Are transmitted memories "true" if the typical means of assessing historical accuracy do not or cannot apply? And true in what senses? Part of the debate around the validity of group histories rests on such questions of discipline and scholarship. Yet such questions also mask the partisan nature of any historical project. I understand history and memory to be one process with different emphases and interests. Historians are more concerned with evidence and verification, with concrete data, memorializers with story and symbol. But in the end, history is also remembrance, and evidence is used both to advocate for and challenge a particular narrative. This brings me back to my grandmother's stories. My father challenged my grandmother's recollection by pointing to what he thought was historical fact: women were not allowed on the altar platform and therefore could not lead the recitation of the Creed. My grandmother stayed true to her memory that was ultimately verified by the picture of nuns wearing deacons' stoles. That picture may have remained "unnoticed" had it not been for my grandmother's turning over of her memory to me.

For those whose stake is in the dominant culture and its master narratives, such movements for change and empowerment will be seen as threatening. A countermovement often ensues that challenges the "truth" of the retrieved memories and seeks to reinstall a narrative of social control that serves the dominant interests and maintains the status quo. Arguments against multiculturalism are designed, in part, to resist the cultural institutionalization of the practice of multiple and particular perspectives and stories in curricula and cultural productions.

In the rest of this chapter, I intend to explicate further such questions, processes, and dynamics by examining briefly two contemporary movements of historical retrieval: women's history and African American history.

Women's History: A Story of One's Own

The old adage that children are to be seen and not heard could be applied to the history of women twofold: women in the annals of history have been neither seen nor heard. The field of history, up until very recently, included little attention to women's lives. Women were invisible and silent. Indeed, Elisabeth Schüssler Fiorenza entitles her groundbreaking book *In Memory of Her*, for the woman in the Gospel of Mark who anoints Jesus. Jesus says of her: "What she has done will be told in memory of her." Schüssler Fiorenza points out, however, that this has not happened. The action of this anonymous woman has been lost in Christian history. Judith Plaskow, incorporating Elisabeth Schüssler Fiorenza's perspectives, looks again at the formative Jewish event, the giving of the covenant, to ask whether women were present. The text points to their absence, or at least invisibility. How would Judaism be transformed, asks Plaskow, if women were included fully as covenant partners?[4]

The quest to uncover women's history, sometimes referred to as "herstory," began with such awareness of exclusion and the desire, if not demand, for inclusion. Women wanted to be seen and heard. As historians have pursued such goals, however, the field of women's history has itself grown and changed. Indeed, the goals themselves have changed from simple inclusion to transformation, from identifying as women to questioning woman as an identity, from claiming power to analyzing the way power is produced and maintained through gender definitions and constructions. In my view, what has remained constant and what is shared is a political agenda of empowerment, though there are differences in what is meant by that as well. To name women's history as feminist history makes the political agenda visible and clear.

In other words, we are reminded once again that history is the story of power. There are, however, very many approaches to telling that story. How it is told, the discursive strategies historians use, shape not only the story, but the lives of those whose story is being told and of those who do the telling. Women, as subjects, are discursively produced through the doing of women's history. It is with this understanding that I will survey some key trends and issues in women's history.

Simone de Beauvoir wrote, in *The Second Sex*, a foundational text of the contemporary feminist movement, that in patriarchal society, women "have no past, no history, no religion of their own."[5] Women are fundamentally Other, passive participants, but not subjects of history.

De Beauvoir's perspective shaped much of the initial scholarship of the second wave of modern feminism. What did it mean to be Other? Was de Beauvoir's assessment of women's lack accurate? Were there no ways for women to be subjects within the confines of patriarchal cultures? Was it possible for the "other" to be included? The pursuit of answers to such questions took several different directions.

One path sought the full inclusion of women in history as it was understood. Though the field of women's history dates from the late-1960s and especially the 1970s, Mary Beard's *Woman as Force in History*, first published in 1946, is often cited as the first major publication in the field. Beard's book seeks to demonstrate that women were present and active in history, that the invisibility and silence of women in available historical records does not accurately reflect women's lives and actions. Beard followed the dominant model of doing history, by examining the lives of "great" women, those who wielded power as commonly understood. Her work begins an approach that has been referred to as the history of "women worthies" or "women's contribution history." This mode of inclusion highlights the agency of women, the ways in which women have contributed to the so-called making of history. An example of this approach from the field of women's religious history is the collection of articles in the volume, *Women of Spirit*, edited by Rosemary Ruether and Eleanor McLaughlin. Its subtitle, "Female Leadership in the Jewish and Christian Traditions," reveals the focus on leadership and on the stories of women who exercised power and so might serve as foremothers or role models for those who want to be included in leadership today.[6]

The authors in *Women of Spirit* find examples of women's leadership despite, or alongside, the patriarchal structures of Judaism and Christianity, which sought to exclude or limit women. Their motivation is the full inclusion of women within those religious traditions. Other historians, similarly motivated, seek to enlarge the historical narrative to recount the agency and contributions of women.

Yet others probe and enlarge the meaning of women as other. If women are always the other in the patriarchal narrative, then their lives in that history are fundamentally ones of victimization. Much work has been done to tell the story of what women have suffered through the rule and power of men. Phyllis Trible's *Texts of Terror* is aptly named as an example of this approach. In *Texts of Terror*, Trible recounts stories from the Hebrew Bible in which women are victimized.[7] Mary Daly, in the Second Passage of *Gyn/Ecology*, offers examples of women's victimization, which she argues demonstrates that women have been victimized in all times and in all places. For Daly, there is no other story for women in patriarchy than victimization. A key example that Daly and other feminists point to is the massive extermination of women in the witch burnings of the early modern era in the West. The witch craze branded women as dangerous others and persecuted them for it.[8] The sufferings of women in history have produced a legacy of trauma that defines women by their victimization and their wounds. The patriarchal history is meant to render women powerless.

Daly's response, and that of some other feminist scholars to what they understand to be the pervasive and harmful dominance of patriarchy, is to embrace the "otherness" of women and seek alternative histories and realities to inform and form women's lives. They see no way for women to be empowered in the dominant culture. Some find alternative traditions within the dominant history by looking for evidence of women's greater participation in religious movements deemed heretical, such as Montanism or Gnosticism, or suppressed religious movements such as witchcraft. Others go further still to claim an alternative gynocentric or matriarchal past, that predates patriarchy and in which women exercised power and perhaps even dominance. For example, Merlin Stone argues for such a different women-centered world.[9] Carol Christ seeks to substantiate the historical antecedents of her Goddess theology in archaeological research and historical evidence that prove there were cultures in which women were central.[10]

In *The Creation of Patriarchy*, Gilda Lerner writes that it is important to posit a beginning in time to patriarchy, so that it is fully historicized and an alternative can be imagined. If we grant that women's lives in patriarchy are always ones of oppression, if women are always constructed as other, then the possibility of something other than patriarchy becomes vitally important to women's sense of self and power. The search for alternative histories is one way to allow for that possibility; another is to question the dominance and/or nature of patriarchy itself.

In other words, history should not be ceded to men. Such a concession in itself works against empowering women. Rather, historians of women need to assert that women were and are in history, and to truly understand history, women's stories have to be heard and included. Women are to be the subjects of history, not only objects. They are not only passive victims, but active agents.

Yet we still need to ask what it means to remember women and tell the story of women. Given the silence and invisibility of women in the available historical records, alternative sources or means need to be used to narrate women's history. Some women's historians turn to different sources to learn about women's lives and experiences. Such sources include diaries, letters, oral histories, art, and archaeology. Other historians and theorists question the way history is done and offer different historiographical approaches. Standard schemes of periodization are questioned, as are categorizations of women's lives into separate spheres.[11]

The Hermeneutics of Remembrance

Since all historical knowledge is interested knowledge, since it is all remembrance and interpretation, historical method is essentially hermeneutics. How the story is reconstructed and what interests the remembering become key factors in trying to narrate the history of women. In her development of a feminist biblical hermeneutics, Elisabeth Schüssler Fiorenza offers a complex and multifaceted approach. For Schüssler Fiorenza, a feminist biblical hermeneutics includes a hermeneutics of suspicion, a hermeneutics of proclamation, a hermeneutics of remembrance, and a hermeneutics of creative actualization.[12] All four are necessary, she argues, if the Bible witness is to be saving memory for women. A hermeneutics of suspicion assumes that biblical texts and their interpretations are androcentric and serve patriarchal functions. They must then all be approached and evaluated critically. A hermeneutics of proclamation chooses to proclaim as the Word of God only those biblical texts that serve the liberation of women. A hermeneutics of remembrance looks at all the biblical traditions and texts to uncover the history of women as a "dangerous memory."[13] The exegete recognizes, however, that the biblical texts do not include the full historical narrative of women's lives in biblical history, so the work of historical reconstruction must include other sources. It proceeds on the assumption that women were present as full and active participants, as well as victims of patriarchal oppression. In other words, a hermeneutics of remembrance reconstructs the truth of women's historical memory as that of struggle: women were both victims and agents in history. They were able to exercise power and agency, and were also marginalized and submerged. Finally, a hermeneutics of creative actualization extends and amplifies the biblical narratives to tell a fuller story of women's lives. Such imaginative reconstruction makes clear that the process of remembering for a specific purpose—for example, the empowering of women in the present—is the key and critical concern.

Schüssler Fiorenza argues both that we need to find women's stories within the biblical narrative and that such an enterprise is not sufficient. Given that the recorded narratives are androcentric in their contents and purposes, women's religious remembrance must extend beyond the available texts if it is to be saving memory for women. For Schüssler Fiorenza, continuity of tradition is maintained not in adherence to particular texts, but in an ongoing process of communal "traditioning." Such continuity is in and through the community of women (and men), the *ekklesia* of women, women-church.

Schüssler Fiorenza's assertion of continuity and connection assumes that Christian women across times and places are related. She grounds such connection in women's shared participation in the Christian community; for example, in a shared historical experience. Other historians would question such an assumption. For some historians, the search for women's story leads them back to such issues as women's identity and women's experience. What is it that women, across times and places, have in common? If too much claim is made for women's experience as particular or shared, or for the nature of women's identity, are not the terms of women's history confining women just as much as the histories that are being challenged? When women's experience is made the subject of history there is a tendency either to focus on the victimization of women—all that has been done to them and all they have suffered—in a way that overemphasizes passivity, or to focus on what women did—the agency of women—in a way that tends to valorize their behavior. What are deemed to be "women's characteristics" are viewed as better, or at least key, to historical explanation. For example, one line of argument has suggested that women's relational nature makes them more caring and nurturing, and this is why women have been so involved in philanthropic work. Others have disputed such explanations as reinforcing characteristics of women that are not inherent, but are the result of social position and conditioning. Still others have tried to explore these "women's worlds" to discern how much women were conforming to social expectations and how much they were engaging in resistance to and subversion of expected patterns of behavior.

The more women's historians have laid claim to the field and its contours, the more complex the question of women's experience and what it means to remember the history of women has become. As women of color in America and women in other parts of the world have begun to give voice to their own histories, they have criticized the field for its white, first-world, and privileged biases. The emergence of so many voices raises even more profound questions about what the terms "woman" or "women" might refer to and if there is any unified or even related content. The quest for inclusion of women in the historical narrative, in order to fill in the missing elements of the past and provide women with empowering memory, seems naive in the face of such complexities. As a result, some historians have shifted their goals from inclusion of women, and even from simple transformation, to a new focus on transforming our understanding, not simply of women as subjects, but of how gender and power function in historical narratives to construct certain significations of "woman."

In other words, the category of woman is in itself empty of content. It is understood as a vessel filled to represent and play out the workings of power. Denise Riley argues that "'women' is historically, discursively constructed, and always relatively to other categories which themselves change."[14] The history of women then reveals not continuity, but instability and temporality. In contrast, the political goals of feminism and the drive for solidarity value and require a common woman's identity, and appeal to a shared experience.[15] Do not such requirements pose the danger of entrapping women further into imposed identities? For Joan Scott, such dilemmas take on the character of paradox:

> Feminism was a protest against women's political exclusion; its goal was to eliminate "sexual difference" in politics, but it had to make its claims on behalf of "women" (who were discursively produced through "sexual difference"). To the extent that it acted for "women," feminism produced the "sexual difference" it sought to eliminate. This paradox—the need both to accept *and* to refuse "sexual difference"—was the constitutive condition of feminism as a political movement throughout its long history.[16]

"Agency," argues Scott, is not a result of the actions of an "innate human will," but of "discursive processes . . . that produce political subjects, that make agency (in this case the agency of feminists) possible even when it is forbidden or denied."[17] Persons, women, then, are sites of such discursive processes. She argues: "To figure a person—in this case, a woman—as a place or location is not to deny her humanity;

it is rather to recognize the many factors that constitute her agency, the complex and multiple ways in which she is constructed as a historical actor."[18] Scott also suggests: "If lines of difference implement relationships of power, they also create identities which can be strategically deployed for resistance and change."[19] For Scott, feminism and feminist history are complex and critical practices.[20]

Theorists and historians, such as Riley and Scott, have elicited strong reactions from other feminist historians who think that women's agency and historical experience are undermined by such theoretical approaches to human subjectivity. These critics suggest that deconstructing women as distinct subjects leads back again to women being rendered invisible and silent. Ultimately, it could play into the hands of those who would argue for a master narrative, albeit a different one from that which excluded women altogether. This time perhaps women's voices will be co-opted by dissolution. Linda Gordon, who debates Scott over the tasks of feminist history, takes a strong political stance: "Only the continued existence of a strong feminist movement will make our own work remembered long enough to contribute to other generations."[21]

For Gordon and others, the history of women is the story of domination and resistance that reveals the ways in which women have exercised power and have been denied power. It is a complex history in which women have been both agents and victims. Scott would not disagree, but would add that power needs to be understood not as a direct expression of agency but as that which produces the agent in an ongoing interplay of social forces and phenomena.

Thus, women's history, which began as a movement to uncover women's presence and voice in history and so empower women today, has come to challenge the term "women," itself. The challenge is a political and theoretical one. The voices of nonwhite and nonprivileged women have raised fundamental questions not only about any claims to a common women's experience, but about the relationship of gender to race, class, ethnicity, and sexuality. They point to an ever-broadening range of experiences and the complexity of factors that contribute to them. Meanwhile, modes of postmodern and poststructuralist thought challenge the very terms "experience" and "woman."

Such arguments change how memory is understood and reframe the question of "false consciousness." As Anson Rabinbach suggests: "The problem of false consciousness gives way to the problem of how representation is organized."[22] It also cuts through the tendency, found in theorists such as Mary Daly, to categorize women as real or not real, subjects or subjected. Rather, every historical context is analyzed for the ways in which women's identity is produced and represented, along with the ways in which women conform to, subvert, and/or transform given definitions and situations. Such analyses reveal multiple forms of women's victimization, resistance, and struggle for life.

Clearly, if we let go of the notion of a unified narrative of feminist and/or women's history, there are dangers of endless splintering and oblivion. One of the lessons of the past is that a feminist agenda is easily lost and forgotten. The doing of women's history is ultimately a dance between analysis and claim, assertion of presence and power, and manifold challenges to such assertions. Some of the challenges may lead to more graceful dancing; others may maim. The task of analysis and historical discernment is to name the difference.

Only through such dancing may history be claimed as memory that informs the struggles of women in the present. The continuity, it seems to me, is in the struggle. It begins in a political commitment to exercise power in order to transform the social order for the good. It is rooted in, and results in, faith—a faith in the process and possibilities born through struggle. In a circular fashion, such faith becomes the basis for claiming the past as memory for the present and future. The remembering engenders connection among women and not vice versa. Women's history is first and last a political struggle for what shall be remembered and how. The problem of women's history becomes a resource when the tentativeness and contradictions, which always attend struggle, are embraced. For women in Christian history, Christianity is revealed as a hegemonic discourse serving the interests of dominating powers at the same time that it is claimed as an oppositional and subversive discourse. The production of women's history in Christianity as memory for today is a way both to unmask Christianity's hegemony, as well as to discover and expand Christianity's transformative potential.

Contradictions attend understandings of what is meant by women, by experience, and even by subject, in history. Some would claim that a common women's identity, the self-evidentiary nature of experience, and a unified and stable notion of subjectivity are necessary for the writing of women's history and for the project of empowerment. An analytics of power, however, raises fundamental questions about each of these claims and whether, rather than contributing to empowerment, they do not lead to reenacting some of the dynamics and discourses of exclusion and domination that are being contested. As Judith Butler argues: "To establish a set of norms that are beyond power or force is itself a powerful and forceful conceptual practice that sublimates, disguises, and extends its own power play through recourse to tropes of normative universality."[23] To posit women as subjects and agents in a nonhistoricized way is to risk reinscribing problematic and disempowering definitions of identity and society. To understand the project of empowerment as including an analytics of power, so that all definitions and significations are questioned and subject to analysis, is ultimately to safeguard agency. Then the contradictions and paradoxes that history offers become not simply problems, but possibilities.

The field of women's history, which began as a quest for "herstory," for memory of and for women, has come to a much more complex understanding of memory. Feminist historians are now arguing that women's past is not to be read only as a story of suffering and oppression, meant to indict the dominating powers and remind women of all that has been endured and lost. Neither is it simply the story of women's resistance and alternative practices of agency. Rather, the past is a field in which women and men were being defined and confined by relations of power. The transformative power of memory is realized through women's recognition that remembering is for the sake not only of recalling, mourning, honoring, and celebrating the past, but of constructing lives today. The measure of women's historical practices will be whether they produce memories that enable life and wholeness for women.

When I saw the picture of Armenian nuns who were also deacons, I "read" us as sharing a history in which women struggled for religious leadership. I produced their identities as continuous with mine. My reading met my need for a sense of women forebears, but it said nothing about how those women saw themselves or would see me. The memory that women's history produces is for today, even as it looks to the past for resources and insight.

African American History: The Legacy of Slavery

The biblical injunction, "remember, you were slaves in Egypt," holds special meaning for African Americans. The great majority of African Americans share a common heritage: their forebears came to this continent as slaves. This history of slavery is a defining factor in the narrative of African American presence in this country. It is a root experience. The imperative to remember grows from that root, planted deeply in soil that continues to be fed by oppression and racism. Remembering the experience of slavery and its historical legacies is both a problem and resource for African Americans today. How African Americans remember their slave past and relate it to the present, how they tell the story of who they are as Africans and Americans, is a complex and highly charged political process. How white Americans remember slavery and relate it to the present is critical to the process and its dynamics. The failure of contemporary white Americans to accept responsibility for the slave past keeps slavery in the national consciousness. It reinforces the need for African Americans to remember the horrors and sufferings of slavery, at the same time that they look in the past for resources that might nurture life after slavery and beyond oppression.

The legacy of slavery and the era of Jim Crow left African Americans with an inheritance of trauma and oppression. The threats that African Americans feel are to their persons, their identity, their social existence, and even their souls. At the same time, numerous African Americans can claim a quality of life, even a flourishing life, as evidenced in social, economic, political, artistic, and other cultural expressions.[24] As is true for the heirs of the genocides we examined in chapter 2, the descendants of slaves live with the layered realities of historical trauma. The Civil Rights and Black Power movements of the late-1950s, and especially the 1960s and 1970s, generated a political consciousness that shifted expectations and raised hopes for a transformed future. The echoes of Martin Luther King's "I have a dream" and of the Black Power movement's "black is beautiful" reverberated in the souls of African Americans. The black theology movement grew in response, as did more attention to African American history and culture.

African Americans wanted to name and own their history in new and different ways. The backdrop to all such movements and attention, however, was the originating African American slavery experience. How did it relate to the quest for dreams and beauty and power in the present? How were African Americans today to remember and position themselves in relation to that past and its legacies? Looking to the past for resources, African Americans uncovered basic problems as to who they were and what it meant to claim their past.

These problems exist on many levels. I will briefly touch on two as emblematic of the struggles African Americans face in remembering themselves and their peoples. One concerns the status of the history of slavery and whether that ought to be claimed as one's "true" history at all. The other asks: if slavery is a key part of their past, how ought it be understood, told, and passed on? At the end of her novel, *Beloved*, which so vividly portrays and narrates the traumas of slave life, Toni Morrison includes a repetitive refrain: "It was not a story to pass on. . . . This is not a story to pass on."[25] Yet the novel is precisely that, the passing on, in the hope that in the telling and the sharing a new relationship with the past might emerge. In the novel, change begins to emerge from confronting the ghost that symbolizes the heart of the traumatic past. For Morrison and others, it is through the remembering, as horrible and life threatening as it might be, that a healing may begin. As Paul D, a former slave in the novel, says to Sethe, the mother of Beloved: "me and you, we got more yesterday than anybody. We need some kind of tomorrow."[26] Any tomorrow arises from remembering and through sustaining relationships. The characters in *Beloved* mediate life to one another. They support one another. Such claiming of life and care after slavery, which tried to dehumanize African Americans and break the bonds of human affection and commitment, is both a form of resistance and an act of hope.

There is yet another dynamic to the problem of remembering the past for African Americans. Given that the institution of slavery was intended to condition and indoctrinate African Americans into another culture, one in which they had no standing as free and full persons, life in America can be said to carry a certain alienation from their identity and culture. To remember their own history and culture, African Americans ought to draw upon the history of blacks in America and also look to Africa. Afrocentrism seeks to lay claim to an identity, history, culture, and even religion that is authentically African.[27]

Afrocentrism is a recovery movement in two senses of the word. It seeks to recover what was lost or stolen, and it wants African Americans to recover from cultural alienation and live more fully and authentically. Afrocentrism glorifies the African heritage and sees it as a rich source of life for African Americans. African customs are adopted to give expression to this heritage. Historical research seeks to uncover both the roots of the African American experience in Africa and to extol the contributions of African peoples to culture worldwide.[28]

Although Afrocentrism is a fairly recent expression, it has connections with past movements among blacks in America. There have always been those who advocated a return to Africa as the true home of those brought here in chains.[29] In the extreme, advocates of Afrocentrism tend toward the contention that black life in America is false. The history of blacks in America is seen as a distortion of what it means to be African American.

For the most part, however, proponents of Afrocentrism are not that extreme and have no intention of leaving America. Rather, they are seeking to replace or augment the remembrance of African Americans with a cultural legacy that is not Eurocentric. In that sense, Afrocentrism is a strategy of resistance, which rejects accommodation to the perceived dominant American culture.

The history of slavery is viewed as a memory of suffering that needs to be left behind or, at least, moved off center stage. Boldly stated, Afrocentrists do not want African Americans to remember they were slaves, but to remember they were founders of great cultures and leaders of large societies. More gently stated, Afrocentrists want to make sure that the resources for life and flourishing of African Americans include those offered by their African heritage, an alternative history to that of slavery. Afrocentric memory functions as oppositional to that which emphasizes black suffering and oppression. The memory of Africa is most often seen as positive, a heritage which bears good fruit in America.

Afrocentrism may have appeal and offer certain resources, but most African American historians and thinkers remain focused on black life in America, including the history of slavery and poverty, oppression and racism. The contours of African American history are, then, to be mapped on that terrain of trauma and injury, as well as survival and struggle. How is the story of slavery and its aftermath to be remembered and told? And how does it influence the present and the way in which African Americans conceive of themselves? At the heart of such questions are the status and meaning of suffering, and the dynamics of victimization and injury.

Slaves as Victims and/or Resisters

How victimized were slaves and what were their responses to the condition of slavery in America? For many years there persisted a popular conception of slaves as docile and lacking in agency. Whether due to conditioning or natural inclination, being black and being in servitude seemed to go together. Black "adaptation" to slave culture included a type of attachment to and identification with their oppressor.

Christianity, the religion of slaveholders, became that of slaves, and served to encourage their docility. Slaves were taught to believe that acceptance of their earthly condition would be rewarded in the next life. Hopes and dreams of freedom were deferred; heaven became the locus of compensation for present suffering. Negro spirituals were cited as offering evidence for such viewpoints. During my elementary school education, I was taught such interpretations of the spirituals we sang: "Swing low, sweet chariot, coming for to carry me home" was about getting to heaven and yearning for release from the hard lot of slavery in this life.

This view of slave life fits well with the ideology of slavery itself. At worst, blacks, resigned to their situation as God's intent, suffered in silence; at best, they were passively obedient. Occasional incidents of overt rebellion could be used to verify this view. They were not only few in number, but represented a type of heroic action that would remain inaccessible to the majority of slaves. These rebellions most often failed. Insurrectionists such as Nat Turner were defeated; runaway slaves were caught and punished severely, if not killed.

In recent decades, especially since the Civil Rights and Black Power movements, renewed considerations of slave life and culture have produced alternative narratives and views. No longer are slaves portrayed as passive participants in their victimization, or as heroes in a dramatic sense, but as resisters and agents who did their best in very limiting and punishing conditions to maintain life and even value. Reconsiderations of the structures and culture of slave life have resulted in very different readings of the same behaviors and texts. For example, the spirituals are not songs of resignation and deferred desire, but of resistance and clever communication. The act of singing them, in groups together, provided support and soul sustenance during times of hardship. Lawrence W. Levine points out:

> The religious music of the slaves is almost devoid of feelings of depravity or unworthiness, but is rather . . . pervaded by a sense of change, transcendence, ultimate justice, and personal worth. The spirituals have been referred to as "sorrow songs," and in some respects they were. . . . But these feelings were rarely pervasive or permanent; almost always they were overshadowed by a triumphant note of affirmation.[30]

Moreover, the words of the spirituals served as a coded language to pass information along about secret meetings or plans to run away.

"Canaan" was a reference to the north; "home" meant freedom in the north. The singing of spirituals was a form of communication and sustenance that slaves could practice right in front of their masters.

Albert Raboteau's work on slave religion has also affected previous perceptions about Christianity and slavery. He shows that slaves did not accept Christianity right away; slaveholders were often wary of allowing their slaves to become Christian, because of the implications for freedom and even equality. When slaves did embrace Christianity, they fashioned their own practices. What Raboteau called the "invisible institution" has become a label for the hidden ways in which slaves took Christianity and made it their own. Secret meetings for prayer and singing helped them express their injury and sorrow; Bible stories, especially that of the Exodus, offered a type of coherence to the inexplicable nature of their condition in life; and particular practices, such as conjure, provided ways to survive and assert themselves.[31]

Recent scholarship has turned to other dimensions of slave life to ascertain how slaves understood their lives and acted in them. Available slave narratives recount how blacks in slavery remember their experiences. Some reveal dramatic stories of resistance, even when such resistance produced its own suffering. For example, Harriet Jacobs (pseudonym Linda Brent) runs away from a master who tries to exploit her sexually, and hides in a crawl space for almost seven years. As M. Shawn Copeland observes in her treatment of Jacobs's and other slave women's stories: "These are narratives of affliction, but not narratives of despair; the women may be caught, but they are not trapped."[32] Copeland goes on to survey the resources of resistance these women display in their narratives, such as "sass"—the use of language to challenge and claim authority and power.[33]

The authors of *Cut Loose Your Stammering Tongue: Black Theology in the Slave Narratives* also examine slave narratives to find what they reveal about black life, theology, and ethics. Dwight Hopkins finds displayed in the narratives a "culture of resistance" characterized by an ethic of taking/not-stealing, which allowed slaves to "steal" what they needed; a "duality of survival," which consisted of "a conscious false display of the slave self in the company of the white master and an authentic expression of the true African American self in the presence of fellow enslaved blacks"; and a "discourse of solidarity," which meant that slaves did not tell on one another and covered for one another.[34] In the same volume, George Cummings claims an even bolder purpose for looking at the slave narratives and practices. They are resources, providing "raw data" for "a counter-hegemonic theological perspective."[35] Cheryl Sanders offers a somewhat different perspective. The evidence of the slave narratives is not so unambiguously clear to her. She implies that it is our contemporary lens of liberation that hears and reads these testimonies in a particular way. Her own reading of four narratives suggests a diversity of responses to the experience of slavery, from somewhat positive, to ambiguous, to negative, usually depending on the way the slave was treated. What these testifiers do agree upon, however, is that slaves did not view Christianity as supportive of slavery. Sanders found not an ethic of submission, but one of liberation.[36] Thus whatever the experience of slavery and however it might be witnessed to, there is little evidence that slaves accepted the condition of slavery with submission and passivity. When submissive behavior is deployed, it is part of a strategy of resistance, supported by and expressed through Christianity.

Contemporary scholarship claims to have uncovered yet other forms of resistance used by slaves that have been overlooked or misinterpreted in the past. For example, tales about trickster figures, such as Brer Rabbit, narrate strategies of cunning and ways to outwit those with more power. Voicing a shared perspective, David Goatley observes: "The trickster tales were obsessed with the weak manipulating the strong, reversing the structures of power. . . . Trickster tales were particularly used to redefine the realities of life in bondage."[37] Other folk tales and myths are also read as supporting resistance and alternative visions and memories. Practices of acting deceitfully toward masters and cooperatively among themselves reveal a distinctive slave ethic. In all these ways, the lives of slaves witness not only to brutality, but to resilience, not only to a traumatic past of suffering and tremendous loss, but one of effective agency for survival. "Slave folk," writes Lawrence W. Levine, come to be viewed "not as inarticulate, impotent historical ciphers who were continually being acted upon by forces over which they had no control but, rather, as actors in their own right who, to a larger extent than we previously imagined, were able to build a culture, create alternatives, and affect the situation they found themselves in."[38]

Remembering the Slave Past Today

Remembering slavery in the contemporary struggle for liberation from oppression and racism seeks to maintain both emphases—to indict the dominant culture for the suffering of black people, and to claim black life as a positive resource. Such remembering attempts to find ways to empower African Americans in the present, for the future, in relation to the past. Such memorative practices are not without challenge, both from within and without the African American community. From within the African American community, such challenges are rooted in the question of empowerment: what kinds of remembrance do indeed empower? What status should past suffering be afforded? These questions cannot, however, be divorced from the racist context that continues to prevail in America. In this sense, African American thought is reactive and shaped by outside challenges.

Cornel West outlines four traditions of African American response to racist discourse: exceptionalist, assimilationist, marginalist, and humanist. Exceptionalist responses assert the uniqueness of African American culture. Some exceptionalists claim black superiority; others assign moral good to the community because of what it has endured and survived. Assimilationists argue the opposite: that African Americans are inferior, either ontologically or sociologically, and their culture ought not to be embraced. Marginalists suggest that African American culture is too narrow and constraining. Humanists argue for the distinctiveness of African American culture, which neither regrets nor romanticizes the past as the other approaches do. The humanist response enables a critically evaluated reconstruction of the past. The other traditions tend to approach the past uncritically and simplistically—either to embrace or reject or delimit it. All forms of response are dealing with the dynamics of remembering, but not always, West would argue, in a way that enables appropriate empowerment. West sees the humanist as the most adequate for that task. He concludes by positing: "A present challenge confronting black theologians is to discover and discern what aspects of Afro-American culture and religion can contribute to a counterhegemonic culture in American society."[39] Since the racist culture persists, empowerment must be framed as counterhegemonic. The other responses do not adequately challenge the racist context and, therefore, West would suggest, produce distorted practices of remembering.

Among those who question the nature of what ought to be remembered are many Afrocentrists. An adequate remembrance of the past, they argue, ought to include the African heritage. In that sense, the history of slavery in America is either marginalized or shrunk in importance. What African Americans need today is not to focus so much on the history of slavery, except as fuel for rejecting the hegemonic American culture, but to embrace and enhance the distinctive forms of African and African American culture.

Other internal challengers question the status and value afforded to suffering in black thought. These challengers ask whether and how memories of suffering ought to be emphasized. So much of black theological and social thought, especially as informed by Christianity, assigns meaning and redemptive significance to suffering. Contemporary thinkers are beginning to question such remembrance. Anthony Pinn, rejecting any approach that gives positive value to suffering, sees the notion of redemptive suffering as incompatible with a goal of liberation. Surveying the long tradition of black redemptive suffering from the spirituals to contemporary black theology, Pinn embraces black humanism as the more adequate response. Black humanism "seeks to intimately connect Black Americans to the larger web of human existence."[40] For him, the remembrance of suffering as having value and purpose and "redemptive qualities" gets in the way of the community's energies being totally focused on social transformation.[41]

Victor Anderson questions the status of suffering and the remembrance of suffering from another approach. He argues that the ways in which the African American community remembers its past and thus itself are not adequate to the realities of African American life today. Anderson proposes that "ontological blackness," the concept by which African Americans understand who they are, is formed in and through the past of slavery and suffering, poverty and oppression, in a way that reifies race. For Anderson, "ontological blackness signifies the blackness that whiteness created."[42] He goes on to argue that African American thinking is stuck between poles of slavery and freedom, struggle and survival, that remain eternally oppositional and that make it difficult for African Americans to achieve "cultural fulfillment."

Black theology is caught in the same dilemma: "The new being of black theology remains an alienated being whose mode of existence is determined by crisis, struggle, resistance, and survival—not thriving, flourishing, or fulfillment. Its self-identity is always bound by white racism and the culture of survival."[43] For Anderson, this situation constricts African American life. Cultural fulfillment, on the other hand, seeks satisfaction and is rooted in hope and the possibility of human flourishing. Not all blacks, Anderson contends, experience the same thing or the same kind of oppressions. The pluralism of black experience needs to be recognized in a way that ontological blackness does

113

not allow. For Anderson, what is needed is "cultural transcendence from the blackness that whiteness created."[44] There is similarity here to the feminist historical project of questioning and emptying the identity of woman from any specific content. Anderson is suggesting that racial identity has not only been constructed with a specific content, but one that is determined by whiteness and its cultural categories, including notions of genius and heroism. The realities of postmodern black life stand in contradiction to these definitions.

Thus the practices of remembering that emerged in the face of threats to social and historical existence, to body and soul, are themselves being questioned and viewed as problematic by those who seek to define the present and future differently. These challenges complicate the task of remembering, even as they suggest different possibilities. An issue that cuts through a number of the challenges is the status of Christianity. Much of the earlier scholarship on black life viewed Christianity as integral to what it meant to be African American and the church as the central institution not only for religious but also for social and political life. Debates have raged about how much African elements were and are preserved and present in the Christianity practiced by African Americans. Debates have also raged about the role and efficacy of the church. The view that seems to be emerging, which is argued by such theorists and theologians as Donald M. Matthews and Dwight N. Hopkins, is that remembering African American religion requires naming and claiming the African elements that make it distinctive and that support an identity that is not Eurocentric.[45] This challenge is posed not only to the historical black church, but to the black liberation theology movement. Another perspective being given voice, as exemplified by Cheryl Sanders, is the need for black liberation theology to move beyond exclusive concern with suffering and victimization, in order to develop "an ethics for blacks who are 'in charge' of their own institutions and resources."[46]

Meanwhile, external challenges have not disappeared. Many would argue that African American life continues to be threatened and that the hegemonic discourses that produced this racist culture continue to function in overt and subtle ways. Those who argue for black inferiority and weakness persist. The type of thinking that condoned and supported slavery gets updated and translated into more scientifically and sociologically sophisticated forms and is regularly reproduced in this country.

Those who challenge affirmative action and so-called entitlement programs imply that there is no institutionalized racism in this country. Some would even argue that such programs reinforce racism.[47] The recent debate over apologizing for slavery raised numerous issues, including the argument that slavery is in the past, over and done with, and should not be "brought up" again. A related argument is that the forebears of the majority of Americans today did not even come to America until after the era of slavery. All these arguments intend to silence and make invisible African American voices that would indict this country for its racism and would seek to hold in remembrance the suffering and oppression, as well as the resistance and ongoing struggles, of black people. Donald H. Matthews refers to the "amnesia of white America" and "the privilege of power" that allows it.[48] Yet, Matthews argues, the trauma birthed in slavery is an ongoing legacy: "Any offense, from the Rodney King beating to the Mark Fuhrman testimony, can revive the memory of a centuries-old psychological trauma that America has yet to atone for in any meaningful manner."[49]

Toni Morrison's novel *Beloved* draws on such tensions. The ghost of Beloved, whose dying represents the exacting toll of the brutalization that was slavery, continues to haunt Sethe. Nothing is right. Even though slavery is over and the black characters in the book are theoretically "free," they carry around with them the legacies of that past as if they are chains. These chains keep some of them, such as Sethe and her daughter, Denver, bound to one place, while others are bound by hatreds and haunting memories. Any promise of salvation exists beyond the property that Sethe and Denver inhabit.

In the novel, the church is a marginal institution, providing service only at the time of death and other moments of transition. Even the clearing, where Baby Suggs, Sethe's mother-in-law, would preach her own hybrid of Christian and African "gospel" is empty now. No one gathers there anymore. The community has dispersed due to resentment that emerges after an event reminiscent of the heavenly banquet but whose effect is the opposite. The sharing of bounty does not knit the community members together, but reveals all the rips and tears in their social fabric, which then unravels into a heap of tangled and loose yarn.

The threads begin to be gathered again after Paul D's arrival. The story of the past emerges in a memorative retelling, as Sethe "rememories" it. Paul D has his own past to remember and share. He thinks his arrival has banished the ghost, but she reappears, alive, in mourning, and with "new feet." She takes up habitation and torments them all in different ways. The path toward the possibility of healing, toward feeling hope, is not easy or direct; the past has to be faced in new ways. This requires courage and risk on the part of everyone. It requires connection. Denver goes out to make the first connection. Those who dispersed in resentment and judgment gather to exorcise and bless. Paul D returns "to put his story next to" Sethe's.[50] The novel ends with the sense that tomorrow will be gentler and more whole than today, though the past will never disappear. Its scars are like Beloved's footprints, which "come and go, come and go."[51]

When Toni Morrison describes Baby Suggs's preaching she writes: "She told them that the only grace they could have was the grace they could imagine. That if they could not see it, they would not have it."[52] The retrieval of history by African Americans, especially the history of slavery, is a struggle for imagination. Sometimes African Americans seek to look away from Europe and the United States and toward Africa; sometimes they cannot bear to look too closely at the sufferings of the past, and at other times they cannot seem to turn their gaze away. Sometimes they put the search light out for heroes and role models; other times they look for clues beneath and beyond the available cultural forms. Yet other times they are distracted by voices assaulting them in the shadows and wonder if there is light enough to see toward the horizon. Their sight is often restored by religious and cultural resources, and relationships with family, ancestors, and one another. And they go on, weaving remembrance with imagination, in the knowledge that grace is both gift and struggle.

Summary

I have tried to demonstrate the importance and difficulties of retrieving cultural histories by those who have suffered in history and whose stories have been submerged beneath dominant discourses serving other interests. The complexities of such historical reconstruction and narration are many and strong, as are the differences among and even within particular movements and groups. What is shared, however, is the claiming of memory as both problem and resource in the struggle for identity and hope. The initial problem of memory as erasure and silencing gives way, in the processes of retrieval, to other questions about remembering, especially those of authenticity and effectiveness. What are the legacies and stories to "pass on"? How will remembering make a difference? The initial claim to memory as a necessary practice in the face of threats to existence and identity leads into more complicated questions about what constitutes identity and what kind of existence is desirable. Questions are also raised about the nature of history and the relationship of history and memory.[53] A group may be preoccupied with the status of memories of suffering and with the pain of the past and its ongoing legacy, or it may focus on the resilience and agency of those victimized. Sometimes the desire to claim agency leads to grander notions of heroism. Group narratives then chronicle past glories and powers. Debates rage about the mythic or historical nature of such deeds, exploits, and accomplishments.

Yet what also emerges from this complex chorus of conflicting and competing voices that wane weak and grow strong is the desire to make a way toward transcending the past and its pain, its losses, it oppressions, its trauma. The desire is even to transcend the practices of resistance toward connection, imagination, new definitions, and renewed identities. The truth and validity of such connections, visions, and ways are tested by their ability to enable life and hope, delicately held in the midst of ambiguity. The project of remembering the past is for the sake of finding oneself and one's people in the present and for the future. This is remembering for life connection and wholeness. As Albert J. Raboteau witnesses in a retrospective essay: "I felt that in the recovery of this history lay the restoration of my past, my self, my people."[54] He concludes with the assertion that memory, story, and ritual are "all ways of re-membering a community broken by hate, rage, injustice, fear."[55] Such losses cannot be made up for or undone, only possibly healed. Such healing results in different life connections and communal narratives.

Vitally important for those of us who seek to listen is the need to attend to the multiplicity of voices coming from different groups and from within particular groups. We should not shy away from the complex challenges they pose to our society, our sense of history, and even our own identities. Baby Suggs may be right that grace comes only to those who can imagine and see it. Such seeing, if grace is to be shared, needs to embrace the differences and the complications, the ambiguities and even the contradictions, before us. What is at stake is not only our understanding of those who are different from us, but of ourselves. As Albert Raboteau exhorts: "the neglect of black history not only distorted American history, but distorted both white and black Americans' perceptions of who they were."[56]

The Armenian church I attended as a child with my family was in inner-city Philadelphia. Around the corner was what I then called a "holy-roller" church housed in a storefront. I never set foot inside that church, but sometimes when we parked and made our way toward our more conventional church building, I would hear the assembled congregation, singing and clapping. The exuberance and the rhythms frightened me. And as is often the case when we are frightened, I judged these black worshipers as strange and even inferior. I can now only wonder what they would have thought of the Armenian church service, so ritualized and formal. Our chanting was controlled and reflected the haunting qualities of minor keys. The air was filled with the smells of incense and burning candle wax. Everyone's movements were minutely choreographed. I imagine the worshipers in the neighboring church would have found us strange indeed. They and we were so different in style; neither did we know one another. Yet we were not so different or foreign in our desire for a relationship with God that would grant us grace and life abundant.

Meanwhile, at my public, white, lower-working-class elementary school we regularly sang hymns and spirituals, such as "Faith of Our Fathers" and "Swing Low, Sweet Chariot," without much understanding of their origins or their meanings, let alone of the contradictions present in singing Christian hymns in a public school. Neither were we conscious of the ways in which these hymns were informing our (limited) understanding of citizenship in a white, patriarchal, classist society.

What difference would it make if children were exposed to and taught about the pluralism in our society from the beginning of their education? What would it mean if we learned to celebrate differences rather than be frightened by them? How might we understand the nature of knowledge and knowing, itself, if we were schooled in a critical consciousness that discerned the relationship of power to truth? What might it mean to talk about God, to remember God's saving actions, in such a way that we do full honor and service to the different experiences of those who have suffered among us, the multiple practices of remembering that are emerging from their stories, and the reflections on those experiences?

Conclusion

Remembering for Life:

Memorative Practices

My family's charge to me, communicated directly and indirectly, to remember their suffering and the suffering of the Armenian people, was in many ways simple and straightforward. I was to be their loyal witness. Yet even then the command contained a thirst for healing and wholeness that began to complicate my compliance. The charge was motivated by a desire for redemption, for a type of acknowledgment, vindication, and even restoration that stirred up restlessness and sent me on a journey that led me in directions neither my family nor I imagined. I have come to the deep realization and appreciation that there is nothing simple or straightforward about the command to remember and to bear witness. As I have tried to show and explicate in the preceding chapters, those who seek to witness to and remember suffering are engaging in a complex and multiform process. What remains striking—and what I seek to honor—is both the immensity of the pain and trauma endured, and the resilience of human beings, body and soul. In listening to these voices of pain, I have discovered the presence of hope birthing possibility, even in the midst of the worst degradation and suffering. The wonder for me is that in the process of looking at suffering and evil head-on, I have learned so much more about hope and the amazing power of life itself. But I get ahead of myself.

In these chapters, I have focused on the remembrance of three types of victimization: the sexual abuse of children; programs of genocidal extinction; and the oppression and persecution of groups or categories of people who are less powerful in a given society. In each case, the victimization has caused much suffering and trauma. Victimization threatens not only individual persons, but society and life itself. In that sense, we are all responsible for and vulnerable to the threats. The legacies of these traumas continue to be manifest, long after the originating event of victimization has ended, especially if the traumas are not worked through. I have learned from those who study trauma that it can be passed on through generations, if it is not remembered and witnessed to fully, appropriately, and adequately. The preceding chapters were intended to be a witness, revealing the contours of such remembering. They draw on the work of other witnesses: therapists and historians, activists and scholars, who seek to bring these memories of suffering to light. The desire I share with these witnesses is that our communal narrative come to incorporate these remembrances in a way that might transform us all. Such a communal narrative needs to reflect the complex processes of remembering.

The witnessing to and remembrance of suffering in these chapters reveal a number of commonalities and characteristics, evidenced in each of the cases of victimization. Remembering is experienced as and remains both a problem and a resource for survivors/heirs and those who bear witness. The problem initially is one of naming and claiming the memory: remembering the original victimization. In each of the instances, we saw a form of forgetfulness—repression or denial or burying or distortion or silencing—at play. Whether witnesses are seeking to uncover their own pasts or that of their people, this problem of lost, hidden, distorted, or silenced memory has to be confronted. Sometimes, as in the case of flashbacks for survivors of childhood sexual abuse, the memories arise from a place of hiding to confront. Often times, changing social patterns bring them to light.

The process of naming and claiming remembrance allows remembering to begin to be a resource for dealing with victimization and suffering. As a resource, remembrance provides survivors and witnesses with a narrative of suffering. Yet in the process of narration, new problems and threats need to be faced. What is to be remembered, why, and how?

As we have seen, it is not enough to remember suffering and trauma. There is more to the past and to history, personal or group, than a narrative of suffering would convey. What emerges from attending to the memorative processes of those who testify and witness to suffering are three distinctive types of remembrance: of suffering and loss; of resistance and agency; and of connection with life and wholeness not defined by the suffering. Each of these types call for remembrance. Suffering and loss must be remembered and mourned. Mourning means allowing oneself to experience the harm and the hurt, to accept the irretrievable nature of the losses, and to grieve. Although the loss is never forgotten or restored, grieving and mourning eventually allow the pain and losses to be less dominant. Remembrance of suffering requires acknowledging that the victimization happened in the first place. To the extent that those who are victimized, their communities, and society itself, avoid or deny the reality of the victimization, it cannot be mourned. The suffering may be held in memory, but not remembered in a way that honors it.

Yet if all that is remembered is the suffering and loss, then those who remember are still caught in the victimization. As we saw in the cases studied, key to transforming memories is finding instances of resistance and agency and incorporating them into the testimony and witness. Being able to name and claim what people did to survive, even in seemingly impossible situations, is vitally important to their own process of healing and transformation, and to the process of witnessing. Even in the worst cases of persecution, even in the concentration camps of Hitler's Germany, Jews were not only passive victims, but resisters. Most often the possible modes of resistance are not heroic. They may even be antiheroic, problematic, or perhaps considered unethical under "normal circumstances." Slaves stole from their masters. Jews and Armenians also stole to stay alive. They lied to and, when able, bribed those in power. Abuse survivors dissociated, as I imagine did many slaves or those in concentration camps. These behaviors can all be claimed and remembered as strategies for survival. Both the tendency to emphasize powerlessness and the shame attendant to some of these practices get in the way of such remembrance. Part of the process of giving testimony and bearing witness is to hold up these practices as legitimate modes of resistance and as expressions of power in situations in which no other avenues were available. Remembering resistance enables resilience, the ability of human beings to go on living.

When remembering is focused on suffering and resistance, the narrative is still defined and determined by victimization and oppression, by threats to existence and meaning. Ultimately, the purpose of remembering and of witness is to expand the narrative for the living. I mean "for the living" in two senses of the term: (1) the obligation to those who survive and their heirs; and (2) for the sake of human flourishing and life abundant beyond surviving. Remembering in this way serves as a resource for life. Such remembrance entails making connections between the particularities of the experience of victimization and other experiences, between oneself or one's group and others. It means transcending the suffering to something more that holds the promise of hope and life. This can be accomplished in a variety of ways, but it is an ongoing struggle and process.

Remembering continues to be problem and resource. The three modes of remembrance outlined each serve to empower in their own way. Together they form a multiple memorative practice for healing, witness, and transformation, responsive to the ongoing threats to remembrance. As we have seen, these threats arise both internally and externally. Internal threats are rooted in the trauma and its attendant fears. In a very real way, no one, including survivors and those who

122

witness, wants to face the suffering, pain, and loss produced by victimization and suffering. Yet there is also a sense in which often the suffering is all that does get remembered. Survivors and witnesses feel a kind of loyalty to what has been suffered and lost. To remember anything else seems like a betrayal, a leaving behind of what has been lost. Ironically, the interest of perpetrators and oppressors is also often in the remembrance of suffering and oppression, because then their power is confirmed and strengthened. At the same time, such remembrance of suffering can challenge their power. The claim of any family, society, worldview, or ideology to goodness is undermined by awareness of those who are harmed by it. Thus the dynamics of threat and remembrance are complex and need to be discerned in each instance. These dynamics may change as power shifts.

The remembrance of resistance is both threatened and threatening as well. The internal threats come, first of all, from the pulls of loyalty to the suffering. To name the situation as other than powerless is seen as compromising the horror and as mitigating the indictment against the persecutors and oppressors. Remembering resistance also may necessitate changing our perceptions of effective action and facing the shame that might emerge in claiming certain behaviors. The kinds of behaviors that seemed necessary for survival may well be deemed unethical or shameful once the threat is passed. Or it may be that behaviors and attitudes that were functionally helpful and necessary for survival in the midst of victimization become dysfunctional once the threat is past. For example, dissociation and psychic numbing might enable surviving the horrors of abuse, but they get in the way of forming attachments and relationships. How can these practices be claimed and remembered as examples of human agency and a resource for life at the same time that they are left behind? Part of the process of remembering resistance is answering this question. External threats to these memories come from those who seek to reinforce victimization and powerlessness. Hitler wanted Jews to believe they were powerless; abusers want their victims to think they are helpless; and slaveholders wanted to believe that slaves were passive and contented.

For those who struggle with a past of suffering, remembering connection and expanding the narrative is perhaps the most difficult aspect of remembering. Again, the threats, internal and external, are legion. It is difficult for those who have been victimized, especially if their suffering has extended over time and/or invaded all aspects of their lives, as is characteristic of the examples studied, to believe that any other way of life is possible. It is as if the suffering fills the whole canvas of their lives. Any other living takes place on top or alongside, almost as a separate reality. The purpose of remembering connection is to shrink the victimization so there is room on the canvas for other images, other stories. The issue of loyalty to the suffering, the past, and the loss remains, as does the necessity of finding new ways to understand self and life. The external threats are strong and persist, especially if there is no adequate communal or public acknowledgment of the victimization itself.

The challenges to the remembrance of suffering posed by those who advocate the False Memory Syndrome, those who deny the Armenian genocide and the Jewish Holocaust, and those who refuse to hear and include voices excluded from our common historical narrative or who would interpret these histories for their own advantage, are very real and present dangers. Equally real and present are the internal threats that such challenges strengthen and feed. It is difficult enough to believe or want to face these experiences, histories, and legacies of trauma. Any challenge is like a frontal assault. The instinct is to run and hide. It takes tremendous courage to face the suffering, let alone the attacks.

What makes it possible to remember, despite the threats, internal and external, is not only courage and hope and the desire for life, but relationships and communities of witness and shared remembering. In the foregoing chapters, we have consistently seen the importance of those who will recognize the trauma, hear, hold, and affirm the suffering and the surviving, and accompany and share in the process of remembering. Indeed, bearing witness is precisely about hearing and accompanying; it is fundamentally a relationship. Through these relationships and through sharing in community, it becomes possible to imagine connection and transcendence of trauma toward a flourishing of life.

All three modes of remembering contribute to empowering for life. The suffering is never fully transcended; it ought never be forgotten. Through such remembrance of suffering, the dead are honored and the losses are recognized as unredeemed. Resistance will always need to be practiced and remembered, because the threats and dangers will not disappear. Yet the call of life to something more than suffering and resistance also persists and woos all those who survive to wholeness of life. The practice of remembrance in all these modes is continual. It is rooted in an epistemology of ambiguity that is, in turn, nurtured through the practice. Such knowing holds truth delicately, for it too is both threatened and ambiguous. The "certainty" of memory is grounded in a commitment to life and empowerment. We come to know our selves and our living as constituted through memory and narrative.

In this section, I have invited the reader to pay attention to memories of suffering and to listen for the word that emerges from those who struggle to remember. Through this process we have come to discover a richer and more complex narrative that contains much more than suffering. It is the story of life, ever-threatened and yearning to be realized, to be made whole, to be redeemed. This multiple memorative practice is a process of redeeming memories. The process of redemption involves preserving and paying due honor; resisting and surviving; and creating transcending connections. What would it mean to narrate the central memories of Christianity in a way that is responsive to these memorative practices? What would it mean to talk about redemption in a way that incorporates them? How might the church be a community of remembrance, holding and honoring the memories we have heard? I turn to these questions in the following chapters.

Section Two

To Know by Heart:
Theological Construction

Introduction

Remember?

Remember me?
I am the girl
with the dark skin
whose shoes are thin
I am the girl
with rotted teeth
I am the dark
rotten-toothed girl
with the wounded eye
and the melted ear.

I am the girl
holding their babies
cooking their meals
sweeping their yards
washing their clothes
Dark and rotting
and wounded, wounded.

I would give
to the human race
only hope.

I am the woman
with the blessed
dark skin
I am the woman
with teeth repaired
I am the woman
with the healing eye
the ear that hears.

I am the woman: Dark,
repaired, healed
Listening to you.

> I would give
> to the human race
> only hope.
>
> I am the woman
> offering two flowers
> whose roots
> are twin
>
> Justice and Hope
>
> Let us begin.[1]

"Justice and hope. Let us begin." What is the nature of the hope that this wounded and healed woman offers? How is she able to move from a plea of remembrance to a gift of justice and hope? What transformation makes possible the shift in her rhetoric from "me" and "them" to "us"?

Justice and hope are at the heart of Christianity. They are foundation and fruit of Christian memory. How are we to understand the justice and hope that Christianity offers? What makes them possible? In order to answer such questions, Christians need once again to remember Jesus Christ. The originating Christian experience was to remember Jesus Christ with a kind of recognition and revelation that turned Jesus' followers toward a different future: "Were not our hearts burning within us while Jesus was talking to us on the road, and opening the scriptures to us?" So mused Cleopas and friend, who encountered the resurrected Christ on the road from Jerusalem to Emmaus. They did not recognize Christ at first. Only after their companion told them the story of redemption, only through the sharing of bread, and through remembrance, did they realize the Christ they had met on the road. Their remembering literally turned these disciples around and sent them back to Jerusalem to share this revelation.[2] They became witnesses to the resurrection. Hope was born in the declaration that Christ was risen; hope rose out of remembering. The past and the future, the story of salvation, were renewed through remembrance, filtered through resurrection sight.

The story of the encounter on the road to Emmaus appears in the last chapter of the Gospel of Luke. Toward the beginning, in the second chapter, at Jesus' birth, the Gospel writer offers another portrait of memory and hope. Mary, the mother of Jesus, takes in all that happens and all that is declared by shepherds and angels: "Mary treasured all these words and pondered them in her heart" (Luke 2:19). What could be a more fitting description of Mary as witness? What could be a better image of memory and hope? Mary knows by heart who Jesus is. She remembers the declarations, not only as birth narratives, but as affirmations of the future and as promises of hope. She too practices remembrance and hope, held by heart, for future revelation and realization.

The Christian story is remembrance and hope. Christianity, as revelation, practice, and religion, arose from the memorative narratives and practices of those who followed Jesus. It promises redemption and renewal, of persons and of the world. It is also a religion of justice. Wrongs will be named and made right. God's intent is for all to live in right relation and harmony. What would it mean, then, for the Christian story to attend to the narratives of suffering and transformation, in all their complexities, that were surveyed in the previous section? Is it possible for the hearts of Christians to burn with the remembrance of those who have suffered victimization and trauma, and who yearn and live for healing and transformation? How might Christians witness, as did Mary and the followers on the road, to the birth and life, death and resurrection of Jesus Christ, but do so in relation to these other narratives of life, death, and life renewed?

The chapters in this section explore such questions in an attempt to construct a Christian theological response to the calls for memory. The initial chapter reviews the importance and meaning of memory in contemporary political, liberation, and feminist theologies, and sets these theological perspectives in relation to what was suggested by the studies in the previous section. How do social calls to remembrance relate to and compare with the attention to victims and the "turn toward memory" in current theologies? The next chapter looks at the work and life of Jesus Christ as a multiple memorative practice, in order to develop a soteriology of remembering. In other words, how does the remembering of suffering and resistance, agency and connection in social contexts relate to the remembrance of Jesus Christ as Savior? The final chapter considers the church as a community of remembrance and outlines the practices of such an understanding of the church. What does it mean for the community to hold and pass on these memories, for the sake of remembrance and hope?

I have already indicated that this theology of redeeming memories is an expression of feminist and political narrative theology. As displayed in the structure of this book, I understand theology to be reflection on the experiences of those who struggle for life. That reflection both shapes and is shaped by the Christian story. The goal is effectiveness: in this case, a memorative narrative witness that leads to healing, justice, transformation, and hope. This goal and method are rooted in certain foundational and anthropological principles, which will be discussed. These principles are the fruit of an understanding of revelation as gracious divine energy present and active in creation and history. The divine is then revealed in and through human experience.

This theology also recognizes Christianity as not only resource but problem. As we have seen, Christianity is complicit in social structures, practices, and ideologies that produce suffering and victimization. Christianity also serves as resource for those who suffer. There is ample testimony to its effectiveness among many oppressed and victimized people. But Christianity cannot simply be claimed as a healing and salvific memory without attention being paid to the ways in which it is used in support of cultures of oppression and abuse. In other words, Christianity and Christian theology need to be problematized in order to discern what does and does not contribute to salvation. The following chapters are meant to offer such an analysis of Christianity as saving memory.

4

The Call to Remembrance and Witness in Contemporary Theology

I read Johann Baptist Metz for the first time, in any depth, during my doctoral studies. When I came across the phrase "dangerous memory," I felt as if the vocation to remember, bequeathed to me so many years before by my family, finally might have a name and a mission and even a theological context. I felt recognized and understood. I also felt theologically excited. Metz was suggesting that at the heart of Christianity and Christian witness was memory, a memorative practice. Christians were bade to remember suffering. Further, this practice was dangerous, which is to say it was not in the interests of the dominating powers in the world. Indeed, dangerous memory might even change the world. My family legacy and my theological/ethical commitments seemed to converge into one, simple phrase, "dangerous memory," which resonated deep inside. Yet, as I soon learned, this theological "revelation" was only the beginning of this long and increasingly enlarging study. In the end, I have come to question the adequacy of the term, "dangerous memory," to hold the complexities of remembering for salvation.

It would not be difficult to make the case that there is a "turn to memory" in those strains of contemporary theology that seek to attend to suffering in the world. In their attempts at correlation between Christian faith and historical suffering, these theologies use memory as a category of connection. Johann Baptist Metz remains the primary and chief theologian to do so, but others have adopted the concept and even the phrase, "dangerous memory." For Metz and other theologians, dangerous memory is a saving memory. In section 1, I argued that there is a redemptive motivation contained in the social memorative practices. How do these intents and claims to redemption—theological and social—compare and connect? In other words, what is the relationship of dangerous memory to the memorative practices that were evidenced in the remembering of abuse, genocide, and cultural histories? In this chapter, I respond to these questions first by reviewing Metz's theology of memory and then surveying several feminist theologians' use and development of memory as a theological category. Finally, I set these theologians alongside what was discerned in section 1, in order to develop more nuance in understanding dangerous memory, as well as to lay some anthropological and theological foundations.

The "Dangerous Memory" of Johann Baptist Metz

In many ways, Johann Baptist Metz begins where I do: with the problem of human and historical suffering. What does it mean to do theology, Metz asks, if we attend to those who are victims in history? Metz's response to that question is to develop a practical fundamental theology, containing the categories of memory, narrative, and solidarity. His purpose is to construct a narrative theology of memory in solidarity with those who suffer. In Metz's theology, memory is not a function of reason abstracted from history, but is a concrete historical, political, as well as religious, mystical activity.

Metz's theology is done in acute awareness of the crises of modernity and postmodernity that he sees evidenced in the world today. He regards the existence and survival of the human subject, history, and religion as all threatened. For Metz, to be saved is to be a subject in history before God. Given contemporary threats to the human subject, history, and religion, Metz wonders how we can speak today of salvation. His practical fundamental theology is an attempt to respond meaningfully and effectively.

Human existence is threatened because of poverty, oppression, and degradation, the effects of human evil in the world. Metz fixes on the reality of the Holocaust as symbolized by Auschwitz and the suffering of the poor, especially the peoples of the so-called Third World, as concrete examples of the depths of suffering and the need to attend to victims. The Holocaust and the poverty of the Third World also represent two specific sites of suffering for which Christians are particularly responsible. Metz points out that Christians bear "responsibility, not only for what we do or fail to do, but also for what we allow to happen to others in our presence, before our eyes."[1]

Metz writes of a new subject of history: the victim. This subject is also the new bearer of Christianity. Metz repeatedly stresses that the present crisis in religion and theology is not a crisis of the contents, but of the bearers of Christianity, its subjects, and institutions. In response, he seeks to do his own theology not only on behalf of those who are most victimized in history, but in relation to them. In other words, Metz begins with remembrance of the suffering of others, which he understands as "a basic category of Christian discourse about God."[2] He then insists that we need to see ourselves, our church, and our culture through the eyes of our victims.[3]

When looking through those eyes, Metz sees indicted before him certain aspects of modernity and postmodernity that breed forgetfulness and timelessness, complacency, and a dissolution of human responsibility into forces beyond human control. These pose their own threats to the human subject, history, and religion. Among the threatening aspects of modernity are bourgeois capitalist society where the principle of exchange reigns supreme; Marxist ideology that asserts a revolutionary future that expunges the present and past; and technological reason that has no feelings and ultimately no commitments. Postmodern thinking adds further threat through its tendency to question and eliminate the human agent and to destroy history as an arena of the struggle for justice.

Since these threats to the human subject, history, and religion threaten memory as well, Metz understands memory as both problem and resource for salvation. Some memorative practices contribute to complacency and lack of a sense of history and responsibility. Threats come, then, not only from forgetfulness, but from forms of nostalgia and historical triumphalism that hide or explain away the memories of suffering and loss. In the end, it is to memories of suffering that Metz turns to save us. By remembering victims and their suffering, we are resisting false claims to progress and the dehumanizing strains of modern and postmodern culture. Our remembering helps keep us human in history before God. Without such memory, we cannot speak of salvation.

I understand Metz's overall theological project to be the effort to reenvision the relationship between history and salvation in a way that might promote the emergence of all persons as subjects. Yet Metz will not allow that emergence to be over the dead bodies of those who have suffered in the past. In that way, the promise of salvation remains always outstanding. There is no justification, resolution, or explanation for the suffering: "no struggle of the living, however passionate," can reconcile "past suffering."[4] Memories of suffering withstand historical resolution. The narrative remembrance of suffering and of unanswered hope, in solidarity with victims, is the practical response to this dilemma of history and salvation. Remembering serves to "remind" us of the suffering, which we would just as soon forget, but which might help save us.

Thus, remembering is not the solution; it does not constitute salvation in and of itself. But it is a resource for salvation. It honors those who have suffered and maintains the future as open. It grounds hope. Memory is a category of salvation of human, social, and religious identity. Our remembering tells us who we are and allows us to say "no" to all that negates us. In this way, remembrance of suffering supports resistance; it acts as an "organon of an apocalyptical consciousness" that breaks in and enables us to negate and resist.[5] Metz does not explicate why memories of suffering and loss lead to resistance and not to resignation, but it seems to be because of a basic anthropological desire for freedom and liberation.[6] Such memories point to outstanding promises and engender solidarity that provide support for resistance and hope. To further underscore the disturbing nature of such remembrance, Metz turns more and more to the language and concepts of apocalyptic thought, which stress historical discontinuity. Correspondingly, religion is interruption.[7]

To make clear this form of memory that is resource for salvation, Metz introduces, into theological use, the term, "dangerous memory." Dangerous memory indicts our desires for facile or abstract resolutions to historical oppressions. It fights against complacency and timelessness, forgetfulness and distortion. It critiques the status quo, resists forgetting, recalls what has been lost, and enables hope. Dangerous memory carries the potential for salvation of the human subject, history, and religion. At the heart of the Christian story, Metz argues, is a "dangerous memory"—that of Jesus Christ—more specifically the *memoria passionis et resurrectionis Jesu Christi*, the memory of the suffering, death, and resurrection of Jesus Christ. More specifically still, it is the memory of Jesus' suffering that Metz deems dangerous.

Metz does not clearly define what he means by the term "dangerous." He adopts and adapts the term from the Frankfurt School, especially the works of Walter Benjamin and Herbert Marcuse.[8] He uses the term in an evocative way, almost as a rhetorical device: to say a memory is dangerous is to say it disturbs us and makes demands on us. Metz's goal is to have people experience the danger and be stirred into remembrance, solidarity, and liberative praxis.

There are four phrases that he uses along with the term dangerous memory. (1) *Memory of the dead and vanquished.* As we have seen, Metz points to a number of historical developments that characterize Western modernity and breed forgetfulness of those who have suffered. For Metz, only a theology that keeps the lives of those who have gone before, especially their suffering, in memory can do justice to those lives. To honor the dead is to remember the dead. This may be all we can do for those who have suffered and died. (2) *Concrete memory of suffering and freedom.* Concrete memory is narrated memory, which is to say it has a specific content. Not only are we to remember the dead and vanquished, but we are to narrate their stories of suffering. Though Metz uses the phrase "concrete memory of suffering *and* freedom" his emphasis is on suffering and memories of victimization and loss, rather than of agency and freedom. Such memories of suffering are, according to Metz, likely to inspire solidarity and resistance. (3) *Memory as eschatological hope.* Memory also serves as a foundation for hope that holds the future as promise and sees time as unfulfilled. This hope is lived out by a memorative narrative and imitative following of Christ. (4) *Memory of the suffering and resurrection of Jesus* or *memoria passionis et resurrectionis Jesu Christi.* Christian identity is formed by the telling and retelling of the story of the passion, death, and resurrection of Jesus Christ. In fact, for Metz, this is *the* concrete memory. Because Metz understands all memories of human suffering to be, in some sense, part of Jesus Christ's suffering, he also uses the term *memoria passionis* to refer to human suffering. That participation in Jesus' suffering gives human suffering meaning, structure, and place in God's ongoing care for the world. The cross represents God's solidarity with all who suffer so their pain is never forgotten, but retold in the story of Jesus. This identification of human with divine suffering does not, or ought not, cause people to accept or negate their suffering. Rather, Metz contends that it leads to an active resistance and to future hope. He writes: "Resurrection mediated by way of the memory of suffering means: The dead, those already vanquished and forgotten, have a meaning which is as yet unrealized."[9] Because the memory of Jesus is a redemptive memory, it is above all a memory of freedom, a tradition of liberation.

These five terms and phrases—dangerous memory; memory of the dead and conquered; concrete memory of suffering and freedom; memory as eschatological hope; and memory of the passion, death, and resurrection of Jesus Christ—are interconnected through the concept of danger and salvation. Their center is the memory of Jesus' suffering and death: the concrete memory of suffering, which for Metz can hold all other memories of suffering. Memorative witness, then, is located at the cross, the site of suffering and hope. Jesus' death is one of solidarity with suffering humanity.

Metz is attempting to deal with the theodicy problem without resorting to explanation that tends to minimize the suffering, or to eternalizing the suffering by suggesting that suffering is in God.[10] Jesus' suffering is not in or from God, but *unto* God.[11] So is human suffering from evil and oppression unto God. It has mystical and political dimensions. Both these dimensions come together in the cross and in Jesus' death, which is also site of solidarity with the totality of the human condition. Metz points to Jesus' descent to hell as a sign of God's not forgetting any who have suffered and died.[12] For Metz, the cross does not "solve" anything; it births freedom and hope, but not resolution. Its salvific potential is as dangerous memory. Soteriology remains "fundamentally memorative and narrative" in the form of "a dangerous and liberating memory of redeemed freedom."[13]

This narrative is preserved and transmitted by the church, which ought to be the bearer of dangerous memory and witness to redemption. The church as a community of remembrance witnesses through its liturgies, dogmas, pastoral practice, and action in the world. Religious orders, which, because of their apostolic witness, Metz sees as the vanguard of the church, lead the way in practicing these forms of remembrance. The base communities of the church in South America and elsewhere are also practicing forms of memory, narrative, and solidarity that Metz sees as models for the church as a whole. These "emergent churches" are following and imitating Christ in a way that contributes to salvation.[14]

Metz deserves credit for focusing theological attention on memory as a theme and category, for articulating an understanding of memory for the contemporary world—that is, one which is historical—and for pointing to the potential of remembering as a salvific practice. Metz insists that we remember and remember historically, concretely, and specifically. The measure of our humanity is in the ability to remember and to allow ourselves to be disturbed by those memories. The measure of our historical responsibility is our willingness to remember suffering, and the measure of our faith is how much our hope is grounded in remembering in such a way that the invitation of salvation for all remains open, even for those who seemingly have no hope.

Metz is most strong in his insistence that the concrete reality of suffering in history must not be forgotten or compromised or sacralized. The losses endured cannot be recovered, but ought to be mourned. Mourning is the proper response to the horrors of the Holocaust and of the injustices done to the poor and oppressed. The ability to mourn is also for Metz a measure of our humanity, which is threatened in modernity/postmodernity. In that sense, mourning is a dangerous and, I would add, necessary activity. It honors the dead and lost; it holds them in memory forever. However, as survivors tell us, mourning is not sufficient. What comes after or along with the mourning to make life possible for the living?[15]

I would argue that Metz's approach to memory is not, in the end, practically effective for victims. I offer six reasons for this claim: the voice Metz speaks in; the valuation his approach gives to suffering; his use of the eschatological proviso; the paucity of narrative in his theology; his exempting of Christianity from ideological bias; and his lack of clear definition for the term, "dangerous memory."

Who is Metz's subject? In whose voice does he write? Metz attends to two subjects. One is the bourgeois and first-world citizen whose identity is threatened by alienation and apathy. The other is the victim with no power—the dead, oppressed, suffering, poor, silenced ones. Actually, both subjects are victims for Metz, even though their suffering is not equivalent. The first is victimized by his or her inability to suffer; the second by his or her suffering. The first is to be saved by turning from apathy to accountability, from a lack of guilt and feeling to feeling guilt and responsibility in response to those who suffer. But such turns require a focus on memories of the victimization and suffering of others, in order to convict toward redemption. Such a focus underplays and makes less important the resistance and active agency of the victimized.

Metz speaks not from the perspective of the victimized, but on their behalf. In that way too, he undercuts their agency. In some of his more recent works, Metz seems to struggle to understand those who suffer on their own terms. He wants to grant them voice and insists that authority belongs to those who suffer, but only as long as they are victims, only as long as they are suffering. For him, what gives authority to the poor and those who have died in the past is their suffering, not their resistance; the fact that they are victims, not that they are active agents on their own behalf.

Another way in which this problem of dual subjects emerges is in Metz's epistemology. For Metz, true knowledge comes from otherness: we come to know through unlikeness, rather than likeness. True memory then is "the remembrance of the suffering of *others* as the basic category of Christian talk of God."[16] The focus on otherness and difference is, for Metz, necessary as a guard against the self-focus that is evident in "identity politics" or what might be called "identity suffering and remembrance." For example, he suggests that the violence in the former Yugoslavia is based in "the purely self-referential memory of suffering in particular ethnic groups." Metz contrasts that violence with the gesture of the Israeli Rabin and Palestinian Arafat, who agreed to pay attention to the suffering of the other's people.[17] What is missing in this epistemological and, I would add, political approach is both an understanding of the relational nature of our knowing, and the reality of trauma undergirding the animosities evident in both Eastern Europe and the Middle East. Metz's observations seem to me facile and not attentive enough to the dynamics of power in relationships, in the production and reproduction of trauma, and in the processes of knowing.

These perspectives are echoed in Metz's insistence that we see ourselves through the eyes of our victims. Such a gaze remains fixed on those with privilege. The victims still serve the interests of those who need to be jolted out of complacency and into feeling and memory. The witness of memory is twisted around in this odd way. I do not think Metz intends this, but there is a way in which his interests blind him to what he requires of those who suffer. It is as if what gets our notice, and even God's notice, is their suffering. He states: "The Christian *memoria passionis* articulates itself as a memory that makes one free to suffer from the sufferings of others, and to respect the prophetic witness of others' suffering, even though the negative view of suffering in our 'progressive' society makes it seem as something increasingly intolerable and even repugnant."[18] Metz's chief concern remains the devaluing of suffering and its implications for dehumanization and, therefore, the need to preserve freedom for suffering.

As a result, suffering is given a positive valuation. It is effective for redemption. Just as Jesus' saving action is his suffering and death, the ability to suffer is a measure of our humanity. The memory of Jesus' passion will save us—in this case, not by satisfaction and substitution but by returning us to our lost humanity. Even though Metz includes the memory of resurrection and freedom in the category of dangerous memory, he does not emphasize or develop these dimensions. They remain in the background, as shadow images, lest they produce a theology of glory that forgets the dead and those promises that remain outstanding.[19]

Although I understand Metz's motivations and his fear of enthroning any future resolution that "forgets" the past, I think his emphasis on the remembrance of suffering might well reinforce the hopelessness many victims feel. Metz is wary of pointing to any historical movement as evidence of resurrection. He holds all human history under an eschatological proviso. That may be an effective strategy for curtailing the forces of domination, but it does not empower the victimized. The eschatological reservation severely compromises the possibility of positive historical action. Yet hope for those who have suffered and been oppressed needs to be concrete. The resurrection is one symbol of hope defeating despair.

Another concrete symbol of God's presence in history is the incarnation and life of Jesus, which do not even appear in Metz's remembering of Jesus. Indeed, Metz's narrative theology incorporates very little narrative. The story of Jesus is not included in Metz's presentation of the saving work of Jesus Christ. Even Jesus' preaching receives little attention. The closest Metz comes to attending to Jesus is in advocating an apostolic lifestyle, modeled on Jesus, for those who would be followers of Christ. Given this lack of a fuller narrative, Metz's emphasis remains on the remembrance of Jesus' suffering and death. In that way, Metz's theology underplays Jesus' active agency, as well as that of the victimized.

Metz also assumes *a priori*, a correlation between the memory of Jesus Christ and what is dangerous memory for those who have suffered. And therein lies another problem. Metz does not apply his principles of critique of ideology to Christian faith itself. Instead, Christian faith is that by which ideology is to be judged. What makes Christianity liberating is that it is distinct from and cannot be derived from history, social theory, or psychology.[20] In other words, I imagine Metz would be suspect of the project of this book because it presumes that we can learn something about how liberation and transformation work by attending to these so-called "secular" disciplines.

I, in turn, would contend that Metz presupposes the truth of Christianity and so does not go far enough in rendering it a practical knowledge in history.[21] For him, the Christian story, indeed Christian dogma, is subversive, dangerous, and liberating memory. Locating ourselves within that story is what will help us see and respond to the threats to person, history, and religion in the modern and postmodern worlds. I find this insufficient.

Also insufficient is Metz's development of the term "dangerous memory." I have already indicated that he uses this term primarily in a rhetorical way. The "danger" of memory is meant to challenge, interrupt, and even disrupt us, to turn our attention to those who suffer and are in need. Danger and interruption are seen as good things; they

correlate with Metz's perspective on the value of apocalyptic understandings of time and religion. In and through the danger is the possibility of redemption, which is more rescue than transformation. Metz
offers little elaboration, however, on how danger is experienced or
understood. As we have learned from those who suffer the eruption of
traumatic memories and from those who study trauma, the "danger"
contained in the return and interruption of memories may be necessary
for healing and may carry the potential for redemption, but such danger is not good. Traumatic interruption brings back terror and pain so
immense that they have to be blocked from memory. Such return causes its own suffering. Even though such suffering is entered into for the
sake of redemption, it is in itself not redemptive. Religion understood
as interruption and memory imaged as danger does not offer sufficient
resources for the necessary tasks of rebuilding connection and moving
toward integration.

In the end, Metz's witness to "dangerous memory" falls short of
attending fully to the lived experiences of those who struggle with
memories of violence and oppression. Metz's main goal is to get Christianity to attend to the historical reality of suffering and its attendant
losses, and to respond to those. This is an invaluable contribution, but
one that does not offer enough hope to the victimized for whom the
memory of their suffering is necessary, but not sufficient for healing or
transformation. Metz's community of remembrance emphasizes preservation in the face of social and political threats, and the honoring of the
dead. Again, these are vitally important goals, but they do not focus
enough on transformative possibilities. As stated, for Metz, there is a
particular kind of danger in asserting any historical reality as redemptive. Yet for those who struggle for life, who seek to honor the living,
there is danger in not committing to concrete historical achievements.
Those who have been victimized yearn for remembrance of more than
suffering. They desire to be subjects and not only the subjected. Metz's
understanding of memory does not offer sustenance enough for the living, for the going on with some measure of realized hope.

Johann Baptist Metz turned the focus of contemporary theology to
reflection on remembrance. This theme of memory echoes through many
other works of contemporary theology that are seeking to respond to the
violence and oppression that seem so evident in the world. Particularly
strong are the echoes among feminist theologians who vary considerably
from Metz, even when they acknowledge his contributions.

Feminist Theologians

Many feminist theologians seek to do their theological work in witness to the victimization and oppression of women. Their starting point is quite different from that of Metz. They begin not with the problems of modernity, but with an analysis of the suffering that women have endured and continue to endure in history and society. Feminist theologians write not only on behalf of women, but identify as women for whom the oppressed are not only "other." Though aware of the privilege of being educated and elite, and in many cases white, they see through their own eyes and listen with ears tuned into their own experiences. In other words, many feminist theologians attempt to construct theology from the perspective of the victimized themselves.[22] This perspective changes what they see and hear and to what they bear witness. For several feminist theologians—namely, Elizabeth Johnson, Elisabeth Schüssler Fiorenza, Sharon Welch, and Rita Nakashima Brock—remembering is central to their witness. All except Brock draw on the work of Johann Baptist Metz, yet they seem to hear different strains in the call to remembrance. They not only seek to honor the dead, but to support the living. When they look at the victimized they see not only victims needing rescue and sufferers who must be mourned; they see survivors and resisters, struggling to be full subjects in history and before God.

Elizabeth Johnson

Although Elizabeth Johnson adopts Metz's language to construct the Christian story in a way that can work as saving memory for women, she enlarges the scope of dangerous memory to include women's memories of suffering, survival, and agency. She outlines four practices of memory employed by those who seek to remember women. These practices "recover lost memory, rectify distortion, reassess value, and respeak the silence surrounding women's lives before God."[23] They uncover and reinterpret the stories of women in Christianity. They restore women to the Christian story in a way that is reflective of their lived experience. For example, in describing women martyrs, Johnson seeks to correct the emphasis the church has put on suffering and dying as good and holy by holding up survival as a "holy choice."[24] Resistance should be valued as much as sacrifice, and the struggles of women to keep life going need to be honored: "Living for the faith is as crucial a witness as dying for the faith."[25] These are ordinary women to whom she points, not heroes: "Spinning out strategies to keep death at bay, such women make present the redemptive possibilities of life in the concrete."[26]

Together these practices of memory form a "subversive memory"; they offer women a heritage capable of challenging "the interconnected biases that continue to press down on their lives in church and society."[27] This heritage is dangerous and empowering. It feeds hope and action for justice. Using Metz's categories of memory, narrative, and solidarity, Johnson weaves a "narrative memory in solidarity" that might contain and communicate the subversive and dangerous memory. The "symbol" that holds all these memories for Johnson is the communion of saints.

Johnson tries to be much more precise in her use of terms and seeks to define danger in a way that clarifies Metz's usage. Echoing Metz, she states that subversive memory is dangerous because it "challenges the absolute power of the present and brings to mind a future that is still outstanding."[28] It is an "eschatological memory." She, however, goes on to distinguish the "danger for those who dominate and thus benefit from the status quo" from what is dangerous for the oppressed. The dominants and complacent ones are threatened and shocked out of complacency; the oppressed are empowered, but still in ways that can "be costly and even life-threatening."[29] Danger continues to designate possible suffering, as well as potential for a different future. Johnson points out that such subversive, dangerous memory is at the core of Christianity in the memory of the suffering, death, and resurrection of Jesus Christ. Again, she echoes Metz's own claims, but gives them broader and clearer definition.

Johnson holds up Jesus' life and ministry, which resulted in his death, as the reason the remembrance of Jesus is dangerous: "his ministry, his compassionate and liberating preaching and behavior enter into the meaning of his destiny in death and beyond death."[30] In other words, Jesus' death and resurrection are to be understood in relation to his life, which threatened the dominant forces of his time by offering hope and liberation to those who heeded. Further, not only is the memory of Jesus subversive, but so is that of women who witnessed to liberation and hope, women who were actors in the Christian story.

Again, adopting Metz's categories, Johnson points to the narrative structure of memory and the powers of narrative to shape and transform identity and action. Narrative memory is communicated through

and engenders solidarity, which knits people together through difference and even death. Solidarity is communion and connection that honors the living and the dead. The communion of saints—friends and
prophets of God—is the theological locus for this narrative memory in
solidarity. All stories not only find their meaning in the story of Jesus
Christ, but the Christian memory is made real, and enacted through the
myriad women and men whose living and dying witness to suffering,
struggle, and joy.

For Johnson, then, it is not sufficient to remember victimization and
suffering. Such remembrance may honor the dead and remind us all of
the evil loose in the world, but living is inspired and made real through
resistance and survival. For example, the witness of the Madres in
Argentina keeps alive the memory of the disappeared and so honors the
dead, but the witness is itself an act of resistance and defiance of erasure. It says that hope and justice cannot be killed.

Thus, while drawing upon Metz, Johnson expands and redefines
Metz's categories to create a richer canvas of memorative witness. Yet
she still tries to frame the canvas with the term "dangerous memory."
She does not question its sufficiency. Redeeming memory remains cen-
tered on the cross, as site of Jesus' solidarity in suffering and as source
of "transformative action."[31] Jesus' life and ministry are led in; the resurrection follows as anticipatory hope.

Elisabeth Schüssler Fiorenza

Elisabeth Schüssler Fiorenza also adopts Metz's term "dangerous
memory," but expands its meaning. In her project of historical retrieval
and reconstruction of women's memory, dangerous memories are not
only of suffering, but of women's resistance, leadership, and agency. If
the Christian story is to be redemptive for women today, then it must
yield and include women's own stories. As I have indicated in the previous section, in *In Memory of Her,* Schüssler Fiorenza laid the foundations of how to read the Christian story on behalf of women. Such a
reading is multiple: a series of readings and interpretive practices that
both mine the story for the ways in which women have been ignored
and maligned, and then reinterpret and reconstruct the Christian memory for the sake of women's salvation. Biblical authority is afforded
only to that which enables women's full humanity. For Schüssler
Fiorenza, this "remembered past" has "subversive power" and is "dangerous memory."[32]

Schüssler Fiorenza wants neither to ignore the ways in which women suffer and have been oppressed, nor to ignore the ways in which women have resisted marginalization, asserted power and leadership, and claimed place and role in Christianity. Her witness is to women's presence and struggle, throughout Christianity, to make real God's saving work for all. She understands remembering to be a complex process of historical recovery and present action. Remembering is a dialectical weaving between past and present, data and interest, community and commitments. It is engaged hermeneutics for the sake of salvation and liberation. Through such remembering women re-member themselves and their histories. Remembering engenders solidarity and committed action.

What is dangerous and subversive about memory for Schüssler Fiorenza is the capacity of remembering the past to reconstitute women in the present in such a way that they envision and enact Christianity differently. Although remembering is both problem and resource, Schüssler Fiorenza's goal is to turn the problems into opportunities and resources in the struggle to empower and liberate women. Women's remembering is always threatened in cultures and institutions that serve kyriarchal interests. Women's remembering is submerged and/or constructed to fit into an androcentric narrative. The process of historical reconstruction and remembering is ongoing, a continuing struggle for empowerment. As women remember the struggles of foresisters and realize there has been a continuous history of resistance and resilience, they will be strengthened in their own resolve to struggle, resist, and eventually dismantle the kyriarchal system. Remembering is for the sake of agency. It is to enable women to be subjects and actors, rather than objects and victims of history. The locus of such remembering, women-church or the *ekklesia* of women, is the community of remembrance that practices retrieval of women's stories, reconstruction of a saving message for women, and envisioning of a transformed future. The remembrance of Jesus cannot be authentic, claims Schüssler Fiorenza, unless women's memories are included and given due place.

Schüssler Fiorenza's witness to the role and presence of women in history and their ongoing struggle to be agents and full partners in Christianity is indefatigable. She remains committed to a continuous community of vision for freedom and hope. However, her concept of struggle does not provide a means to mourn victimization and its attendant loss. Struggle always suggests activity for change. Awareness of pain and suffering is cause for more commitment to struggle for liberation, but not for grieving and acceptance of loss. The remembrance of suffering is in order to tell the whole story and to indict the historical record. Whereas Metz gives too much status to memories of suffering, Schüssler Fiorenza tends to give them shorter shrift lest they undermine women's sense of historical agency. Thus, she takes the term "dangerous memory" from Metz, but changes the emphasis from remembrance of suffering to that of struggle. Dangerous memory is that which enables the reclaiming of a past other than silence and oppression, and therefore a more open future. Schüssler Fiorenza does not make clear this different use, however, and the term remains suggestive.

Sharon Welch

Sharon Welch also employs the term dangerous memory, but expands its meaning. Drawing even more on Foucault than Metz, she understands memory as a strategy of resistance. It is an "insurrection of subjugated knowledges." Welch points out that the term "subjugated knowledges" refers to "the history of subjugation, conflict, and domination," which has been excluded from the prevailing discourse. It also refers to "a whole group of knowledges that have been regarded with disdain by intellectuals" and to strategic struggles of power.[33] For Welch, dangerous memory is an encompassing term that speaks to the eruption into conscious struggle of the sufferings and hopes of the oppressed. In liberation theologies, memories of suffering critique the false universality of the dominating "reality." They also indict Christianity for its failure to address human problems. In those ways, memories of suffering are dangerous to the status quo, as are memories of struggle that serve as "witnesses to protests."[34] In Welch's use of the term, dangerous memories also include those of hope, freedom, and resistance, which enable the oppressed to be subjects. The ability even to remember suffering implies a sense of self and an experience of something other than degradation: "In order for there to be resistance and the affirmation that is implied in the preservation of the memory of suffering, there must be an experience that includes some degree of liberation."[35] Resistance and struggle are fragile and rare, but necessary occurrences in history.

Welch's intent is to highlight human resiliency, especially in dehumanizing and oppressive contexts. Remembering, practiced in and through communities of resistance and solidarity, is critically important in the struggle to be human. This hope for the future does not, however, make up for the suffering of the past. In that way, such suffering seems irredeemable.[36] Welch tries to balance and hold together the diverse challenges of memory: the irreconcilable and tragic memories of past suffering; the importance of memories of struggle and resistance to give grounding to human subjectivity; and the value of remembered hope to give meaning to liberation and life. Her goal is a theology of liberation, rooted in memorative practices, expressing mourning and joy, as well as fueling ongoing struggle in history.

These memorative practices are all dangerous memory. Despite Welch's ability to weave a richer tapestry of what is to be remembered and why, she tries to hold it all in the frame of this term, which remains ambiguous. What makes memories dangerous is not so much a specific content, but their use: "Memories of oppression and defeat become dangerous when they are used as the foundation for a critique of existing institutions and ideologies that blur the recognition and denunciation of injustice."[37]

Dangerous memory is practiced in communities of accountability. Such communities employ an epistemology of solidarity, which "posits the determination of judgment by concrete, specific relations."[38] All points of view are partial and particular. All knowledge is ideology. Rather than seeing ourselves through the eyes of our victims or grounding all knowledge in our own experience, Welch points to the importance of and need for different viewpoints: "Thus the condition of overcoming ideology is difference, a mutually challenging and mutually transformative pluralism."[39]

Even though Welch draws on Metz's work, she offers quite different views on epistemology, ethics, and community, as well as memory. Welch leaves much more room for effective action, albeit partial, limited, and fragile. The remembrance of suffering is not a sufficient motivation for resiliency and resistance. There is "danger" in either remembering only suffering and so being rendered hopeless, or remembering only struggle and victory and so forgetting the dead. "Dangerous memory" avoids both.

Herein lies another ambiguous use of the term "dangerous": it is used in reference to dangers to memory and dangers of memory. This confusing use begins with Metz, but is carried through to Johnson, Schüssler Fiorenza, and Welch. Their attempts to expand and shift the meaning of the term do not, in the end, resolve the ambiguity. Before turning to attempts at clarification, there is yet another feminist theologian to consider.

Rita Nakashima Brock

Rita Nakashima Brock does not draw upon Metz, but remembering is central to her theological work. It is important in relation both to suffering and to healing: "To heal ourselves and to liberate a suffering world, Christianity must find a healing image that leads us to dangerous, empowering memory and a theology grounded in such concrete memory."[40] Brock also begins with the human condition of suffering and what she terms "brokenheartedness." She deals explicitly with suffering caused by abuse, especially violence in families and against women and children.

For Brock, at the "heart" of life is connection. Existence depends on connection and relation. Connection is broken by sin, evil, and suffering, which produce damage and loss of heart. Brock writes: "Finding our heart means remembering how we have been damaged. It means facing the past squarely, ambivalent and whole, without nostalgia, without romantic heroes and heroines, and without numbness."[41] Memory has the capacity to restore: "Memory that emerges from the heart of ourselves binds us to the suffering of others and provides us the routes to empowerment and self-acceptance. Such memory also makes us hungry for collective memory, for the stories of our own people, and of the truth of the life of the human species."[42]

Drawing on process theology and object relations theory, Brock's perspectives on the human condition of suffering and the process of remembering are more relational and existential than historical. The process of remembering for healing is through relation and the restoration of heart. Memory creates and is created by connection, which expressed as erotic power, "is the divine dimension of human existence" and "the energy of incarnate love."[43] Salvation is healing and empowerment in and for remembrance and connection. Living by heart takes us on a dangerous journey of "witness against all powers of oppression and destruction."[44] Trusting "in heart, in erotic power, is a dangerous act" and "dangerous memories are frightening."[45] Through courage and "heartfelt connections," we can face fear and threat, and experience transformative power. In these ways, we witness to the power of erotic love, the power of remembrance of heart, to restore life.

Brock attends with care to the journey of healing from injury and trauma. Yet she also does not elaborate sufficiently on the ambiguities of remembrance. Because she does not fully historicize human relations, erotic power and love remain idealized in a way that does not do justice to the complex dynamics of power present in the practices of remembering.

These feminist theologians — Johnson, Schüssler Fiorenza, Welch, and Brock — each in her way bids us to remember. Remembering is a narrative action in solidarity. It both requires and creates community. Remembering is a process that leads to re-membering of persons and society. These feminist theologians, along with Metz, lift up dangerous memories as potentially powerful and effective for salvation. Yet the danger remains ambiguous; the process not clearly delineated. What is the process of remembering for redemption? What is the nature of witness and solidarity?

Pluralizing Dangerous Memory

In the end, the term "dangerous memory" is not adequate for the complex processes of remembering that we saw emerging from the experiences of the victimized. If we are to listen and respond to those who have suffered persecution, abuse, torture, and oppression, then we need to pluralize the process of remembering. The witness of remembering requires us to attend more carefully to the multiple memorative practice that was outlined in the first section of this book. In other words, danger does not tell the whole story of redeeming memories.

We have seen that the threats to remembering are multiple and real. They operate both externally and internally. Remembering is not only dangerous, but endangered. Sometimes what is endangered is the remembrance of suffering, as Johann Baptist Metz argues. In other instances, what is endangered is the remembrance of resistance to oppression and of acts of historical agency. This is the concern of the feminist theologians I surveyed. Even more often, what is endangered is remembrance of a vision of life — whole, connected, fruitful, joyful, even if fragile or imagined. Sharon Welch and Rita Nakashima Brock especially seek to remind us of such visions. Because remembering may be endangered in all these ways, it is not enough to bid the Christian community to remember suffering. The community must also remember resistance and agency, as well as the yearning for and practice of fullness of life.

When memories of suffering are threatened, then remembering them may itself be an act of resistance. This is Metz's point. In his world—Western, first-world, elite, male—suffering is excluded or manipulated. To hold up in memory the experience of the victimized is to challenge the dominant worldviews and to practice resistance. From the perspective of the victimized, however, the remembrance of suffering does not necessarily change anything. Such remembrance may arouse fear and/or anger by stirring the trauma from its hiding place. It may offer explanation for the ongoing pain in their lives. It tells the truth and leads to wounds that have to be found, identified, and opened in order to be treated and healed. For such reasons, remembrance of suffering is necessary and important, but what nurtures resistance to the degradation and oppression is recalling that the victimization was not total. Taking such a step asks of the victimized that they remember their own acts of resistance, agency, and struggle in the midst of the victimization itself. Feminist theologians, in particular, are pointing to the importance of women claiming their own experiences of agency, as well as mining historical records for evidence of women's full presence, participation, and resistance. The recall of struggle and historical action, however compromised or seemingly insignificant they may have been, breaks the stranglehold of narratives that tell only a story of victimization and suffering. Such recovered memories offer resisting readings of history and experience. The witness of such memories is to the resourcefulness and resilience of human beings who choose life, however they are able, in the worst of conditions.

Not all those who have been victimized had opportunity for such choice or any choice. Not all survived. By not letting death and loss be the last word of narratives of persecution and annihilation, resisting readings also bear witness to all that has been lost. Memories of resistance, resilience, and survival threaten any claim that victimization is total. These memories are dangerous to those in power because they harbor and nurture insurrection. They are also threatening to the victimized because they call for rethinking the accommodations that were made in order to survive. They recall the traumas in different ways and they offer the possibility of hope. For those who have been starved of hope, such an offer can be frightening.

Yet it is hope and the desire for life that motivates remembrance. Even remembrance as loyalty to past trauma is a form of desire for life. Remembering is a human, historical activity, reflecting the divine. It makes us human, situates us in history, and connects us with one another and with the divine. Remembering for life and salvation expands beyond the frame of suffering and even survival to call for an abundance of life, as inheritance from the past and vision for the future. Interconnecting memory recalls alternative histories and imagines transformed possibilities. When Sharon Welch writes of the web of life, fragile, yet strong and Rita Nakashima Brock points to erotic power seeking connection, they are affirming relation and living and wholeness. The power released through remembering calls for a witness to more than threat and even more than resistance. It seeks birth and actualization; relationships of intimacy and mutuality; embodied structures of justice; fruitfulness, and joy—not only as imagined, but as realized, in however partial form. Surviving is not life enough for those who want to be fully alive. Surviving is about getting through; living is about embracing and laying claim to the whole of life.

Remembering of life connection and wholeness requires a narrative that is not controlled by the history of victimization. It means finding other stories to tell that mediate fullness of life. When my grandmother told me the story of a woman leading worship and a girl speaking before the class, she connected us in a way we had never before been connected. Alongside the inheritance of the memories of my family's and my people's suffering and survival, she was telling me it was good and right for me to choose to be fully who I felt called to be. And she was suggesting that my life choices validated her and fulfilled her witness. Through her telling and my hearing, through both our remembering, we were giving each other gifts of life. My father had told her these events could not have happened. Neither did I get the full import of her story for many years and even doubted its truth. Given how strong the forces are that would choke life, there is danger and threat even in remembering connection. Such forces threaten from the outside: there are those who would want the suffering to continue or who act out of ignorance and forgetfulness. And they threaten from within, from the stranglehold of trauma.

In order to respond to threats and dangers and to tell the full story of suffering, survival, and life wholeness, remembering needs to be multiple. The multiple memorative practice I am advocating understands distinctive modes of remembering as preserving, resisting, and life-connecting. Remembering for redemption includes all three modes as ongoing processes. They are not sequential, nor do they replace one another. These modes of remembering function as narrative threads to be held and woven. Such a weaving produces a different understanding of coherence.

No one narrative can tell or hold the full story of remembrance. Narrative adequacy and effectiveness are to be measured by a narrative's ability to communicate multiple and even conflicting remembrances; and to do so in the face of threats—psychological, social, and political challenges. These threats persist. Even when the acts of victimization and oppression are long past, for survivors themselves and for their heirs, the challenges, distortions, and denials, internal and external, remain. At times of change and transition—personal and political— they will be particularly strong. Each practice of remembering may be endangered and/or experienced as dangerous, depending on the circumstances and the situation. Remembering, then, has to be attended to with great care and with continuing vigilance in relation to threats and shifting dynamics of power. Bearing witness is the faithful and ongoing practice of remembering as preserving, resisting, and connecting in full awareness of the complex and conflictual narrative field in which we remember.

Beyond Solidarity with Victims

Political, liberation, and feminist theologians share a common commitment to the oppressed and victimized. Their theologies are done in awareness of the suffering and degradation that seem to characterize the world of the poor, the persecuted, and the abused. For these theologians, theology is to be done for the sake of, on behalf of, those who suffer. It requires witness and solidarity. Theology seeks to be effective.

I see a fundamental contradiction between the way the commitment to victims is articulated in many of these theologies and the desire for effectiveness. Whether it is liberation theology's claim to God's preferential option for the poor, or political theology's commitment of solidarity with victims, it is the condition of need that turns divine and human attention to the poor and victimized. To offer solidarity with victims is to suggest that it is their victimization that elicits our witness. For example, even though Metz includes in his understanding of solidarity an assertion of human togetherness and interdependence, what he stresses is human need: "above all indigence (need) is the decisive presupposition for recognizing the subjectivity of others."[46]

I do not understand this contradiction to be intentional. It arises from problems long set into Christian thinking that affirms God's

154

power and human's powerlessness and sees salvation as rescue. The rhetoric of "preference" and "option" suggests choice from outside the situation by those with more power. God chooses the poor, presumably among "options," and it is right and good that we do the same. Solidarity is understood to be a form of moral witness, originating in God's care for the dispossessed. Many liberationist appeals to biblical views of justice affirm that moral witness. God requires care for the stranger, the one in need, the "least" among us. Although we are bid to identify with those in need, they remain as "other." Even though liberation theologians appeal to Jesus' identification with those in need, by citing Matthew 25 — "what you do to the least of these, you do to me" — there is still a sense of separation and otherness. Jesus may be one with those in need, but his hearers are not.

What I am proposing is a different understanding of witness and solidarity. It is a position of "withness," that is grounded in a vision of living and a celebration of relationship that does not dissolve difference. Such witness is rooted less in moral choice and more in recognition and affirmation of a common, yet multiple humanity. The mystery of grace, offered by God in creation and redemption, is that we are all profoundly and inextricably interconnected one to another. Our witness must ultimately be to such life. We are all diminished by the suffering in our world. Grace is mediated to all whenever life is renewed and transformation is realized. So we enter into "solidarity" for the sake of life. This practice of solidarity is grounded in incarnational thinking. It contrasts with other theological approaches that emphasize following Christ as an imitation that leads always to the cross.

Solidarity is most properly a relation of empowerment through presence, alliance, partnership, and advocacy. Witness in solidarity requires a rethinking of power that critically analyzes Christian understandings that are grounded in dynamics of domination and of control versus liberation. Christian views of liberation have developed as "correctives" to views of domination. In such debates, power is moralized as good and bad. The power of domination becomes bad power. God is on the side of the good power of liberation. Yet power, as Foucault has shown, is not inherently moral, good, or bad. It is energy and force that is used for domination and regulatory regimes, but is available for resistance. Power is necessary for living, even if it is used to delimit the possibilities of life. It may be made inaccessible by social arrangements. People within social systems may be made to feel they cannot do anything and are powerless. But human beings also find ways of resisting and subverting. Evaluations of power ought then to assess how power is being deployed and what types of regimes it is supporting or keeping in place. Attention should also be given to sites of resistance and subversion. In recognizing that power is always being manifest in ambiguous, conflictual, and contested ways, and that internal and external threats remain, witness in solidarity requires ongoing analysis and intentionality.

Even though the interrelationship and connectedness of all is of divine purpose and design, it is not an ontological given. Rather, it is historical promise, partially realized and always elusive. It is constituted narratively and enacted in practice. The multiple memorative practices of preserving, resisting, and relating that I have outlined are intended to help realize connection and life, as well as mourn loss, and support resistance. Witness as "withness" is a listening and holding with loving care and effective empowerment.

Foundational and Anthropological Affirmations

For centuries, theologians and philosophers of being and existence have asked the question: why is there something and not nothing? That question led them to the reality of God, as source of being and ground of existence. I am also concerned about being, but in a different way. Given the history of my family and my awareness of victimization and oppression, I wonder: why do people choose life and not death? Why do people in situations of extreme suffering and trauma not give up on life completely? This questioning also leads me to God. For me, the miracle, the divine mystery, is in the resilience of the human spirit that is able to choose life again and again in the midst of death; the human spirit that does not give up and lie down to die (even if that is all some are able to do); the human spirit that says no to the horror of what is and imagines other possibilities (even if these split the person into pieces). This human spirit craves freedom and love and works endlessly for change, renewal, and right relation, at the same time that it is deeply wounded.[47]

Trauma causes injury. Traumatic situations are much too common. The responses people make to trauma are about taking care of themselves and finding ways to survive and trying to make sense of the senseless. We have seen how sometimes, especially if these responses continue after the trauma no longer threatens, these behaviors may become dysfunctional and themselves harmful. But the motivation at the heart of traumatic responses is to live and do what it takes to go on living. In the experiences of those who have lived through trauma, degradation, and oppression, we then may see evidence of power and desire for life. The resilience of the human spirit is manifest even in the worst of circumstances. In the witness of those most degraded are resources for hope and even joy. These are seeds of life, fertile and struggling to be realized.

The woman in Alice Walker's poem, which opened this section, displays such resilience and desire for life connection. That woman begins with the question "remember me?" and ends with the promise of life renewed and transformed. She is transformed by her articulated remembrance into someone able to offer flowers of hope and justice. Alice Walker's poem demonstrates that human existence and reality are constituted narratively. As the woman in the poem tells her story, she changes. She creates herself. She does not do this alone. The poem is addressed to an other, who moves from being "you" to being included in "us." In a very real sense, as the poem indicates, we make ourselves through the stories we tell ourselves and others, as well as through the stories we are told.

There is much discussion in intellectual circles these days about the nature of human identity and agency and the ways in which human beings are constructed through social, political, and/or discursive practices. Postmodernists debate about whether there are such things as subject and agents. Some would suggest that the human person is being deconstructed into nothingness. What I am suggesting is that we cannot posit what it is to be a human person *a priori.* Rather, the human subject is constructed discursively through narrative and acts narratively. Sociologist Margaret Somers writes of "ontological narratives," which "are the stories that social actors use to make sense of—indeed, to act in—their lives . . . the relationship between narrative and ontology is processual and mutually constitutive. Both are conditions of the other; neither are *a priori.*"[48] Such narratives "make identity and the self something that one *becomes.*"[49] This formation is social: "Identity-formation takes shape within these relational settings of contested but patterned relations among narratives, people, and institutions."[50] The ability to develop narratives is limited by available stories, plots, and representations. Somers argues that: "Which kinds of narratives will socially predominate is contested politically and will depend in large part on the distribution of power."[51] Narratives can and do change, as well as serve as battlegrounds for social power.

The multiple memorative practice I propose is about enlarging the narrative repertoire of what it means to remember suffering. It is also about redistributing power by changing cultural narratives of social relationships. Challenges to and denials of these memories provide evidence of the power that is at stake and the potential for cultural change made possible through these emerging narratives.

The starting point for my theological construction is the human person, victimized, resilient, able to act and affirm life. In that way, I am in accord with the modern "turn to the subject" in theology. I concur with Karl Rahner that "theology is anthropology." However, I do not hold to his modern notion of subjectivity. I agree with those strains of postmodern thought, such as that of Somers, which understand human subjectivity as both socially and narratively constituted within a web of relations of power. This subject is not fixed. Agency is not located in an individual actor, but is a function of the ability of a person to interact with and among a web of relations. This understanding of agency and identity is truer to the experience of survivors, even though they are not always able to express it in available narrative forms. The proposed multiple memorative practice is meant to offer more adequate and complex narrative possibilities.

I also understand all knowledge—including theological—as subject to the play of power. Christian theology is not innocent knowledge. If Christianity is to be a religion of justice and hope, the question, then, becomes what kind of regimes are created and supported by its ideologies and institutions. Ultimately, the liberating and transformative potential of remembering is measured by what that remembering makes possible. If Christianity is to be redeeeming memory, then its theology must support the kind of remembering that honors the suffering, yet makes life possible. The Christian story must be one that heals and liberates through its memorative narratives and practices.

This claim holds many implications for the Christian narrative. In the following chapters, I explore what it means for Christian understandings of Jesus Christ, redemption, and the church. Here I suggest how it might affect our understanding of the human condition. If Christianity is to be a religion of remembering for witness and transformation, then it needs to change from its focus on sin and death to an affirmation of creation and life. Such a transformation is not to compromise the reality of evil or the persistence of sin. There is no question that we live in a world of sin. Human beings are ceaselessly perpetrating harm and

violence against one another, the world, and the environment. Such violence takes on a life of its own through institutions, structures, practices, and ideologies that justify it or naturalize it. Persons pretend that
they are not responsible or that they are powerless. They may even
believe in the "rightness" of the behaviors and attitudes. They develop
ideological justifications to support their position and enlist God on
their side. God is called in to give divine sanction to social arrangements that oppress and do harm. Therefore, God cannot be innocently
recruited on the side of liberation without problematizing and challenging such ideologies and practices.

Those who are victimized are often complicit in their condition of
victimization. I do not presume innocence or purity among those who
are victimized.[52] There is much that attests to their inability to escape
from the traumas that trap them. They practice destructive behaviors,
directed toward self and others; their lives reflect this brokenness. In
order to understand the dynamics of their "sin," however, we need to
see their lives through the lenses of trauma and oppression and their
aftereffects. The effects of trauma and oppression can persist long after
persons are safe and free. The struggle for wholeness entails working
through these effects. It requires much attention, care, and support.
Christian perspectives on sin, suffering, and redemption have made it
more difficult to recognize trauma and its impact on the victimized
because these perspectives tend not to differentiate between those who
perpetrate harm and those who are harmed. In other words, the narratives of what it means to be culpable and responsible will be different
for those who sin and those who are sinned against.[53]

Christian theology also needs to attend more to human participation
in redemption. The ways in which discussions of will and nature and
grace have been framed tend to hold human beings responsible for
whatever befalls them, but offer little by way of empowerment. Attention to practices of resistance and resilience will open up new ways of
viewing the dynamics of redemption. For example, African American
theologians are mining narratives to uncover the ways, alongside the
language of dependency on God and Jesus, in which African Americans portray their own agency and resistance. M. Shawn Copeland, for
one, highlights the use of "sass" by enslaved black women, "to guard,
regain, and secure self-esteem; to obtain and hold psychological dis-
tance; to speak truth; to challenge . . . and, sometimes, to protect
against sexual assault."[54] Copeland suggests that at the same time that

these women relied fully on God and God's power, they entered into a partnership of redemption with God.[55] They used their resources to survive and to claim life for themselves and others.

To argue that we need a Christian narrative that affirms life does not mean that it will forget death and those who have died. Life includes the tragic. Hope does not turn its back on injustices that can never be justified or made up for. There is nothing that can adequately answer or compensate for what has been lost, whether that be thousands of human lives or the trusting openness of a child. Such losses cannot be redeemed. As Michael S. Roth has stated: "Mourning, or the historical consciousness that results from it, is not a reparation; it is not replacing the dead but making a place for something else to be in relation to the past. . . . We allow ourselves to experience what we have lost, and also what we are—that we are—despite this loss."[56] Such mourning is done in community. Any claiming of life embraces the lost and preserves them in memory and mourning through community.

The mystery of God's presence bears the seeming contradiction that witnessing to suffering in narrative and community both remembers and also "forgets" the terror and trauma. As Roth and psychologists of trauma have pointed out, to speak of trauma is to begin to let go of it, to loosen its hold, and, even, in a sense, to lose it.[57] The narrative telling is necessary for healing and such integration, but it is also an experienced loss. In the beginning and at the end, remembering is a risk requiring courage and trust. What makes the risk possible is the affirmation that with God, nothing is lost. With God, our remembering may pay due honor to the dead and the living.

For those who live with a legacy of trauma, remembering makes possible a type of coherence, but it is also disruptive and interruptive. This is most dramatically experienced in the kinds of flashbacks that abuse survivors experience that are also common with other trauma victims. Johann Baptist Metz has emphasized the interruption of history in apocalyptic terms. His interest is to indict history and notions of historical progress lest the dead and suffering be forgotten or left behind. Scholars of the Holocaust argue in a similar vein that the reality of the Holocaust created a kind of historical rupture that negates any positive evaluation of history. I come at these concerns somewhat differently, by focusing more on the interests of those who suffer, for whom interruption—or more descriptively, eruption—is necessary but not welcome. It contains both threat and promise. The task of historical negotiation is to establish coherence, in the knowledge that full integration or resolution is not ultimately possible. History remains ruptured, without continuity or even stability. Ironically, but in truth, hope—and the type of transformation it makes possible—is born when one is able to live into such an ambiguous and precarious existence.

A multiple practice of remembering is intended to account for these seeming contradictions. Through suffering and loss, resistance and resilience, and the embracing of life, wholeness and connection are held together. To be human means to remember in history. To be human with God means to remember as God remembers, for redemption. To be human in community is to bear witness to oneself and others and especially to those whose own witness is buried in silent pain or death.

For Christians that witness is through Jesus Christ. The promise of redemption is told through the story of the birth, life, death, and resurrection of Jesus Christ. Yet too often when Christianity has remembered Jesus Christ, it has not told a fully redeeming story. As a result, Christianity is problem, as well as resource, for those victims who seek to find redemption there. We need to retell the story of Jesus Christ in such a way that our narrative witness speaks to the complex processes of remembering revealed in attending to those who suffer and struggle for fullness of life.

5

Remembering Jesus Christ, Remembering Redemption

When I was about nine years old, I asked my Sunday school teacher why Easter was more important than Christmas. I said that, after all, if Jesus had not been born, he would not have died or been resurrected. Whether this was the linear and literal thinking of a child or the musings of a young theologian, I remember it as my first theological question. My Sunday school teacher replied that it was a good question and that he did not know the answer. This lack of response left me with my question and quest unfulfilled. As with many issues of Christology, my question was rooted in a soteriological concern. What was it about who Jesus was and what he did that was the work of salvation?

A couple of years or so later, while still a young child, I had an experience that I consider a mystical encounter. I was sitting in the living room. Since my family lived atop my parents' grocery store, this room was on the second floor. As I looked out the window at the rooftops of the row houses across the street, I began to envision roof upon roof stretching around the world. I felt lifted out of myself for an instant: I was in the world of all those roofs and no longer on the couch in our living room. My center moved outside of myself and I felt one with the world and its inhabitants. Though the experience startled me, I experienced no fear. Though it was but an instant in time, it has stayed with me in a haunting way ever since. I cannot re-create it and can barely describe it, but I can recall it. For me, it contained something of redemption: not only the promise, but the experience, that my life was part of something beyond myself that was very real and deeply connecting. And this something was worldly. This was no nature mysticism or direct encounter with the divine. The connection I experienced was in and through the world, the concrete lives of people, literally joined by rooflines. For me, these apprehensions point to the truths of incarnation and redemption, truths that seem to elude Christianity itself.

My goal in this chapter is to explore such truths by enlarging the frame of the redeeming work of Jesus Christ. For too long, Western Christianity has focused its soteriological attention primarily on the cross. It has asserted that we are saved through Jesus' suffering and death, vindicated in the resurrection. The memorative narrative of Jesus has been shortened, essentially to Johann Baptist Metz's phrase, *memoria passionis*, memory of the passion. Even if "and the resurrection" is added, the emphasis remains on the passion. In the end, Metz's saving narrative of Jesus is all about the cross. Metz is not alone in this. He stands in a long line of Western theological thinking that emphasizes the cross as the site of redemption and stresses the redemptive value of suffering and sacrifice.

This is not adequate. A theology of redemption that focuses on Jesus' death as *the* saving event is not able to incorporate the multiple memorative practice necessary to speak fully of salvation, especially to those who struggle with suffering, trauma, and loss. Jesus was not born only to suffer and die. To tell of God's redeeming love, it is necessary to narrate a story of the fullness of divine presence, imaged and encountered in Jesus, who lived among us, as one of us, to the point of abandonment, torture, and death. During his life, Jesus laughed and cried, walked and ate with his friends, preached and healed, became weary and rested, felt love and fear, grew in wisdom and understanding, listened and changed, touched and was touched. He offered a vision of God's reign and lived into it with deep respect and care. The torture he was subjected to killed him, yet the power of life made him alive. Jesus' life did not end with the suffering he underwent. He lives on in the community of resurrection, making life possible again and again. He is present even now among us through our remembering of him and our being re-membered through him. The Spirit enlivens our remembering and re-membering in an ongoing process of redemption. The "event" of Jesus Christ—his birth and life, death and resurrection—is made real through our own salvific activity. Christ lives in and for the community that proclaims the good news of transformation and reconciliation. The community remembers Jesus Christ for the sake of salvation. This whole process is what I mean by incarnation. Incarnation, then, is not a singular event in the past, but an ongoing process and experience of divine presence.

This chapter moves toward such an understanding of incarnation by explicating what it means to remember Jesus Christ in such a way that we are re-membered and redeemed, even in relation to the most horrific suffering. I begin by looking at theologies of the cross and why they do not provide an adequate redeeming memory. Then I expand the witness to include the resurrection and life of Jesus, and God's incarnated presence. I conclude by offering a narrative of redemption, inclusive of a multiple practice of remembering Jesus Christ.

The Scandal of the Cross: Historical Developments

Jesus—prophet and teacher, healer and friend—was condemned to die by crucifixion, a torturous and ignoble death. Jesus' followers were confused and frightened. Many of them fled from the cross. Only a few of the women remained. Whatever it was about Jesus that had drawn these men and women to him, it did not include this kind of death. What were they to do with this scandalous turn of events? They had followed him around the countryside and to Jerusalem. They had witnessed him performing healings and exorcisms that were hailed as miracles. They had sat at table with him, and had practiced the vision and power he showed them. How could they now face his death? What hope could there be in this?

The cross was a crisis for Jesus' followers and those who came after. I would suggest that the crucifixion of Jesus was a traumatic event, for Jesus himself and for the community around him. It terrified and confused Jesus' friends. It left them bereft and abandoned. They did not know how to respond and deal with this loss and trauma, especially since they seemed more interested in sharing in Jesus' power than in his defeat.

Rather than remembering Jesus' death as a traumatic event, Jesus' followers looked for ways to justify it and, indeed, to make it their justification. That process began with Paul and the other New Testament writers, who looked for images and metaphors to give shape to the unimaginable and to give meaning to what was experienced as scandalous. Though the narratives they wove were in light of the resurrection, that light was directed toward, and shown on, the cross. Though the early Christian community came to be through the power of the resurrection, it was the sign of the cross that seemed to consume its attention.

The resulting process turned more and more to the cross as meaningful and effective for salvation. The cross was remembered and witnessed to as *the* saving moment: Jesus giving up his life as ransom, in expiation or propitiation, to reconcile or make sacrifice. A whole array of metaphors and descriptions were appropriated to narrate the death as accomplishing a good. Jesus' suffering was increasingly seen as something Jesus chose, indeed, the reason for his existence. Jesus gave up his life and died, for the sake of our salvation, for us. The need for such an offering was explained and justified by the reality of human sinfulness. Jesus died to set sinful humanity into right relation, to make atonement.

Over time, a narrative thread was spun consisting of the cross, Jesus' undeserved suffering, and human sin. Jesus' sacrifice was required because of the sinful human condition. Suffering was good, a thing of value that was effective. This narrative took a number of forms, with shifting stress on the different ways to understand or symbolize what Jesus did. Was it ransom or sacrifice? Did the death reconcile or make offering?

Symbols clashed: Jesus was hero and victim, warrior and scapegoat. However else he was depicted, Jesus was innocent and sinless, undeserving of death. The scandal of Jesus' death magnified as his divinity was proclaimed more and more. What did it mean for the divine one to die? How could that be? Especially for the Greek mind, death and divinity could not coexist. God was immortal and unchanging. God could not suffer or die.

Early church theologians strained and struggled in relation to what seemed so inconceivable and unreconcilable. Motivated to proclaim what they knew as saving grace, they held tightly to the principle: that which is not assumed is not healed. If suffering and death were to be "healed," to be part of God's saving work, they had to be known to God in Christ. But how? These theologians turned to Greek philosophical categories of being to find ways to describe the incarnation and to affirm the presence of God in the Christ event. Their desire for an adequate ontological explanation moved them further from the narrative structure of early Christian witness.

Christian practice developed its own responses to these dilemmas. Faithfulness to God meant imitating Jesus. If Jesus suffered, then human suffering could be seen as a way of following him. Martyrs and ascetics adopted the passion of Jesus Christ as a trope to understand and narrate their own experiences. Their goal was participation in Christ: his suffering and that of his followers were read as one narrative. The martyrs imaged Christ in their tortured bodies. The language of martyr texts speaks of the martyrs, not as victimized, but as empowered through suffering. In later years, as Christianity became more established and, indeed, became the religion of the empire, the focus shifted to asceticism and suffering as a means of discipline and penitence. Ironically, suffering became the means of both making an offering to God and reflecting the divine. For both martyrs and ascetics, the "suffering self" became the cornerstone of what it meant to be Christian: "to be a Christian was to suffer and die."[1] Jane Strohl suggests two primary ways of accounting for suffering in Christianity: "The Christian tradition has attempted to explain suffering under two broad rubrics: suffering as *imitatio* and suffering as discipline."[2] For martyrs, suffering was imitation for participation; for ascetics, it was discipline for combat.

Meanwhile, the category of sin grew more encompassing. It began to consume all other forms of alienation, pain, or lack—even finitude. Sin was the cause of evil in the world. Human suffering was a result of sin. Rebellion against suffering could then be read as further sinful behavior. In that sense, suffering was deserved. Such thinking did not differentiate sufficiently among the types of suffering humans might endure.

Thus suffering came to be understood as necessary, valuable, beneficial, and redemptive. Jesus himself was the model of suffering for the sake of redemption. Some theologies even emphasized the passiveness of Jesus' death: he was as a sheep led to slaughter; he offered no word of protest; he offered his suffering fully to his heavenly "Father" who, it was even said, demanded it in retribution for the wrongs perpetrated against "Him" and "His" power and majesty.[3]

Jesus' passivity reflected back onto the human condition. Not only did human beings have no capacity to participate in their salvation, but their suffering and acceptance of suffering might well be necessary for salvation. Jesus' passion and death had become the model for devotion to God: a dying of self and a positive valuation of suffering, for the sake of redemption, which was granted solely by God's grace.

Over time the remembrance of Jesus' death evolved from the original experience of trauma and scandal to a soteriology of the cross as purposeful and effective action, ordained by God, for the sake of salvation. Theological works like Anselm of Canterbury's *Cur Deus Homo* reinforced the idea that Jesus' passion and death were a necessary and even loving action. Even protests against Anselm by theologians such as Abelard or Walter Rauschenbusch, writing centuries apart, continued to uphold the redemptive value of Jesus' suffering love. Suffering served as model for Christian love.

The fear and confusion experienced by Jesus' followers were forgotten; their mourning aborted. The experience of death was denied, in a way, by later theological developments that celebrated Jesus' death as a good thing. The memory of Jesus' death was glorified, even as it continued to be heralded as scandalous. Its scandalous nature was itself reinterpreted. The scandal became ours: that our sin necessitated such an action.

As Christianity gained power and position in the world, the valence of Christian theological affirmations about sin and redemption shifted. In the hands of those with social and political power, Christianity could be used as a useful system for social control. In such an environment, the political function of talk about sin and redemptive suffering could be developed to serve the interests of Christendom. The cross became a symbol not of scandal, but of conquest: God conquering sin and colonizers conquering "sinners." The cross came to stand for the power of those in positions of domination. This sign of defeat became a banner of triumphant power. It was proclaimed as the sole avenue to redemption—for everyone. Those who suffered could at best find consolation in a savior who offered redemption through suffering.

Political, Liberation, Black, and Feminist/Womanist Theological Critiques and Constructions

Political, liberation, black, and feminist/womanist theologies critique such theological developments; they acknowledge the ways in which the cross has been used to conquer and control, to encourage passivity and compliance. The cross is itself challenged and contested: the immensity and depth of human suffering raises questions about whether a suffering Christ can help. Yet for political, liberation, global, and black theologies, and for most feminist and womanist theologies, the cross still stands as site of redemption. They argue that what has been amiss is not the value of the cross for redemption, but the way it has been understood and interpreted. They tend to reinterpret the cross as an action of solidarity and saving love, and connect Jesus' death more closely with his life praxis. Emphasizing the political nature of Jesus' death, they view Jesus' death as a result of the challenges he posed to the reigning powers. Jesus' suffering is not passive, but is an active engagement for the sake of justice and liberation. The suffering of the oppressed has place and significance in and through Jesus' passion; such sharing in suffering opens up to hope. Suffering is thus meaningful and effective. The cross is central to God's redeeming (and suffering) power and presence with the poor and oppressed. It represents God standing with them in compassion and empowerment.[4]

More extensive critiques of the redemptive value of the cross are coming from feminist theologians. Some of these theologians, even while pointing to the problems in a model of suffering love, continue to embrace it. Chung Hyun Kyung, writing from a Korean perspective, notes that "making meaning out of suffering is a dangerous business."[5]

Yet she sees the cross as a source of empowerment for Korean women.[6] Elizabeth Johnson views the cross as an act of divine compassion and love, but her careful thinking differentiates modes of suffering and the relationship of suffering to redemption. She turns to women's own experiences of suffering—through childbirth, anger for justice, grief and degradation—for metaphors that might illuminate "the power of the suffering God."[7]

Other feminist theologians are wary of assigning any redemptive value to Jesus' death. Chief among these are Joanne Carlson Brown, Rebecca Parker, and Rita Nakashima Brock. Also advancing this perspective is womanist theologian Delores Williams.[8] Each in her own way points to the potentially harmful effect on those who are victimized and oppressed of viewing suffering as redemptive. Each seeks to do away with classic understandings of the atonement. Brown and Parker state bluntly: "Suffering is never redemptive, and suffering cannot be redeemed."[9] Surveying the various approaches to the atonement, including those proferred by liberation theology, they conclude that any view of the cross and suffering as redemptive reinforces the acceptability of violence and is abusive theology. Rita Nakashima Brock also accuses traditional atonement theories of supporting "cosmic child abuse." Atonement theologies breed theologies and relationships of dependency. They make good a result of suffering and so make suffering a good.[10]

Womanist theologian Delores Williams's commitment is to African American women's survival and quality of life. Her critique is rooted in an analysis of surrogacy as emblematic of black women's experience of suffering and oppression. Atonement theologies tend to read Jesus' death on the cross as an act of surrogacy and so reinforce surrogacy and suffering as good and redemptive.[11]

Elisabeth Schüssler Fiorenza, surveying many of these critiques and constructive efforts, turns our attention back to the New Testament interpretations of Jesus' death. She contrasts the "empty tomb" tradition of the women with the "visionary appearance" tradition associated with the male disciples. It is the visionary appearance tradition that has provided the language of sacrifice and atonement. She concludes that because much of feminist criticism has been formulated in relation to this androcentric and kyriarchal tradition, it cannot find new ways of thinking about Jesus' death, or "hear" those who still find the living among the dead.[12] She proposes that as we continue in struggle, we will encounter the Resurrected One who goes ahead of us and calls us to life.

One of the contributions of Schüssler Fiorenza's work is to remind us that contrasting and contradictory views of Jesus' death were present from the earliest of responses and formulations—that death was indeed a crisis for the followers of Jesus. One set of responses tried to make sense of the death within available systems of meaning that attributed ultimate power and dominion to God. In critiquing this approach, Schüssler Fiorenza points to a key and critical concern in any theological consideration of the cross and suffering—namely, power.

The Power of the Cross

Though most theologies of the cross are about justifying God, I see them also struggling with human empowerment. The move to make meaning out of suffering is in part due to this interest in empowerment. Whereas that move seems to be about God and God's power, it is our human need that drives it. More traditional versions, whose main interest is in affirming God's power and sovereignty, attribute causation to human sin: Jesus had to die on the cross to save humankind. Human beings are then responsible for the death.

Ironically, holding humanity, as a whole, responsible for Jesus' death is a way to give human beings a kind of control and power. This dynamic is similar to the behavior of oppressed and abused people who would rather take on the responsibility for their victimization than feel utter powerlessness and lack of control. Sinfulness serves as a justification. It provides for a kind of coherence. Meanwhile, those who are most responsible and have power can claim a kind of innocence and nonculpability. Justifying the cross—and all suffering—as the result of human sin can serve the interests of domination.[13] It allows the dominators to ascribe to others the need for sacrifice and obedience for the sake of salvation. Political, liberation, and feminist theologies have rightly challenged this setup (pun intended). They often argue that the cross is not about the sin of the oppressed and victimized, but about their suffering, their undeserved and innocent suffering. They contend that the dynamics of power and responsibility must be named rightly. When that is done, God emerges as the one who sides with those who suffer, even to the cross. God's power is redefined as expressed not in domination, but in suffering love.

I am suggesting, therefore, that what motivates the emphasis on

God's solidarity with the weak and powerless, and the value of suffering love, is empowerment of the oppressed. When womanist theologian JoAnne Marie Terrell proclaims that there is "power in the blood" and when South American liberation theologian Jon Sobrino extols the contributions of "crucified peoples," they are interested in affirming those who suffer and helping the victimized toward liberation.[14] They are trying to find ways to empower those who are in situations of extreme powerlessness. They are seeking to right the relations of power that have been distorted and misused in those forms of Christianity that for centuries have provided ideological justification of violence against peoples and the earth through colonization, exploitation, slavery, abuse, and oppression.

Although I am sympathetic with these theologians' motivation and agree with the need to right not only relations, but understandings of power, I do not see their strategy as sufficient for empowerment or even for resistance. The primary value of affirming God's presence with and on behalf of those who suffer is to offer comfort and enable survival in situations of extreme victimization. In other words, God's presence in suffering may help one live with pain and suffering that cannot be changed, but such presence is not enough to enable one to change the situation of suffering. What I hear in the testimonies of those who claim the power of the crucified Jesus' presence in suffering is the affirmation that those who suffer are not ultimately alone and that God has not turned away from them. Rather, God is radically present even in seeming absence.[15] There may be comfort in knowing that even Jesus felt despair and abandonment. In that way, God does know their pain.

Such witness and "withness" is absolutely necessary for survival, but it does not change the conditions of victimization. Indeed, it does not really alter the terms of power. Delores Williams offers a similar argument in *Sisters in the Wilderness*. She points out that God's presence with the slave woman, Hagar, enables her and Ishmael's survival, but it does not change her condition of slavery. God's empowering presence in suffering is about endurance and survival. A different form of empowerment is necessary in order to assure quality of life. Such empowerment comes from being able to express agency and to change the conditions of oppression, not only endure them.[16]

Another motivation underlying the assertions of those who see the cross as empowering is to attribute agency and even virtue to those who suffer. This too is dangerous because it tends to give a positive value to suffering and may even romanticize the victimized.[17] As will be discussed, agency is to be attributed not to suffering but to being human. The "crucified peoples" participate in salvation because of their humanity, not their oppression.

I see danger in any move to relate undeserved and unchosen suffering to effectiveness or virtue. Suffering is suffering. It does not empower, even if it is necessary to endure it for the sake of empowerment. However, suffering, salvation, and power are so connected and embedded in Christian thinking focused on the cross, that it is difficult to think differently. In order to do so, we ultimately need to change the way we think about power. To move toward another understanding of power, it is necessary not only to challenge the notion of absolute dependency on God's power, but to question the redemptive value of the cross. It is not enough to shift the meaning of the cross from sacrifice to solidarity and witness. Neither is it adequate for the oppressed and abused to identify with Jesus on the cross or to reinterpret atonement in a more relational way. As long as salvation is dependent on God's sovereign power and the site of salvation is the cross, then suffering will be redemptive. To affirm the soteriological contribution of those who suffer—such as crucified peoples, as well as crucified Savior—is not so much to change these terms as to try to redistribute them.

Just as remembering suffering in and of itself does not redeem from abuse, genocide, or cultural oppression, remembering Jesus' death does not redeem in and of itself. Jesus' death ought to be remembered precisely as a memory of suffering, rooted in trauma. Trauma that is not remembered and dealt with appropriately finds expression in distorted relationality and arrested living. So too with the cross. Suffering, pain, violence, and degradation get in the way of full humanity. Victimization, especially when it becomes a condition of existence, can block access to one's own resources and constrict life tremendously. Many persons who have sustained ongoing violation have developed mechanisms for avoiding and dissociating from pain. Such dynamics operate with groups of persons, as well as individuals. Communities that are oppressed may socialize their members in practices of distrust and avoidance.

The memory of Jesus' suffering on the cross may serve to "remind" the victimized that there is no way out but through the pain. Just as Jesus had to face the inevitability of his death, those who seek to remember for redemption must face the necessity of experiencing and dealing with the hurt and pain that are split off and buried in their memories of suffering. That process will feel as painful and lonely as the cross must have felt to Jesus. Jesus' experience of crucifixion can offer witness in that way too. But such witness is only effective if the crucifixion is set within a larger narrative that includes Jesus' life and resurrection. The pain of facing one's torture can only be endured if one knows, even if one does not feel, that it is not the last word, that there is new life on the other side of the pain. The crucifixion by itself is not effective for redemption; it can only provide a partial message of salvation.

For the cross to be a redeemed and redeeming memory, Christianity has to face the crucifixion in a new way, as a traumatic event, embedded in a web of relations. The fixation of the Christian tradition on the cross provides centuries of evidence of what happens when one tries to make something good and meaningful of what is not good or meaningful or transforming. The danger of distorting the cross is always there. It is a kind of ambiguous space that has been claimed too often on behalf of the interests of domination. Remembering the cross as an endangered memory of suffering is one way to stay alert to the danger.

The memory of the cross must be preserved precisely as tragic. It is a death and a loss that needs to be mourned. In the Christian story, the narration of Jesus' death is an invitation to all those who have suffered unjustly and unremittingly to add their testimonies. The witness of Jesus' death is made real through such testimonies. In that sense, all suffering and loss find place in the cross, and the cross is kept real through such witness.

The cross is not about God executing (pun intended) a plan of salvation for humankind, but about God taking responsibility for the degradation and tragedy of the human condition.[18] God is thus present in the worst of human pain. Such presence does not transform, but it does support. It is an act of solidarity, as well as of witness. Those who choose to stand with the abused and oppressed in witness may find themselves also facing threat, persecution, and even death. In this way, there may be suffering for the sake of witness and healing.

In the end, the cross is not a source of empowerment or transformation. Acknowledging the cross, however, is a necessary condition for the possibility of empowerment and transformation. Suffering is not good, but neither is it meaningless. It is real and needs to remain part of our redemptive memory. Suffering effects not salvation, but loss: the loss of all those who died because of violence and injustice, and the losses that those who survive violence carry with them. Such suffering and loss ought to be mourned and given due honor. To give due honor suggests that the suffering not be justified or made to stand for more than it is. In that way, suffering is kept in its proper place.[19]

Resurrecting Hope: Remembering Resistance, Resilience, and Agency

The Christian story does not end with the cross. Very soon after Jesus' death and burial his followers began to report encounters with the risen Christ. The two on their way to Emmaus were but a pair in a growing number of those who proclaimed that Jesus was risen and had appeared to them. The Gospel accounts, written long after the event of resurrection, report the story of the women who found the tomb empty, as well as numerous instances of the risen Christ appearing to the disciples and other followers but not being recognized at first. Only through these encounters and interactions do the followers come to know the one present with them as he who had lived among them and was crucified, died, and was buried. The resurrection was of the body. It was not only Jesus' spirit that continued to live, but the embodied person whom they had known. This resurrected body did not erase the suffering endured: Jesus' scars remain as evidence that the crucifixion was real. No future hope or restoration negates the reality of past injury. The hope is real nonetheless: Christ is alive among those who had followed and befriended him.

Those earliest followers came slowly to this resurrection faith. Only as they were able to recognize Christ more fully could they proclaim with joy and conviction that the one who had died, lived again. This proclamation and faith became grounds for hope and for their commitment to continue to preach and teach in Christ's name. Their remembrance of Jesus, the retelling of the story, came to include the affirmation that torture and death were not the final word. There was life beyond the horror and degradation of the cross. Indeed, their testimonies to faith and hope were fed by the experience of Christ, alive among them. They were empowered by the Spirit to invite others into such hope.

How has the Christian memory accounted for this power and such hope? How has Christianity claimed the resurrection as saving memory? The resurrection is pointed to as evidence of the power of God to overcome threats to life. It is an act of resistance and resilience that effectively makes life possible, even beyond death. Jesus is not simply a passive victim, but the one able to break through the bonds of evil and death. This power of the resurrection is manifest among those who encounter Christ as risen: they are able to live into hope beyond fear; to be empowered beyond all that seeks to oppress and kill.

As I have indicated, Elisabeth Schüssler Fiorenza compares and contrasts the revelatory traditions represented by the empty tomb accounts, which feature women as witnesses, and those represented by the visionary appearance proclamations, which feature men.[20] She argues that in the empty tomb tradition, the "Resurrected One" is present to those who struggle for survival and liberation; the resurrection is vindication of struggle. In contrast, the visionary appearance tradition serves to authorize those (males) who claim to have seen the Resurrected One, who is now absent.[21] That tradition tends to empower those who claim the authority of witness, rather than empowering all to be witnesses. This visionary appearance tradition came to be the dominant one in Christianity. On the basis of being witness to the risen Christ, the apostles claimed authority to preach Christ crucified and risen, and the coming reign of God.

As the testimony of the early church developed, it took the symbol of the kingdom of God, which Jesus had preached and to which Jesus had pointed, and applied it to his person: the promised new realm was being ushered in by Jesus' resurrection. In Jesus the Christ, the reign of God was inaugurated. God's day, when all would be subject to the rule of God, was imminent. Faithfulness meant living in eager anticipation of Christ's return and the ultimate consummation of God's intent for the world.

The eschatological and apocalyptic tones of the early Christian witness shifted as the days stretched out and the second coming of Christ remained only a promise. Early Christians turned their attention to the future on earth and looked for different ways to anticipate God's reign. Hope shifted both forward and backward. The decisive victory had already been won in the resurrection. The promise of resurrected life would not be realized in this life, but in a life to come.

There is a way in which delay in the anticipated return of Christ might be read as another traumatic event for the early Christian community. This return and the hope it symbolized seemed no longer in view. In dealing with this disappointment and the challenge it posed to

God's power, the early Christians sought to continue to have faith in God's promises and effectiveness. Resurrection faith developed as an affirmation and confirmation of the mighty power and glory of God, who was able to conquer sin, evil, and death. In other words, though the historical evidence seemed to contradict the faith that God was in charge of history and was bringing it to consummation, early Christians continued to proclaim, and do so even more strongly, the power of God to accomplish all things.

The salvific power of the resurrection has been underscored in what is referred to as the classical or patristic tradition of soteriology. The resurrection vindicates Jesus as the Christ and affirms God's power over the devil and the forces of evil. The metaphors of bondage and ransom serve to emphasize redemption as freedom and liberation. In the twentieth century, writing between two world wars, Gustav Aulén revived this classical model and labeled it *Christus Victor.* In the *Christus Victor* model, the resurrection is the place where God is vindicated, Christ's victory is confirmed, and humanity is liberated.[22]

There are strains of this thinking in those theologies of the oppressed that emphasize the resurrection and seek to uphold the power of God over all other powers and forces in the universe. In this affirmation is hope for the powerless and poor, for whom God has a preferential option. Indeed, the turning to cosmic battle can be read as a strategy of the powerless. Without the ability to effect change through human action on earth, the belief that God is in charge and is powerful may provide assurance and comfort. In addition, if evil is a real power, not of God, then explanations can be found for human suffering and oppression that do not originate in God and so ensure God's goodness.

The resurrection has always been a symbol of the power of life to overcome death, but its meaning has not remained constant. One set of interpretations underscores God's power as able to overcome all other powers and forces; another has been to portray Jesus Christ as a super-hero in a cosmic battle. Although these affirmations may provide important comfort for those who suffer, they can also lead to problematic compromises of human agency. When divine power and might are emphasized, human empowerment is not. In other words, the Resurrected One no longer goes on ahead and bids the people of God to follow as participants in the struggle for liberation. Rather, Christ's resurrection becomes the symbol of what God is able to accomplish for the sake of saving us. Further, when divine power is aligned with the power of those who conquer or maintain dominion on earth, then it can be used to reinforce oppression and passive compliance.

If the resurrection is to be an effective symbol of human agency and struggle, it must work to empower those who suffer. If it is to enable remembrance of resistance and resilience, then it ought to evoke life-sustaining powers within human beings. The ability of the symbol of resurrection to accomplish salvation and mediate hope requires that it be viewed as an affirmation of the power of life and not power as might. This necessitates a reconsideration of the way in which power is viewed: God's power and Jesus' power.

Jesus: Neither Victim Nor Hero

Even though Jesus is the "star," so to speak, in the cosmic battle between the forces of good and evil, he may not be viewed as the primary actor. If the action is cosmic, then it occurs, in a way, above and beyond Jesus. The resurrection is not something that Jesus accomplishes, but is what God is able to do to vindicate Jesus' sacrifice. It is God's action. When the resurrection is portrayed in this way, it is difficult to see how it might empower those who suffer on earth. It tends to make their vindication something to be accomplished in the heavens and/or at some future time. Emphasizing God's power or the promise of eternal life too much may contribute to a human sense of power-lessness.

One way to correct such a portrayal might be to emphasize that Jesus is the actor in this drama, a hero who is doing battle on our behalf. But, as Rita Nakashima Brock and Mark Kline Taylor have pointed out, such images of Jesus also compromise human power. Brock suggests that in modern atonement doctrines, "Jesus becomes the spiritual heroic warrior, the single conqueror who defeats death, injustice, or evil."[23] For Brock, such a view of Jesus is problematic because it separates Jesus from us and sets him apart as liberator of humanity. Such a Jesus exercises "unilateral power."[24]

Mark Kline Taylor also shies away from viewing Jesus as a hero. Taylor argues that emphasizing Jesus' singularity and power tends to reinforce Jesus' male identity in problematic ways. He sees Jesus Christ as "leaven" and "ferment," permeating the whole, rather than an individual agent.[25] For both Brock and Taylor, Christ exists in and through the community.

At the heart of images of victim and hero are concepts of power and will. If Jesus is but a victim, then it is only through the action of God in the resurrection that Jesus is vindicated and his divine status conferred. Such a view is especially problematic because it suggests that God's favor is won through obedient suffering. If Jesus is a hero, embracing suffering and then rising from the dead, then his exercise of will is something that eludes, if not indicts, the victimized. Each of these perspectives is problematic, because of the way in which power and will are viewed. For the victimized who are rendered powerless, heroic behavior is not possible and may even be dangerous. If their agency is to be recognized, it needs to be conceptualized not in terms of obedience or heroism, but as that which is expressed through acts of resilience and resistance that enable survival.

The resurrection is not about Jesus the hero breaking the bonds of death or about God the almighty doing battle on behalf of a lost humanity. Rather, the resurrection is about the power of life to persist and to prevail. It is the affirmation of life even when death seems more powerful. Such life is not a personal possession, but participation in a larger whole. The emphasis is not so much on survival of the individual as on the continuation of life itself. The ability to exercise power and will exist in and through a community.

Resurrection Through Christa/Community

The resurrection is an event that happens among the followers of Jesus. Rita Nakashima Brock refers to this as Christa/Community. Christa/Community begins in Jesus' lifetime as the expression of erotic power; the witness of Christa/Community continues after Jesus' death.[26] For Brock, the community resurrects Jesus' memory and his power through erotic power that is divine power.[27] I would propose a more dialectic relationship. The community resurrects Christ, but the resurrection also shapes the community. Resurrection is what happens between Jesus and his followers, manifesting the gracious and hope-filled presence of God. Resilient hope is always made more possible in a community of support and affirmation, a community intent on affirming life. Such hope makes the future possible, even when the present is impossible. It does not negate the suffering: the scars remain forever as reminder of the terror, pain, and loss. Neither does it leave the earth. Hope is embodied here and now. Yet such hope also embraces the unrealized redemption of those for whom resistance and resilience were not possible or not effective for survival.

179

The resurrection is a dangerous, subversive memory precisely because it tells us that evil, suffering, and even death are not the final word. Life is always possible, even if one's personal life comes to an end. Such life is not triumphant in a dominant sense, but it does celebrate resistance and resilience. Resurrection is a remembering of life in the midst of death; it is the struggle for survival. To witness to resurrection is to remember resistance and resilience.

Our witness to resurrection ought to include not only the story of Jesus Christ, but the stories of all those who claimed power, even when they did not know that was what they were doing; who found ways to go on living, even when there seemed to be no way; and who were not heroes in a dramatic sense, but who exercised a kind of resistance that enabled life for themselves and others. The miracle and mystery of resurrection is made manifest when there is "resurrection" from traumatic suffering, when people survive horrendous childhood abuse or genocide or slavery or other forms of degradation. The memorative practice of resurrection is shaped by the story of Christ's rising from the dead, but that story is in turn shaped and contoured by those who struggle for life.

Resurrection is always framed by crucifixion. There would be no need for the resurrection if there were no suffering and death. Resistance is always in some sense reactive; it is over against that which seeks to injure and destroy. Resurrection never gets beyond life as struggle. But life is more than suffering and survival and struggle. The power of life wants more for and from us. Crucifixion and resurrection narrate an incomplete story of redemption. In the beginning and in the end, the power of life must be manifest in embodied human existence, living and working and making whole.

Ambiguous Power

The power of resurrection that I describe is based in ambiguity. There are no absolutes. Indeed, one of the signs of resilience is precisely the ability to live with ambiguity. The narrative remembrance of resurrection ought to contain and foster that ability. The declaration — "we have seen the risen Christ" — is an affirmation of joy, rather than of certainty. There is nothing final about the resurrection. It is the ongoing witness to life that is always challenged and threatened. Its subversive power — that is, its ability to subvert death-dealing powers — is compromised and lost when the Christian community gets too fixated on "figuring out" the "problem" of resurrection. Rubem Alves notes: "It is ironical that the language which for the first Christians was the expression of freedom has become for us today rather a problem to be solved."[28] I would add the further irony that it is precisely in and through the ambiguity that resurrection is able to offer hope most fully. Ambiguity is not the enemy of hope; finality and certainty are. The power of resurrection is for freedom—a freedom that is always elusive and ambiguous, even as it is able to change the world and stir the hearts of all those in captivity and bondage.

It is difficult to live with ambiguity, so the temptation to eliminate it is strong. Such attempts often lead one into sand traps of faith. A potential trap of resurrection faith is precisely the seeking to dissolve the ambiguity, to make resurrection faith be more about belief than hope. Another trap is to make the resurrection a final event rather than a paradigmatic narrative of promise and resisting power. Yet another is to explain it away as wish fulfillment. A more common trap is to view resurrection as a miraculous event that proves God's power to intervene dramatically not only in history, but in nature. Each of these traps, in its own way, compromises the redemptive power of the resurrection. It is for the sake of the redemption and hope that the ambiguity must be celebrated. To read resurrection as resistance means to embrace its ambiguity. The truth of resurrection is not in its status as event, but in its ability to foster and narrate ongoing resistance and resilience.

Resurrection of the Body

Perhaps the most difficult challenge of resurrection faith is the assertion that Christ was resurrected bodily. The tomb is empty, the risen Christ appears as a bodily, albeit transformed, presence to friends and followers. Those who would do away with any ambiguity about this part of the story assert the resurrection of the body as evidence of God's power to overcome all, even the forces of nature of which death is a part. This approach does more to support the triumphal power of God than to communicate hope. Again there is irony: instead of bodily resurrection affirming the importance of embodied existence, God's power is aligned with denial of finitude and death, which define embodied existence.

Resurrection of the body ought to remain an ambiguous affirmation of faith. As Elisabeth Schüssler Fiorenza points out, the empty tomb traditions maintain that ambiguity. Whereas they declare the tomb empty, they say nothing about the body and yet affirm the Resurrected One as going on ahead. The presence of the Resurrected One is real and clearly manifest in and among the community of struggle.[29]

Resurrection of the body is an affirmation that bookends the incarnation. It is about God's full commitment to human existence. Hope and freedom include finitude and death, but are not exhausted by them. The whole person is to be saved; the site of suffering is also site of redemption.

Incarnating Life: Remembering Wholeness in Connection

I began this chapter with two stories from my childhood that reveal my bias toward "incarnation," toward affirming concrete life and relationship as the heart of what it means to be human and divine, as the center of God's redemptive desire. Ultimately, I see redemption as the ability to live into these affirmations of life and relationship, to enter into and experience life with love and power. In other words, redemption is about being alive, fully alive human beings. All else flows from the living: justice, healing, freedom, reconciliation, and harmony. I concur with Irenaeus that "the glory of God is humanity fully alive." To be redeemed is to be human—to remember that we are human, made in God's image and reflecting the glory of divinity.

Yet how difficult this is. Human beings are forever forgetting we are human. We do not remember to affirm living. We do not pay attention to the reality that our humanity is intertwined inextricably with that of others. No one can live fully alone. None of us will know justice or freedom truly, unless and until everyone does. Whereas we all forget these things, those who live with trauma from abuse, degradation, and oppression may make a habit of forgetting to be alive and human. This habit may have been inculcated as an intentional part of the program of the persecutors. It may even seem to be necessary for survival. We have seen how the lives of the victimized become constricted until they cannot see beyond the pain. Or how decades and even centuries of accommodations made for the sake of survival come to shape behaviors and even group characteristics. As a result, persons are disconnected from life; whole parts of their own selves and histories are unavailable.

If the memory of Jesus Christ is to be redemptive then it must help the victimized and all of us remember our lives, re-member our lives, to include love and power and life-sustaining connection. One of the early names for Jesus was Emmanuel, meaning "God with us." God *with* us.

God with *us*. If this be true, then how is God's presence and love and power manifest?

The early church struggled with that question for years—for centuries. It was a long, difficult, and even bloody struggle. The minds that wrestled with these questions were schooled in the ontologies of Greek philosophy and were wary of the earthiness of history. Despite their faith that human and divine were fully present in Jesus Christ, they found it so very difficult to bridge the chasm they knew separated the human condition from the life of God. They could imagine God with us, maybe, but not God like us. Given their mind-sets and the available modes of thought, it is to the credit of these theologians that they stayed with the struggle. As I have indicated, a fundamental commitment to the principle that "what is not assumed is not healed" guided their way. Only if God in Jesus Christ had taken on full humanity would the promise of salvation be realized. For the sake of redemption, these theologians stretched their philosophical thinking to bridge the differences that gaped wide between the life of God and the human condition. The doctrine of incarnation was the fruit of the struggle: Jesus Christ—fully divine, fully human, two natures, one person.

Based on the way these theologians understood the universe and the divine, this creedal formulation was a monumental, though limited, achievement. They affirmed that Jesus Christ was human and divine, but they did not affirm his life. Their Jesus Christ had no life history. For them, what was necessary for salvation was the event and reality of incarnation. Jesus' incarnated life, the story of his birth and life, his ministry and relationships, his teaching and healing, his loves and values, dropped out of the picture in a way. In other words, they were not able to imagine the divine in human terms—vulnerable to suffering, subject to change, involved in relationships, being affected by people and events. Though they attested to the union of divine and human, there was still a world of difference between the life of divinity and that of humanity.

In order to be a fully redeeming memory in our time and for those who are victimized, Christianity needs to live more into the promise of incarnation. At the center of incarnation faith ought to be the affirmation that God is fundamentally connected to humanity and the human condition. God embraces human life fully. It is, therefore, good to be human. Redemption is not in spite of, but in and through our humanity. One way that Christianity can attend more to the promise of incarnation is by reconsidering who God is and the way in which the divine relates to the created order and to human beings.

Expanding the Narrative

In the first section of this book, we saw how one of the signs of resolution of trauma was the ability to connect to a larger narrative, personal or communal, that remembered more than victimization and survival, and that affirmed life. In a very real way, Christianity needs to do the same: to decenter crucifixion and resurrection toward a redeeming memory more inclusive of Jesus' life and the history of God's people. For too long, Jesus' life and, indeed, the history of the people of Israel and of all creation have been read and remembered as a prologue to the crucifixion as saving event. What would it mean to begin to tell the story of Jesus' life so that the crucifixion became one, albeit critically important, moment in that narrative?

There are numerous voices in modern and contemporary Christian theology, especially among liberation and feminist theologians, who have been attempting to do just that. These voices turn our attention to the humanity of Jesus and to his person and mission. They also turn our attention to the humanity of God and the way in which God is mostly known in and through loving relationship. I see four trends emerging in contemporary discussions of God's presence with us in Christ: (1) focusing on Jesus' life in terms of ministry and preaching; (2) emphasizing God's compassion as embodied in Jesus; (3) emphasizing God as being in relation; and (4) imaging Jesus in terms of particular cultural icons. In each of these trends there is an attempt to redefine God's power, especially in relation to God's love and in relation to redemption. God's redemptive work is manifest in a coming together of power and love that reveals God as with us, empowering us to be fully alive humans, to the glory of God. Whereas these trends help us remember Jesus' life and humanity and to think differently about power, a brief consideration of each will indicate how they do not go far enough toward a fully life-giving memorative practice and narrative.

Jesus' Ministry and Ministerial Vision

One set of voices reminds us that Jesus did not preach himself as savior, but pointed to the reign of God, which was already being inaugurated and of which Jesus was a messenger. Emphasis is put on Jesus as a prophetic voice announcing God's intents and calling people into a different relationship with God. All are invited into God's "kingdom," especially those who are disenfranchised or oppressed. Those who accept the invitation are empowered to preach and to heal, to make real the vision of God's "reign." The promise of salvation is about transforming the world toward justice and healing. This promise is actualized in Jesus' teaching and healing ministries, as well as in his social practices. He challenges social arrangements of domination and seems to ignore various social and religious taboos. The way to salvation is to follow Jesus and respond to the power made present in encounter. For those who respond, participating in salvation means to experience and practice such liberation. Their empowerment both changes their lives and engages them in changing the lives of others. They become partners in God's salvific work by joining in the struggle for justice, healing, and right relation.

For theologians of the oppressed, Jesus' special relationship with the poor and marginalized receives particular attention. It points to God's favor toward and preferential option for those who are poor or dispossessed or violated. Jesus is the liberator who comes to change the prevailing order and make clear God's intentions for history and creation. The crucifixion is an act of violence by those forces that would deny God's work of liberation; Jesus' death is an act of solidarity that decisively puts God on the side of the dispossessed. Thus, while attention is shifted in these theologies to Jesus' life and ministry, there is a way in which the culminating point is Jesus' death.[30]

Among theologians of the oppressed, Delores Williams is a clear dissenting voice. For her, the cross is not the site of salvation. Williams keeps our attention on Jesus' life and ministry as portrayed in the Gospels: "the texts suggest that the spirit of God in Jesus came to show humans *life*—to show redemption through a perfect *ministerial* vision of righting relations between body (individual and community), mind (of humans and of tradition), and spirit."[31] She also lifts up Jesus' wilderness experience, during which he "conquered sin in life, not in death. In the wilderness he refused to allow evil forces to defile the balanced relation between the material and the spiritual, between life and death, between power and the exertion of it."[32] In the wilderness, Jesus defined the contours of his ministerial vision of life; through his life and teaching he invited people to live that vision.

The turn to Jesus' life, ministry, and teaching emphasizes the presence of God not only with us, but for us. Jesus is on the side of heal-

ing, justice, and liberation, especially for the disempowered and marginalized. The power that Jesus deploys reveals not only God's choice
for the oppressed, but the evil of the powers of domination. Thus the
Jesus of liberation theology is aligned with "good" power in the battle
against "bad" power. This model does not get away from seeing power
in such a way that God's good power ends up on the cross. As long as
these theologies assert that God chooses to align with the oppressed
because of their condition of suffering, there is a way in which the
oppressed are not empowered for full participation in the work of
redemption. They remain the objects of divine care and attention,
rather than the subjects of transformation.

Jesus as God's Compassion

There are yet other voices who, in turning attention more to Jesus'
life, emphasize the character of his presence to those who suffer as
compassion. Compassion reveals God and God's means of redemption.
It connects Jesus' life with his death and keeps both united with God,
who is the source of loving compassion. Compassion reflects a fundamental witness of care. It is the way in which God's love and power are
manifest in Jesus and in relation to evil and degradation.

Such themes are especially strong in theologies being formulated by
women, as well as men, in so-called third world contexts, particularly
Asia and Africa.[33] Kwok Pui Lan entitles an article on the subject, "God
Weeps with Our Pain." When Jesus wept over Jerusalem, his desire
was likened to that of a mother hen yearning to gather up her children.
From the weeping emerges compassion for life.[34]

Two North American feminist theologians who develop the theme of
compassion are Wendy Farley and Elizabeth Johnson. Farley begins
her consideration with the challenge of suffering; Johnson seeks to
develop a theology clearly compatible with feminist sensibilities. Both
are moving toward an understanding of power rooted in and expressed
through love—love that absorbs hurt and offers comfort and loving
kindness. Such love is embodied in the incarnation.[35] For Farley, incarnation refers, then, not only to Jesus' person, but to the ongoing presence of God in the world, made manifest in acts of love in community.
For Johnson, compassion reveals divine power as redemptive love,
manifest in relationship. Jesus the Christ is the embodiment of the relational care of God. In Jesus, God's own being entered into the human
condition—not in the mode of triumph, but compassionate power. We

are empowered through God's compassion to endure suffering and transform it whenever possible.

Compassion protects our own humanity, especially in instances of degradation where all hope is threatened. Therefore, it keeps us connected not only with God, but with ourselves, our humanity. And yet, since power for life is still made manifest through suffering love, the question remains whether such power is effective for change and empowerment. Other theologians, especially feminist theologians, come at connection and empowerment more directly, through the concept of eros as the essence of God's power.

Jesus as Embodiment of Eros for Mutual Relation

One of the major contributions of feminist theology to theological discourse has been to emphasize relationality as essential to what it means to be human and what it means to be divine. The goal of such relationship is mutuality and love. Often the energy or power of such relation is written of as eros, erotic power.[36] Such themes are central in the works of Carter Heyward and Rita Nakashima Brock, among others.[37]

For Carter Heyward, God is the power in relation. Divine power is erotic power that realizes relationship; it is a good and positive force. In Jesus, divine erotic power is incarnated and lives among us. Jesus is our brother who embodies erotic power throughout his life and ministry, through his healing and empowering presence. The goal and process of redemption for Heyward is mutual relation, mutually empowering relations, which can create and recreate the world. When human beings act with such power they are cooperating with God to make right relation.[38]

For Rita Nakashima Brock, erotic power is also at the heart of God and the goal is right and healing relation. The metaphor of heart is able to contain, for Brock, both the image of brokenheartedness from suffering and victimization, and a sense of center and holism. Redemption is a healing through erotic power that "creates and sustains connectedness—intimacy, generosity, and interdependence" and "integrates all aspects of the self, making us whole."[39] Erotic power is "the incarnation of divine love. The presence and revelation of erotic power is the divine dimension of human existence."[40] Its "fullest incarnation" is found in the affirmation "that we are all part of one another and cocreate each other at the depths of our being."[41] Power is available in and through our humanity and not despite it. At the heart of ourselves is divine mystery, incarnating love. What is most true of incarnation and salvation is such connection and life-giving power. As was discussed above, Jesus' life reveals participation in such power, but not as an isolated or heroic individual. Indeed, Brock offers a perspective that "relocates Christ in the community of which Jesus is one historical part."[42]

Heyward and Brock are seeking not only to offer empowering interpretations of Jesus' work, but to evaluate and provide moral judgment about what is good power and what is bad power. Erotic power is good power. Empowerment is, then, not only a process, but a movement toward the good, which is embodied in relations of erotic energy. This approach maintains a dualism of power, which I see as problematic from the perspective of those who have been victimized. Survivors have to face moral dilemmas that are not helped by dualistic thinking. Movement toward wholeness of life entails a fundamental embracing of ambiguity that prescinds from such absolute judgments. That may sound like an utter contradiction, since the world of the victimized is shot through with evil, but experientially it is so. The complexities faced by survivors regarding what might be deemed evil and what might be deemed good cannot be reduced to moral judgments that separate the world into good and evil.[43] Those who have been victimized merit attention and care not because they are good or even because they have been wronged, but because life seeks itself.

Jesus as Icon

There is yet another trend in present contemporary theologies, especially those theologies emerging from oppressed groups: connecting with the divine by imaging Jesus in cultural categories that can function redemptively. Theologians of Asia and Africa are particularly adept at seeing God in and through all things. For example, Chung Hyun Kyung offers a survey of images of Jesus for Asian women that includes not only Jesus as Lord, suffering servant, an "Immanuel," but as mother, shaman, worker, and even grain.[44] Alongside the traditional images, African women see "Christ as a woman and an African."[45] Such a Christ is also friend and companion, as well as advocate and high priest.[46] One Ghanaian woman, Afua Kuma, uses story to reveal what Christ means for women in African churches. Jesus is the one who helps them. She even sees Jesus as the "Pensil" used by the teachers to enable learning.[47]

Black theology in America has similarly claimed that Jesus is black, the "Black Messiah."[48] Jacquelyn Grant and Kelly Brown Douglas have extended that claim in order to image Christ as a black woman.[49] Such constructions are motivated by the desire not only to encounter Christ in culturally specific and accessible forms, but also to affirm identity. To say that Christ is black and/or female is to value blackness and/or femaleness. If the incarnation is going to be meaningful for those who are oppressed, then it must include them concretely. As Grant argues, it must contribute to their becoming subjects.[50] Images of Christ as black and/or female go beyond claiming solidarity as cosufferers to identifying with Christ's personhood.

To envision Jesus in particular cultural forms or through experiences that support our humanity is to live into the promise of incarnation — that the divine becomes one with our humanity, concretely and specifically in history. Images of Christ as female affirm women fully as subjects; images of Christ as black or poor affirm the humanity of those who are black or poor. There is much testimony to the effective power of these images. They remember Christ in a way that re-members. They empower through identification and a valuing of concrete cultural conditions. Yet issues persist about how these images function. For example, an "icon" of a crucified woman is a problematic image in a culture that eroticizes violence against women. Women's bodies are sites of male hegemony; they are subject to the male gaze. Though women may find support and even empowerment through such images, they remain cultural icons that reveal the complex and conflicted plays of power.[51] This is true for other images too, even ones that are not so gendered. For colonized peoples, given the complexities of cultural identities and appropriations, any image becomes a site of power dynamics. Afua Kuma's "Pensil" is, in cultural terms, an instrument of the colonizers, as well as of those who seek liberation.

Each of these four trends in contemporary Christology is attempting to understand Jesus' incarnation and life in such a way that the oppressed and victimized are empowered. Such empowerment is for the sake of changing the world and experiencing new life. Yet these trends do not go far enough either in exploring the complexities and ambiguities present in any use of power or in affirming that God's incarnating presence is revealed and realized in life itself. The challenge Christianity has faced from the start—how to embrace Jesus' life fully and tell a redeeming story—persists. It is to that task I now turn.

Remembering Jesus Christ for the Sake of Our Salvation

As we have seen, early church theologians were guided in their thinking about Christ and salvation by certain principles. Whereas Irenaeus declared that "the glory of God is humanity fully alive," Athanasius put it differently: "God became human in order that humanity might become divine." He and others asserted that "what is not assumed is not healed." Ethicist Paul Lehmann offers a more contemporary and political version of such affirmations: "what it takes to make and to keep human life human in the world." For Lehmann, this principle is grounded in an understanding of human beings as fundamentally related and of salvation as a coming to wholeness and maturity in relation. God's presence is "political" action toward this making and keeping of human life human.[52]

Remembrance of and witness to Jesus Christ's saving action ought to be guided by such principles that (1) affirm our being human as the site of redemption; (2) declare God to be on the side of redemption in and through humanity; (3) see the goal of redemption as wholeness and integrity, right relation and full humanity and (4) recognize redemption as political, meaning it is in history and involves community and relationships, as well as the exercise of power. Finally, to be human is to be embodied, so redemption is in and through bodies, individual and corporate. The story of redemption is about embodied, historical remembrance, which is to say, we are saved by the Body of Christ.

The church has not always remembered these principles. These principles also elude those who are victimized, for whom embodied humanity has become a most painful thing. Being human in relation— fully, wholly, rightly—remains difficult for victims and witnesses alike. Lehmann's principle of "what it takes to make and keep human life human in the world" stands as challenge and goal.

The redeeming memory of Jesus Christ ought to incorporate these principles. Jesus Christ is the loving power of God incarnate. In Jesus, the divine embraced humanity totally and declared itself as one with us. The evils that we then do to one another, as well as the joys we share, are known to God embodied. In and through Jesus Christ, God revealed to us that only in relationship can we be human and be made whole. These considerations move us back from the cross as sole site of redemption and toward telling a more complex story of Jesus' saving work. To remember Jesus Christ, for the sake of salvation, is not to speak only of Jesus' death, or only of

Jesus' death and resurrection, but of Jesus' incarnate humanity and life.

"For God so loved the world" that God became one with our humanity in Jesus the Christ. This Jesus was a historical person, who lived in a particular time and place, with all the specificity and limitations that went with it. He was embodied and engendered as a male and a Jew, a member of an ancient race, an occupied people. What we know about him narratively is quite little. His public, recorded "ministry" seems to have taken place over a rather short span of time. The Gospel accounts are our primary guide to his history, and their narrative focus is on remembering him as the Christ, the one who had come to save the people. A central affirmation of those narratives is the power of Jesus' teachings and of his encounters with people. Often these encounters involve healing or some sort of transformation. People's eyes are opened, their infirmities healed, their past mistakes recognized and forgiven. There is a great deal of energy in the power that is exchanged between Jesus and others in these encounters. It changes their lives. It changes him. It is experienced as miraculous.

The redemptive power present with Jesus and those whom he encounters is real. It is effective. What happens is transformative. The narrative accounts witness to this power and its effects, at the same time as they wrestle with how to make sense of it. How can the lame walk, the blind see, the dead live? The transforming power practiced by Jesus is not only about what happened then, but what happens now. As Pamela Dickey Young asserts: "When I hear the biblical witness to Jesus, to his whole life not just to his death and resurrection, I am offered the same grace that was offered to those first followers who experienced him. This is no past act of God once-for-all, but a present relationship."[53]

So we too may ask: How can those whose young and trusting selves have been disfigured by abuse; how can those who have suffered the annihilation of their families and people, and come to the edge of death themselves; how can those who carry on their backs and in their souls the scars of slavery and oppression and degradation; how can all these people continue to live and seek life? How can the dead live? This is not only my question, but the question of all those who witness to such suffering. It is at the heart of the promise of redemption.

In Christ, God's answer is to offer life, again and again, in all its fragility and glory, its terror and beauty, its brokenness and stumbling joy. In Christ, God lives among us, as one of us, as that energy in us that most wants to keep breathing and going on, as flesh of our flesh, forever scarred and yet resilient in its healing. At the same time, in Christ, all that has been lost and all who have died are not forgotten. They are honored forever in remembrance and in promise of redemption. In Christ, hope is reborn in recognizing that death is not the last word, that the forces that seek to entomb may just find out that their tombs are empty, that escape is possible. The images of Christ descending to the dead, opening up their tombs and releasing them, as depicted in Byzantine art, are often entitled *anastasis,* meaning "resurrection." Such resurrection opens up not only tombs, but the historical narrative. As Elisabeth Schüssler Fiorenza reminds us, the resurrected Christ goes on ahead and bids us come. The future is open—for all—even though much of what has been lost will never be recovered or restored.

We are saved by Jesus' life, death, and resurrection, by the story of living and dying, of resistance and resilience, of damaging, defeating, degrading power engaging the power of compassion and connection. But mostly we are saved by Christ's body, by incarnation, by the "in the flesh" presence of the divine. It is from the perspective of incarnation, of Emmanuel, that we can tell again a redeeming story, able to speak to the depths of terror and loss, and find yet a way to hope and live anew.

Incarnation is a historical process. Early church theologians knew only how to describe incarnation in ontological terms, which spoke of being and nature as static and eternal. I understand incarnation as historically and narratively constructed in practice. Incarnation is realized in our choosing life, both for ourselves and for those who have suffered and died. We choose life in and through remembrance that re-members us, not only as persons, but as a community and a society. This is true for survivors and witnesses alike. Indeed, we are all called to be witnesses—either to our own experiences or to those of others. As witnesses, we remember and are re-membered. As we are re-membered, we remember and witness anew. This is the ongoing process of redemption.

The redeeming memory of Jesus Christ includes Jesus' life, death, and resurrection, as three threads of an interwoven narrative of incarnation. In remembering each thread, in witnessing to it in remembrance, we continue to weave a saving story. No thread is to be released or replaced. All need to be held together in order for the redemptive narrative to account for the suffering and loss, the resistance and resilience, and the yearning for and making real of life connections in relation.

What holds the threads together is the power of God, and the way we know the power of God is through incarnation, through God's presence with us, among us, in us. This power is for life. God is on the side of life and the power that enhances life is of God. God's power is not good in and of itself, but it is effective if it enables survival and relationship and commitment to life. There is ambiguity in such power and in its uses. To exercise power for life is always a risk whose outcome is not assured. Yet there is no living without it. This knowledge is central to the witness that emerges from the victimized.[54]

I come back to my "mystical" experience in the living room of my childhood home. I was not lifted out of myself in that moment and connected with the people around the world because I was good or they were good, but just because we existed—because we were human. In that instant, I experienced a commonality of existence that I received as a truth of the universe. Even though the experience contained no encounter with a personal God, I knew it connected me with the divine. It was a fully earthly connection, but not of this earth. It was a moment of transcendence, an experience of life connection, and an intimation of wholeness.

Such experiences of connection and wholeness elude survivors of traumatic persecution and suffering. Their experience is of a fundamental loss of safety and of place in this world that is felt as a black hole in the middle of existence or as a lack of bottom, of fundamental support. It is not enough to say they do not experience the world as a safe place. They never feel safety. There is no foundation beneath them to hold them up. It is as if they live in a constant earthquake or on the edge of a vacuum that may suck them in. To speak to such survivors of the power of God to prevail against the forces of destruction, or the loving compassion of God for all who suffer, or the healing power of Jesus who sought out the marginalized and degraded, may provide glimpses of hope and consolation and comfort, but these affirmations do not touch the depth of the hole, which seems boundless. To speak only in categories of good and evil, of innocence and guilt, is often to throw words to the wind or to get into debates that have no end.[55] Even to affirm the goodness and love of God often feels like a meaningless gesture. There is no justification or explanation for their suffering. Such suffering is not redeeming or redeemable. There is no remedy for the losses endured and the pain borne. Remembering the suffering must acknowledge these limits. Ironically, only when that is done can there be movement toward life again. Only when the tragic losses are accepted and mourned is there a possibility both to remember them and to experience life connection.

Often what begins to make acceptance of the losses even imaginable is a relationship of witness. This witness, "withness" in remembrance, begins to hover at the rim of the black hole and drop in a word or two that may just echo back. The experience that someone else can tolerate what the survivor can barely contemplate becomes a delicate thread of connection from which the weaving of a fuller narrative can begin. When someone can look at wounds long hidden and want to tend them, and when someone will express the outrage and cries for justice and making right that gets forever caught in throats long tightened by silence and choked cries, the thread is strengthened. Witness that is able to hold the complex threads of remembering and continue to weave them is the beginning of redemption.

Such witness is possible because we are fundamentally connected to one another in history. That basic relation simply is; it exists. We do not bear witness because it is a good thing to do. Our bearing witness is not a result of moral decision or an expression of erotic power or a reflection of God's goodness and compassion. But it is of God. Bearing witness reflects God's presence as life and breath of the universe. When we bear witness, we image the divine, whose power is for life, whose power is not finally reducible to good and evil.

Since experience is constructed narratively, changing the story we tell begins to change our experience and change the world. As we witness one to another, we both hear the stories that shape our world and potentially we create space and offer resources for new stories to emerge and be crafted. In that process, dialectic and ongoing, transformation is made possible. Threats, both internal and external, remain. Survivors' experiences can be challenged and lost, as can our practice of incarnation. This is why the role of witness is so important and never ends. This is also why we can never assume truth as given and why we need to maintain all three modes of remembrance in practice. Witnessing is to life-enhancing remembrance, seeking integrity and wholeness.

Thus, redemption as remembering for re-membering is an ongoing and complex process that is motivated by and seeks commitment to life.[56] Re-membering is envisioned as a process of incarnation, which is to say that redemption is participation and incorporation. Through the narrative of Jesus Christ we can not only encounter God, but also participate in the divine. This is the work of the Spirit.

To assert that we participate in the divine means, we have available to us the power of life as fundamentally interrelated and connected. God is the holding in relation. Participation is embodied. Incorporation means that we are "in the body." Our redemption is a concrete process that brings us fully into a different kind of relationship. Such relationship has been described as reconciliation and right relation. Reconciliation implies right relation—that which has been out of harmony or off balance or at odds is brought back into a right relationship. There is a very real reconciliation and righting of relation that happens in the process of remembering, but it does not include harmony or the balancing of accounts. Losses remain unaccounted for; promises remain outstanding. Ambiguity that eludes full harmony will always be present.

Thus far I have said nothing about forgiveness and its place in either the relationship between victims and perpetrators or in the process of redemption. That omission is intentional. Christians often jump too quickly to forgiveness either as offer or obligation. I do not find this movement or command helpful. It tends to short-circuit the complex and multiform process of redemption I am suggesting is necessary, especially in those cases of suffering and abuse when forgiveness may seem most at issue. If talk of forgiveness gets in the way of remembering fully, then it is problematic. If the command of forgiveness results in perpetuating the kind of moralizing of power that I have been suggesting obscures the dynamics of remembering and recovery from trauma, then forgiveness is not redemptive. I would propose that Christians prescind from moving too quickly to talk about forgiveness until we learn better the practices of remembering for re-membering.[57]

Reconciliation does not necessarily have to entail forgiveness. It is movement toward integration and integrity, toward bringing together that which has been excluded, hidden, condemned, rejected. Reconciliation involves a new sense of freedom, in dialectic relationship with a reconciling process. There is, however, no freedom or reconciliation without power. Thus re-membering is most fundamentally a process of claiming and exercising power, in relation. It is grounded in witness.

In the story of the annunciation, when Mary questioned the angel as to how she could conceive and bear God's child, the angel replied that all things are possible with God. The incarnation is about faith in possibility, the amazing possibility that our humanity is a good thing, that life is possible always, that there is healing connection offered through our own lives and through loving relationships of care. In the affirmation that all things are possible with God, God's power is declared as mighty for life, mightily on the side of life. So the incarnation is also about power—God's power as our power, potentially.

A chapter later, the author of Luke tells us that Mary kept all that she saw and heard at Jesus' birth in her heart. As we have seen, toward the end of Luke's Gospel, the author tells us that in their encounter with the risen Christ, Cleopas and friend felt their hearts stirred. The promise of the incarnation is not only that all things are possible with God, but that our hearts contain the seeds of salvation. In our coming to know by heart, as was true for Mary and Jesus' followers, we will encounter and realize redemption. We will become partners and companions in the work of salvation. That partnership is ever to be realized.

To know by heart is to remember. To remember for redemption is to witness to all the suffering and loss endured, to the resistance, agency, and resilience practiced, and to making connections for life in the web of relationships. These three forms of remembering woven all together constitute a saving story. Incarnation is both ground and fruit of this process. It is the transforming promise revealed from our overflowing hearts.

The Witness of Jesus Christ: Telling a Redeeming Story

Jesus' crucifixion and death witness to the persistence and power of violence and degradation in this world. Jesus was killed because he threatened the forces of domination and offered hope to those who were supposed to experience themselves as powerless. Envy, fear, need for control, and other human desires wanted to see Jesus gone. The cross is a site of abuse—the abuse of power against the undeserving. The cross is also the result of human evil. God did not kill Jesus, but rather human and political forces did.

The narrative memory of the cross ought to remember the suffering and degradation Jesus endured because they were real. But they were not unique. Jesus died in ignomy and alone. So have millions of human beings whose only "crime" was that they were children or dark skinned or Jewish or Armenian or female. God knows their pain, but does not redeem it. The cross is not redeemable. It is not redemptive. The cross is horrible and tragic. It must be mourned and remembered. The loss endured must be acknowledged and accepted. There is no going back before the cross. In that way—and only in that way—it changed history. It is a trauma that remains at the center of the Christian story.

Until that trauma is faced more directly, the Christian story will produce distorted and harmful readings of it. But even then, because the forces that killed Jesus continue to find victims in the world, there will always be the danger of distortion and manipulation of the cross.

The narrative of Jesus' death can never stand alone. It must always be remembered along with Jesus' life and the resurrection. The resurrection witness is to the power of life that cannot be defeated. Even death is not able to stop the living. The power of life is manifest in the Resurrected One who lives in the community that witnesses to Christ and to life itself. The power of resistance does not accept the conditions of death or degradation. Within life there is an energy toward resilience, a claiming of agency in the midst of powerlessness. Though all seemed lost, life arose anew. The community bore witness to the power they experienced from the one who went before them and who had called them together and given them hope. They encountered resurrection life again and again, and testified to it.

Christianity has wrestled long and hard with the nature of the resurrection and what type of event it is. It is both cornerstone and stumbling block to faith and it is one of Christianity's claims to uniqueness. The resurrection of Christ is not unique, but it is miraculous. As miraculous as life itself. The miracle of resurrection is recognized each time someone rises from defeat and terror to take a breath and utter a cry. There is much wonder in the capacity of the human spirit to endure and to revive, to seek life again and again. To remember the resurrection is to affirm human resistance and resilience and agency, even in the face of death in all its manifestations.

There is more to be said about life than the resurrection. Jesus had a life history and a ministry. At the heart of his life was the practice of relationship and connection. Jesus preached a vision of society in which there seemed to be fewer hierarchies and more loving-kindness. Those who experienced themselves as outcast were included with special care. There was power enough for healing and for celebration. The life that Jesus lived, what he preached and taught, and the way he related with others demonstrated the power of life itself. Jesus affirmed as well as challenged those around him. He appealed to the part of everyone that sought justice and love. His message was not gentle or nice, but it spoke to those who were eager for a transforming word.

Jesus' life and ministry allowed those around him to imagine and practice new possibilities for their lives and for the life of the world. He helped them form a vision of life transformed and made whole. Jesus would speak to them of God's promise and the coming reign of justice and care and peace. He would tell them their faith enabled them to act and to change.

That faith was in life, which Jesus embodied fully and unconditionally. The life that Jesus lived is expansive energy and power. It gathered people up—not in imitation, but in realization of their own divine humanity. The joy of giving such glory to God produced a kind of euphoria that even the forces of evil, death, and trauma could not ultimately contain.

Neither can they still. Christ lives in and through life-seeking and life-giving humanity. The incarnation is all moments in time in which God is present, making holy, making whole. This is the work of the Spirit. To say that we are saved through Jesus Christ is to live incarnation in our lives. Such incarnation is ongoing. It is the divine presence in life, realized through our participation.

6

The Church as a Community of Remembrance and Witness

A number of years ago, I was invited by an Episcopal church to be the guest preacher on the Sunday when, their rector told me, they commemorated the Armenian genocide. I was surprised and impressed. Not only was this congregation aware of what had happened to the Armenian people, but the genocide was included in its liturgical calendar. I had heard of no other Episcopal congregation holding such a commemoration. I readily accepted. Preparing that sermon was an important experience for me. It gave me an opportunity to reflect on the genocide theologically and to think about how to present it homiletically and pastorally. Two parts of myself, my identity as an Armenian American child of genocide survivors and as an Episcopal priest, were both engaged fully. Rarely did this happen. Preaching the sermon to the congregation strengthened these feelings of connection. The Armenian community did not much acknowledge or have place for my vocation as a priest, and the Episcopal Church did not pay much attention to my ethnic history. On this occasion, I was able to be fully both, one in service of the other.

There were two other places in the liturgy, along with the sermon, where the Armenian genocide was acknowledged that day. During the intercessory prayers, special petitions were included. Then, for the offertory anthem, the choir presented a special arrangement of what is traditionally referred to as the Lord's Prayer. The organist had set the English words of the prayer to the music from the Armenian liturgy. As I listened to the choir, I found myself deeply moved. This music was so familiar, so haunting, so part of me, but I had never heard it before in an Episcopal church. For the first time, these different parts of my history were present and acknowledged in the same place, at the same time. That moment was very powerful for me. That liturgy had become not only an occasion to commemorate the past and witness to it in the present, but to re-member me as well.

To declare that the church is a community of remembrance is, in some ways, to state the obvious. The Christian church came to be in witness to the memory of Jesus Christ. It developed from that group of people, Jesus' followers and friends, who kept his memory alive and shared it with others. This memory was contained not only in the church's narrative and proclamation, but also in its practices and life.

As we read in the book of Acts and elsewhere, the earliest Christians gathered in community for worship and mutual care. They tried to practice a certain lifestyle that was in continuity with the way Jesus called them together and related to them. They preached the Christ whom they had known and/or witnessed. The post-Pentecost life of the church was directed toward the past and the future. In remembering Christ, they anticipated Christ's return. The church's purpose was not only to remember, but to proclaim the good news of redemption and to spread the redemptive memory to others. The church then and now has existence because of and for the sake of the Christian narrative and witness. It is a community of witness in remembrance.

In this chapter, I explore what it means for the church to witness to and be the bearer of redeeming memories, as these memories have been defined here. As we have seen, not all remembering is redemptive. Remembering for redemption is a complex and multiform process. It is a particular practice and witness. Here I further define that witness by examining the nature and purpose of the church as a community of remembrance. I then explore the liturgical, pastoral, and educational practices of the church as a community of witness and remembrance, as well as its mission—its social and political witness.

The Nature and Purpose of the Church

Community of remembrance not only describes what the church is, but what it ought to be. Naming the church as a community of remembrance both describes the church and suggests a theological and ethical proscriptive claim. The church is called to be a community of remembering/re-membering for redemption, formed and reformed in hope. This calling of the church is a religious promise and ethical mission. It is rooted in the identity of what the church is and does. In other words, purpose is formed in relation to nature and practice.

The purpose of the church is to remember God and God's action, especially in Jesus Christ. Again, this purpose is both descriptive and proscriptive. This purpose effects several things. First of all, remembering confers identity, both personal and corporate, and so makes us human and constitutes us as community. Our memories do not only shape who we are—there is a way in which we have no identity if we have no memory. The act of remembering is constitutive of identity and the content of the memories shapes the character of the identity. The church not only needs to remember, but what and how it remembers will affect its nature and mission. The church's defining memory is the narrative of who we are in relationship to God in Jesus Christ. Christian identity is shaped in relation to that narrative.

Second, remembering provides meaning and structure and so informs faith and action. The content of our remembering shapes the way we understand God, and God in relation to the world. The Christian narrative not only tells us who we are, but for what purpose we exist. It shapes our apprehension of the divine. It gives meaning to our lives and provides a basis for faith. That faith informs what we do with our lives and the way we act in the world. Christian memory is historical, which is to say that faith is formed and shaped by and in society and culture. It is grounded in concrete historical events that are read as revelatory. But faith and action also shape meaning. Who we are and the way we are are constituted through what we do. Remembering is fundamentally a practice that produces narratives of meaning.

The third purpose of remembering is a consequence of understanding remembering and faith as historical. Remembering orders time from past to future through the present. Remembering is a historical activity that sets us in time. It is not timeless or eternal. Remembering not only temporalizes existence, but historicizes it. The content of remembrance and, therefore, of revelation, changes with time and circumstances. This is true for the Christian narrative as well. Even though that narrative is about the past, it is a present activity with a future intent. It is made present again and again in the work of the church, for the sake of God's realm. In that sense, the past exists for the sake of the present and the future, which has yet to be realized. For Christians, remembrance is the basis of hope.

Last, in all these ways remembering makes possible liberation and transformation and so it mediates salvation. Remembering is for the sake of re-membering. Christianity affirms this again and again by its witness to the story of God in Christ and through the sharing of sacraments. The community of the church is not only formed, but reformed through its memorative practices. It is constituted by remembering and re-membering.

These four purposes of remembering describe what it means to call the church a community of remembrance. They inform the church's witness. The church aids us in being human and being community, it offers us meaning and guides purposive action, it reads history as the arena of hope, and it helps realize the promise of redemption. These things also form the foundation of what the church ought to do and be as a community of remembrance. But before we can give that purpose more definition, we need to consider some key issues in relation to the church's remembrance.

The Dimensions of the Church

For Christians, the church exists in three dimensions: it is of God and so represents divine mystery; it is made up of people and so is a society; and it exists in the world so it is a historical institution. These dimensions cannot be separated without the church ceasing to be the church.[1] Even though these dimensions are distinct, they operate in relation and are sometimes conflated. When they are conflated, there is a tendency for the church as institution to become dominant and determinative of the other dimensions. The dynamics of power are such that those in institutional positions of dominance and control seek to protect and enhance certain interests. They use their institutional position and authority to serve those interests. They then claim to be the interpreters and vehicles of the church as divine mystery. They are the keepers of revelation. They also determine the nature of the church as a society by regulating membership and ecclesial activity. The purposes of the church enumerated above are then defined in such a way as to serve the institutional interests. The practices of identity, faith, hope, and salvation are all filtered through these interests.

Sometimes concerns about the interrelationship between these three dimensions become embedded in discussions about authority. What is the nature of authority and its relationship to revelation? How is authority mediated and recognized? Where does it lie—with the people or the hierarchy, in texts or in practices? Asking such questions of the church is one way to understand and analyze the operations of authority and power. But these are loaded questions. They have been the center of many controversies about the church. Indeed, wars have been fought over them. The Reformation was as much about the nature of the church and its authority as about anything else. Martin Luther did not challenge the basic tenets of Christianity, but rather how the church was practicing Christianity. In our day, there are similar battles being waged. These include how and what the church will remember.

The theology I develop here is rooted in the commitment and presupposition that authority ought to be granted to those who suffer and who struggle for survival and life. In other words, redemption for those who are victimized and for all of us necessitates that we pay attention to those voices that are often silenced or manipulated. They are not to be granted authority because of their suffering, but because of their struggle for life, and their humanity that has been overlooked and denied. Their struggle may be holding truths that we all need to hear for the sake of redemption. My approach reflects an understanding of authority that is contrary to those who want to maintain institutional authority, often through support of the status quo. Rather, authority belongs to that which promotes effective witness and action and faith. Only that which contributes to healing and transformation should be granted authority.

A crucial site where the discussion of authority and what will be remembered is enjoined is the issue of tradition. Tradition may be defined as corporate memory and witness. In other words, the church's tradition is the corporate memory of the church. The church, then, is the bearer of tradition, which is conveyed through word — in story, doctrine, creed, and confession — and practice. Tradition effects the purposes of the church. It confers identity, shapes faith and action, informs hope, and mediates salvation.

Remembering as tradition is intentional. It intends particular things. Because Israel remembered its status as stranger and its sojourn in the desert, it was obligated to extend hospitality to the stranger in its midst. Because Jesus welcomed all, the church feels a similar obligation. Because the early church gathered to praise and give thanks, so does the church today.

Sometimes a community's or the church's remembering, its perspective on the past, sets up certain expectations. Because Israel told the story of deliverance from Egypt as the mighty acts of God its deliverer, it assumed God would always protect Israel in particular ways. The exile then came as a very rude shock that led to a struggle to rethink Israel's past. For the church too, time and again, it has had to rework its ways of understanding the past and the present because of differing perceptions of what God was about. This process began in the earliest years when the church struggled to define itself in relation to Judaism and its Gentile members. Throughout its history, the church has been challenged by historical events and by the impact of new knowledge. These new circumstances give rise to the need to change, for remembering to be for the sake of re-membering.

It is at this point that the nature of tradition as memory is tested.

There is a tendency for tradition to become static and ossified. When that happens the emphasis is put on tradition as that which preserves identity and faith, and regulates hope and redemption. The past determines the present and future, but not in a way that is dynamic and dialectic. Tradition is replaced by traditionalism. There is no mechanism for hearing new voices or incorporating new memories. Indeed, the active process of remembering is replaced by the static concept of memories.

Related tendencies include nostalgia for bygone days, fixation on a golden age, and denial of conflict and problems in the past as well as the present. That which does not fit the master narratives and their purposes are hidden and submerged. These tendencies are always present in one way or another when we seek to remember. Remembering is by nature partial and perspectival. It is literally from a particular point of view. So memories are always in danger of being distorted or forgotten. But traditionalism rigidifies memories and enthrones a particular perspective as universal and even eternal. In the church, tradition is also given the status of revelation which, according to the traditionalist perspective, cannot be altered or changed. The defining and closing of the canon is but one example of such turning of memory into eternal, unchanging revelation.

The stated motivation for such declarations is redemption through preservation. The truth of revelation as contained in the tradition of the church needs to be preserved and transmitted for the sake of salvation. For some adherents of traditionalism, tradition is threatened by those forces that are understood as denying God's truth. To preserve tradition, then, is to do God's work and protect God and God's people from what is considered evil.

As we have seen, preserving is an important memorative practice. But it cannot stand alone. Preserving tends to be focused on the past and on maintaining the status quo. Often it fights change in any form. Change threatens to expose distortions and hidden truths. Even the potential for change challenges the timelessness and universality of tradition. The battle, so to speak, gets enjoined as one between the forces of change that would destroy Christian faith and those who would preserve God's truth. The forces of change are often portrayed by traditionalists as "outside" and "worldly" forces—for example, secularism, modernity, special interest groups.

The rhetoric of many traditionalists points to a core and hidden dynamic: the exercising and preserving of power and authority in order to maintain a particular set of power arrangements, both in the church and in the world. Ecclesial traditionalists are often not protecting the church from the world so much as supporting certain ways of understanding power that tend to maintain the status quo and serve the interests of those who are already in positions of authority and dominance. In that way, the church may collude, intentionally or unintentionally, with those who perpetuate abuse, genocide, oppression, and persecution. Feminist, black, and liberation theologians have demonstrated this connection again and again. The church tends to support and provide divine sanction for social arrangements that oppress and harm women, people of color, and the poor.

When this happens, it may well be that the institutional dimension of the church has taken over the other dimensions. The institution determines God's revelation and the church as divine mystery. It also regulates the community of the church by defining membership in terms of compliance and loyalty. Authority and power are maintained in and through hierarchies of either position or "truth."

With traditionalists in charge, the church is still a community of remembrance, but its witness is to the interests of those in power. Such a church does not remember for redemption fully. Not only does it not provide means to evoke the potentially liberating memories of those who suffer in the world, but it often actively excludes these memories. In effect, it tells those who suffer that there is no place for them in the remembering processes of the church, except insofar as they are objects of the church's concern and charity. This church does not remember to re-member. Truth as well as salvation are understood as belonging to the church, which also defines and controls their meanings.

Redefining Church

Numerous theological voices today are challenging the church to be a different kind of community of remembrance, one that practices remembering for the sake of redemption in a way that is inclusive, liberating, and transforming. These theologies want to expand and change the church's witness and practice. Indeed, they are seeking to transform the church itself. The impetus for such change often comes precisely from those who have been excluded and/or deemed powerless.

Among these voices are those of liberation, political, and feminist theologies. These theological movements are offering new ecclesial models that change the way we understand not only the church, but the dynamics of power. For these theologies a measure of the church's authority and authenticity is precisely the character of its witness to those who suffer and are oppressed. The church's remembering ought to attend particularly and preferentially to those who are and have been victimized.

For Latin American liberation theologies and feminist theologies these models emerge from particular experiences and practices. In Latin America, the liberation theology movement has been rooted in base community churches, which in turn are derived in part from the Marxist idea of cell groups. Feminist theology has its roots in the feminist movement and its consciousness raising and support groups for women. Both the base community churches and women's groups have provided settings for being "heard into speech" (Nelle Morton), and for the evoking of memories hidden, forgotten, not understood. In these settings people's hearts have been stirred and they have come to new awareness and understanding of the presence of the divine. They have also been strengthened and equipped for action.

The Latin American base community churches have been an important resource in a number of ways. They provide not only a setting for worship and pastoral care, as well as consciousness raising and political organizing, they also offer an alternative experience of church. In many countries in Latin America, the institutional church and its hierarchy have been aligned with repressive and oppressive regimes. This complicity has raised numerous questions about the church's commitment to what is considered the gospel message. The base community churches are places where such questions and contradictions can be explored. The method of Bible study often used allows the gathered community members to comment on texts and to do so from their perspectives and experiences. Participants' voices and understandings are granted authority. The process of *conscientization,* as Paolo Freire called it, evokes and develops the analytical and critical capacities of participants.[2] They remember their lives in different ways. As the Bible and worship are related more to people's lives, those lives become part of the work of the church in liturgy and mission. The community itself is re-membered.

Women's groups operated in a similar way, although they often began in nonchurch settings and focused on women telling one another about their lives. Out of this process emerged long hidden pains and memories, and the claiming of new strengths. Individual women recognized themselves in other women's stories. Deep feelings of connection allowed women to name and claim their experiences for the first time.[3] As these groups spread to religious and church settings, women began to share their experiences and raise questions not only about their religious experiences, but about their participation in religious institutions that excluded them from leadership and other roles. They also began to develop settings in which to explore and practice what is loosely referred to as "women's spirituality"—spirituality that is rooted in women's own self-expressions and experiences. Some of these groups formed into something resembling small communities. For women in Christian churches, they have been providing an alternative ecclesial structure, often referred to as women-church. Women-church is a community of remembrance in witness to women's lives and experiences. It grew out of the recognition that women's lives were overlooked and forgotten in most churches and their experiences were silenced by the practices and theologies of those churches.[4]

Theological reflection on these movements has emphasized the church as a society and as community. God is present in and with the gathering. Divine mystery is revealed in relation. Power is marshaled and increased through sharing and mutual support. The church is to be an active witness in the world. The church works in partnership with God to realize redemption. Institutional structures ought to serve this mission and support the practice of partnership.

Johann Baptist Metz's term for this vision of church is "church of the people." He contrasts it with a model of what he calls the "bourgeois church." This church of a comfortable middle class is not adequate and is, indeed, false. The people of this church do not let religion get to them; they use religion as they need it. Metz calls this the "services church," which people request for services when they need or want them. Otherwise this church does not influence their lives.[5] Such a church takes refuge in particular types of memories. It engages in nostalgia and a forgetfulness of anything distasteful. In contrast, Metz advocates for a church that is guardian and transmitter of those memories that the status quo may find disturbing and challenging, those memories that, as we have seen, he calls dangerous. These memories interrupt complacency and make salvation possible. For Metz, this church is to be found especially in the base community churches of Latin America and all those communities that are trying to live the gospel in full engagement with the world and for the sake of salvation and liberation. This church keeps in mind the subversive memory of Christ, which challenges all social forms that masquerade as what Metz calls "believed-in but not lived faith."[6] The church as an authentic community of remembrance lives by and transmits the dangerous memory of Jesus Christ, by which all other memories are to be judged.

As I argued previously, Elisabeth Schüssler Fiorenza goes further to challenge the authenticity of the church's memory of Jesus Christ. She engages in a more dialogical process of challenging and assessing the Christian story, itself, in relation to the experience of the *ekklesia* of women, which is for her a locus of revelation. A task of the *ekklesia* of women is to recover and imagine a tradition that is resource for women's salvation and so recover memory that functions on behalf of women and, indeed, all who have been oppressed. Authentic Christian remembering must include the reality of women's lives. She asks the question: "How can we point to the eucharistic bread and say 'this is my body' as long as women's bodies are battered, raped, sterilized, mutilated, prostituted and used to male ends?"[7] Thus women's suffering does not find place and meaning directly in the memory of Jesus' suffering, but rather remembering Jesus' suffering is to be through the memory of women's oppression and pain. Women-church, the *ekklesia* of women, as a community of remembrance, provides support and context for women to remember. As it embodies and institutionalizes women's memories, it makes them more real and affects connection between and among women and all those struggling for an authentic memory that includes women's experience.

Whereas Schüssler Fiorenza's project attends specifically to women-church, her arguments apply to other dispossessed groups who are seeking to form communities of remembrance that might retrieve and honor particular cultural memories of oppression and of power, of suffering and of agency. These various expressions contribute to a multivocal, multiform understanding of church. The communities themselves take different forms—from small groups that meet for Bible study or other kinds of sharing, to project groups that gather for a specific purpose, to ritual groups, to more organized institutional structures.

Black theologians look to the historical black church as a community of remembrance. The black church has provided continuity and institutional support for black people's experiences. Many black theologians, however, are challenging the black church to be more truly a community of remembrance and witness for the full liberation of black peoples. They argue that it too has tended to lean toward traditionalism and institutional loyalties that align it with the status quo and preoccupy it with self-preservation. Delores Williams goes even further to challenge the vision of church offered by black liberation theologians, who do not attend sufficiently to the experience of women. She suggests that they compromise church's memory, witness, and effectiveness.[8] Other womanist theologians offer similar challenges and seek to expand the vision of the black church.

Whether it be from the perspective of the base community churches of Latin America or women-church or the black church or other ecclesial communities of those who are excluded or oppressed, a general imperative has emerged to make the church more inclusive and more intentional in its witness. This imperative necessitates shifting from loyalty to the institution and its traditions to understanding the church as a society with a mission in the world, reflective of God's intent. What is also emerging from these groups is a desire for community that is authentic and responsive to the desire for liberation. Women, the poor, those living in postcolonial contexts, African Americans, Native Americans, and many others are offering their stories and their memories for inclusion in the church's narrative of identity and transformation. By expanding and transforming the church's remembrance, they are seeking to re-member the church.

Sharon Welch offers a vision of such communities of resistance, solidarity, and remembrance. These communities practice faith in a way that honors suffering and resistance, and engages in transforming action. They are characterized by attentiveness to the oppressed—not only to their suffering, but to their practices of remembrance and resistance. The ethical practice of these communities is rooted in commitment to life as ambiguous and tragic as well as good. There are no absolutes to fall back on, only the process itself of making and remaking life. For Welch, if these communities are to be authentic and effective then they need to embrace difference, "a mutually challenging and mutually transformative pluralism."[9] Solidarity in community is characterized by expansive love. Borrowing from Martin Luther King, Jr., Welch talks about the "beloved community" as "the matrix within which life is celebrated, love is worshiped, and partial victories over injustice lay the groundwork for further acts of criticism and courageous defiance."[10]

Welch's vision speaks to the desire, shared by a spectrum of movements and groups, to make the church an effective instrument for justice, healing, transformation, and hope. Together these communities are reforming the church and offering alternative models that both include the experiences of their members and move to change the social conditions that harm and oppress, inside and outside of the church. Some of the theologians who reflect on these emerging models also argue that these forms of church have always existed but have not been remembered. Feminist theologians, in particular, look for continuity with the past, in part to affirm that women always sought to be full participants.[11] Elizabeth Johnson retrieves and reinterprets the symbol of communion of saints in order to provide a vision of connection across time and culture.[12] Others look for historical precedents as well. For example, Gustavo Gutierrez's work on Bartolomé de las Casas is intended, at least in part, to establish historical precedents for liberation theology.[13]

Theological Development

The model of church I propose draws on these movements and motivations, but adds a distinctive voice. In this model of the church as a community of remembrance, remembering is not only about establishing continuity or being inclusive; it refers to the work of the church and its redemptive mission. The witness of the church is to remember for transformation. Such remembrance is shaped by the narrative of Jesus' life and ministry, death and resurrection, knit together in the promise of incarnation. The memory of Jesus is made incarnate today through the multiple memorative practice I have identified in this work. The church as a community of remembrance honors and preserves memories of suffering; evokes, recognizes, and validates memories of resistance and agency; and actively supports, embodies, and celebrates memories of connection and life affirmation. These together form the purposes and mission of the church. Its structure and practices are to be defined and measured by how well they enable and enhance the work of remembering as a multiform and ongoing process.

In this model, remembering is not only descriptive of what the church does. Remembering is meant to be at the core of what the church ought to be and do for the sake of a redemption that frees and makes whole. I have already outlined the purposes of the church as a community of remembrance: namely, conferring identity, forming faith,

211

nurturing hope, and mediating salvation. In the church as a community of remembrance the multiple memorative practice would shape the meaning of each purpose. The overall goal and guiding principle is liberation and reconciliation, being made whole in freedom. Remembering and witnessing are the means to achieving these ends.

The church as a community of remembrance is expressed through all three dimensions of divine mystery, society, and institution. Most obviously, it is a society. As a community of remembrance, the church is a gathering of people, intended to be inclusive, especially of those who feel excluded elsewhere. It is a place where the memories that are most threatened are to receive special care, where traumatic memories are acknowledged and held with gentleness. The church ought also to be a place where the deepest fears of those who have been victimized might be recognized and their most elusive hopes nurtured.

This church not only receives and holds memories, but actively witnesses to them. This witness can take a number of forms, as will be demonstrated in the outlined functions of the church. These are shaped by the threats, internal and external, to remembering. On the one hand, the church acts as witness with those who have been victimized to accompany them at every point of remembering in its multiple dimensions. It stands with those who seek to remember, invites their movement through the different modes of remembering, and provides support against the internal threats that forever haunt the remembrance of suffering, agency, and life connections. In so doing, the church needs to make sure that its teachings and practices enable, rather than hinder, full remembering.

On the other hand, the church bears witness to these memories in the larger society, in the world. As we have seen, sociopolitical threats to remembering for redemption do not stop. Indeed, as the voices of the victimized grow louder and the memories of suffering, injustice, and oppression receive more of a societal hearing, these external threats develop new and even more virulent and subtle strains of sabotage, manipulation, and attempted control. These two directions of the church's witness inform one another, just as the internal and external threats are interrelated. In both cases, the witness is active. The church bears witness not only to protect and preserve against threats, but to change persons and society toward a fuller realization of remembering for redemption.

Witnessing for the sake of social transformation requires the ability to discern and evaluate, with a critical consciousness, the necessarily perspectival nature of remembering. Remembering is always subject to distortion. It is partial, subjective, and even elusive. The church needs not only to receive the memories of those victimized, but to test them for the sake of redemption. What is ultimately deemed as redemptive is that which enables healing and transformation. As we have seen, such remembrance is complex and multiple. The church as a community of remembrance and witness is a place where memories are not only recounted, but are subjected to accountability. Bearing witness includes being accountable and holding others accountable.

As I have argued, such witness is a form of solidarity, which is rooted not in voluntary commitment, but in a recognition of connection. Solidarity is a standing with and being allied with through a common humanity held together in God. The Episcopal Church had a mission program a number of years ago that was entitled "Mutual Responsibility and Interdependence." For me, this phrase sums up what it means to claim connection in witness. Solidarity and witness are about mutual responsibility and interdependence, a partnership of redemption.

Such a partnership includes witnessing to ambiguity. In the face of those who challenge memories of abuse and genocide, and who question emerging historical narratives, the temptation is to witness by asserting these memorative narratives with certainty and a certain insistence. Such a temptation ends up serving the interests of those who challenge and threaten the remembrance of suffering. Ironically, a witness of insistence and certainty tends to reinforce the victimization and even stigmatize it toward a victim identity. As I have argued, defensive and reactive responses to groups such as the False Memory Foundation and Holocaust deniers, which are suggesting that the victimization is false, tend to reinforce victim identity. These groups' interests are really in maintaining power arrangements that keep the victimized powerless. I see this dynamic operating in two ways. First, if the energy of those who have been victimized and those who witness to victimization goes into asserting the reality of the victimization—if witnesses are preoccupied with responding to the deniers on the deniers' terms—then there is little energy left to do the work of healing and transformation. In that way, reactive responses tend to reinforce victimization. Preoccupation is a form of being occupied, even colonized, by the interests of those who challenge and subvert. Second, responding to deniers by asserting the certainty and objective truth of victimization serves to support epistemologies that do not enable transformation. As we have seen, recovery and healing require an embracing of ambiguity. The trick of solidarity is to support the victims' own struggle, which is served best by keeping focused on a multiple practice of attending not only to suffering, but to resistance and life connection as well. Such a practice is enhanced by cultivating an epistemology of ambiguity.

In order to carry out this witness of solidarity effectively, the community of remembrance needs to be not only a society, but an institution. As an institution its commitment, as evidenced through its form and functions, should be to empowerment and accountability and to making concrete a vision of the church that is a partnership of redemption. These commitments require the exercise of power, which an institution can facilitate. Institutions are embodiments. They realize and make concrete and ongoing the commitments and values a society holds. They are necessary for the work of changing society and social structures.

It is, however, as an institution that the church most often gets in trouble. It seems to be in the nature of institutions to solidify and abuse power in order to maintain themselves. Hierarchies of power form, even when an institution has it beginnings in challenging and criticizing existing hierarchies. Power is used to enhance the position and privilege of those who already have access to it in the system. All too often, rather than using its power and authority to effect change toward liberation and transformation, the institutional church attends to the preserving function of memory and gives short shrift to evoking and incorporating those memories that might challenge the church itself to change.

Thus, whereas the institutional dimension of the church is necessary, it is also problematic. The witness of the church as a society is always, in part, to challenge and recall the institutional church to the needs of the world and to remembering fully through its multiple memorative practice. Optimally, there would be in the church mechanisms for ongoing self-reformation as institution. But even then the intransigency and yet instability of power would be present to threaten the potential effectiveness of any safeguards. The church as institution must always be held in relation with and in tension with the church as a society and as divine mystery.

What does it means to name the church as a divine mystery in a world where the powers use God for ideological support? The history of the church is replete with times when the power of God was cited to reinforce the hierarchy and "the powers that be" in the institution and in the world. That same history is full of those who challenged the church and its actions in the name of God and God's intents. Calls for reformation, as well as for preservation, always claim divine justification. The implication in these calls is that the church is God's institution.

That is not what I mean by the church as divine mystery. For me, to name the church as a divine mystery is to suggest that it is constituted through remembering for the sake of redemption. Such remembering is rooted in relationship. It is experienced as gift, as well as task and obligation. The mystery that is at the heart of God is life itself: continuous, replenishing, healing itself, and seeking itself in love. The divine mystery is life: created and recreated, shared and redeemed. Remembering is for life. The gift of remembering is life-giving, even when it seems only to encounter pain and death.

The divine mystery of life is a process, a process of coming to be again and again, in history and time, embodied and transitory, yet persistent. The witness of the church to the divine mystery is a witness to life. There is no life without power, so the witness of the church to divine mystery is also a witness to power. That power is there for all. Life also seeks love, a realizing of relationship and mutuality, justice and harmony. Such love requires power as well: power to make real the commitments of love.

Love desires that nothing be lost even while it mourns the losses that cannot be redeemed. Love yearns to realize its promises, even as those promises remain outstanding, never to be fully realized. Love seeks to bring all into harmony, even though it knows harmony only as elusive. Conflict is and will remain as long as life goes on. There is no resting of the powers that both make life possible and make it impossible.

It is to this complex and conflictual universe that the church as divine mystery bears witness. The divine mystery is a process of remembering and re-membering amid all these dynamics. In bearing witness, the church honors the suffering of the victimized in a way that both gives due attention to that suffering, but also empowers precisely through the knowledge that there are no absolutes, no final solutions, no end to struggle. In this way, the church as divine mystery practices an epistemology of ambiguity. Claims to truth are held delicately and tentatively, to be tested in practice. Truth is both effective and fleeting, strong and fragile.

Survivors of abuse and violence, who seek to remember fully, often come to such understandings of knowledge and the way it functions through their experiences. In doing so, they are teaching us all something of the divine.

I see the practice of this understanding of power and knowledge as conflictual and ambiguous, as a potential safeguard in relation to the tendencies of the church as institution to authoritarianism and control. An epistemology of ambiguity challenges and destabilizes any arrangements of power that claim absolute authority. It also calls into question any understandings of truth or of power as unchanging. The church as a society can help mediate the practice of this epistemology. An epistemology of ambiguity emphasizes the social dimension of who we are as well as what we know. Knowledge is not simply a personal possession, but in a very real way it comes to be in relationship. We know and are known in relationship. Our ability to tolerate and embrace ambiguity is aided by relationships and social settings that help us learn and practice such a way of living and thinking. The church as a community of remembrance will then be a society that is not only inclusive of differences, but able to hold and tolerate contradictions and conflicts in a way that retreats neither to absolutism, nor to *laissez-faire* disregard.

The dimensions of the church as society, institution, and divine mystery work together in a community of remembrance to do the work of witness in partnership. This witness would invite and incorporate a range of memories into ongoing narratives that provide meaning and coherence, all the while attending to the dynamics of power and the ambiguities of knowledge. Such a church would be the gathering place for the myriad voices that will emerge when remembering for ourselves is genuinely welcomed. The memories of all would be heard, challenged, and tested, and then perhaps honored and confirmed. Losses would be acknowledged and mourned in community; resistance, survival, and transformation would be recognized and celebrated. The church would evoke and preserve, narrate and formulate, all memories in an ongoing dialogical process. In such communities of remembrance, hope and openness toward the future would be nurtured, and action for change given concrete structure and support. At the same time, there would be an ongoing practice of analyzing power dynamics, in order to understand who has power to define and control the memories, and how this power is being deployed. Attention to the dangers and threats to right and redemptive remembering would be incorporated into the church's witness. All would be held appropriately accountable.

Marks of the Church

The Christian tradition has identified the authenticity of the church by characteristics that are referred to as the marks of the church: namely, that the church is one, holy, catholic, and apostolic. These marks identify, in part, the church's witness. They refer not only to that which marks or signs the church, but to its tasks, to that which the church is to practice. As a community of remembrance, the church also claims to be—and practices being—one, holy, catholic, and apostolic, but these marks carry meanings that are somewhat different than traditional usage. The oneness of the church as community of remembrance witnesses to a unity comprised of plurality. Authentic narrative memory is pluriform. It is a weaving together of multiple and distinct memories. Unity is never uniformity, but relationality—a willingness to stay in relationship and to share and expand the memorative witness.

Holiness is about manifesting the energy and power of God, in and for right relation. It is experienced as a gift. It is not a possession, but a presence that is realized in the practice of right relation. A church that is holy sees itself as partial and provisional. It is very much a community of people "on the way." Holiness is the potential for wholeness that is only possible when all are included and remembered.

Holiness, therefore, implies catholicity. Catholic means universal, which here means inclusive and open to change and transformation. No church can be catholic that practices behaviors of exclusion or silencing. Catholicity seeks out and attends to those who are silenced and invisible, who are lost and weary, who are in danger of being forgotten. The remembrance of this church is also inclusive, as well as provisional. All are included in God's care in ever-expanding and changing circles.

Finally, the church as a community of remembrance is apostolic. The Christian narrative and the practice of the church are to be marked by continuity in witness. For church as a community of remembrance, such continuity is in intent, rather than content. Continuity is through the process and practice of remembering in witness. Apostolicity is in maintaining that witnessing process as dynamic.

These marks together lend an ultimacy to the church's identity. Not only is the church identified as one, holy, catholic, and apostolic, but the implication is that *only* the church is these things. By nature and divine intention, the church is claimed to be a distinctive society and unique institution. Often that claim has functioned to remove the church from accountability in the world. Whereas such a positioning may allow the church to serve a useful function in evaluating and judging the uses of power in the world, I find it problematic. It tends to suggest that the church is somehow exempt from the misuses of power.

I would propose instead that the measure of the church's oneness, holiness, catholicity, and apostolicity is precisely in relation to its use of power. Is the church using its power toward oneness, holiness, catholicity, and apostolicity in the ways outlined above? Are the practices of remembrance in the church serving to give voice to those memories that have been excluded and silenced, distorted and forgotten? The true church, bearing these marks, will be characterized by memorative practices that are redemptive. The witness of the church—one, holy, catholic, and apostolic—is to such redeeming memories. That witness is manifest in and through all the activities of the church: worship, education, pastoral care, action in the world.

Worship and Ritual

The church gathers in worship to remember and re-member itself in relation to God. The worship life and rituals of the church are all in some way about remembering, about being reminded of who God is, who we are, and what God calls us to. They are also about re-membering, bringing us into relation in community as an ongoing process. Paul Connerton argues in *How Societies Remember* that memory is social and is mediated not only cognitively, but also, and even primarily, through commemorative ceremonies and bodily practices. In other words, memory and tradition are produced and reproduced in enactment, in and through bodies. Remembering is communicated and sustained through "habitual performances."[14] Nowhere is this more clear than in the liturgical and worship life of the church. It is through ritual practice that the church passes on tradition and makes it live in the present. Worship and ritual are practices of remembering and of being re-membered. The image of the church as the Body of Christ both reflects this understanding and enacts it.

The liturgies of the Armenian church to which I belonged as a child were conducted in fifth-century Armenian, a language not accessible to speakers of modern Armenian. I had little cognitive understanding of what was going on until I was older and able to follow the liturgy in translation, in a book. Despite my childlike impatience with this lengthy liturgy, I nonetheless absorbed its drama and intensity. The music and the gestures are still deeply part of me. They formed me. Protestant emphasis on preaching and word, along with its pared down liturgical "memorials," may seem to be light-years from this Armenian operatic drama, full of incense and bells, gestures of bowing and crossing oneself, elaborate vestments and ritual vessels. Yet even in Protestant worship, memory is being enacted and produced through what is said and done, and how the worship is conducted. Here too the Body of Christ is made present. Worship, in whatever form, is "habitual performance" and memorative witness. Indeed, the habit, the repetition of the performance, shapes the witness and literally "incorporates" it as memory.

The question then becomes: to what does the church bear witness in its worship? What does the church remember, memorialize, and commemorate in and through its rituals? Does that witness contribute to a process of redeeming memories? Experiences of profound and unrelenting suffering call into question the witness of worship. Sometimes it is the *possibility* of worship itself that is questioned. In other words, worship itself becomes a problem. What does it mean to offer worship or prayer in the midst of oppression and degradation, in the face of the seeming triumph of evil? What does it mean to enter in relationship with a God who seems absent, if not punishing? Witnessing in such settings seems to be more to God's absence than presence. Some survivors of abuse feel so much shame they cannot turn to God in prayer; others experience so much anger at God and what they have been taught about God that worship becomes inconceivable. The experience of genocide raises its own particular issues about the possibilities of prayer and worship.[15]

Others question the *authenticity* of worship. What does it mean to worship in a way that speaks to the situation of suffering? For example, those who have been sexually abused, especially if the abuse was by their fathers or by the "fathers" of the church, may question how God could be addressed as a loving father. How can one make oneself vulnerable in worship to God the Father or God the Mighty One when one's body has been violated in the name of father, in the name of power? Feminist theologians and liturgists extend their questioning to the language and style of worship in general. Worship is not authentic that does not include women and/or affirm women. Ethnic groups question forms of worship inherited from their colonizers and oppressors. They seek to incorporate elements from their own cultural experience and/or to lift up those indigenous elements that have persisted in customs and forms of spirituality.

Questions are also raised about the *adequacy* of the standard rituals to address the needs of those who are victimized. There seems to be a need especially for rites of healing and remembrance, as well as rites of reconciliation and integration. Feminist liturgical projects have tried to expand the range of available rituals and their uses, especially for commemorating women's lives and supporting healing. For example, Rosemary Ruether's book *Women-Church* contains rituals of healing, as well as ones intended to mark women's life events and acknowledge the history of women. The book's liturgical calendar also includes Holocaust Commemoration Day. Ruether is by no means alone in seeking to develop liturgies of healing and commemoration for specific events of victimization, such as genocide or violence against women. Others have focused on remembrance of resistance and survival, as well as transformation. One popular strategy is to expand the calendar of saints to include more women and representatives of ethnic groups, not only as those who suffered, but those who resisted and worked for transformation. Such strategies are meant to address and correct the inadequacies of the church's memorative witness in worship.

These problems and challenges suggest that, if the church is to remember for redemption, its witness needs to be more inclusive and responsive. Marjorie Procter-Smith describes the tasks of feminist liturgy as the reconstruction and enlargement of worship. These tasks require memory and imagination.[16] They are not restricted to feminist liturgy. Reconstruction and enlargement could well describe what is required for the memorative witness of the church in worship to be enacted in a way that works and is authentic and adequate to the experience of those who have been victimized. The church needs to remember multiply, with occasions to acknowledge and honor the victimization. Such rituals might allow for and even evoke anger as well as lament. They also ought to enable mourning and the holding in memory of those losses that cannot be redeemed or justified. Not only do the irretrievable losses in the lives of survivors need to be mourned, but those who did not survive, the dead, need to be mourned for and remembered. The corporate witness of the church could well be a setting for preserving the memory of those who have been lost, for making sure they are not forgotten.

Yet, as we have seen, it is not enough to remember the suffering and loss. The church in worship ought also to provide opportunities to claim agency, practice resistance, and celebrate resilience. Delores Williams suggests the need for African Americans to develop "resistance rituals" that might function "to remind the people of their ancient belief that God supported them and continues to support them in their resistance struggles."[17] Feminist litanies that recall faithful women in history as foremothers and role models are intended to enhance the agency of women in the present. Thanksgiving should be not only for deliverance, but for the power to resist and to survive. Rituals of healing ought to emphasize not only woundedness and need, but the life-restoring power already evidenced through survival and struggle.

The church in worship needs also to offer opportunities to celebrate healing and new life, and to enable integration in and through worship. Such rituals are most truly remembering to re-member. For survivors, these ritual moments set their story of victimization within a larger narrative. For all participants, such rituals weave connections and name God as the power of life abundant and ongoing. We have little practice with such rituals in our church communities. At best, we have liturgies and sacramental occasions that are about restoration, about the return of a sinner or the reconciliation of a penitent. Such liturgies emphasize the power of God to overcome adversity, but they do not give sufficient attention to God's power working through human agency and through relationships.

At its heart, worship is about a relationship of remembering. In and through worship, we remember God and God remembers us. In and through worship, we enact our relationship with God and with one another; we are re-membered. Traditionally, worship is directed toward remembering God and is about offering ourselves to God. It is our relational response to God's presence and grace in our lives, our remembering who we are in relation to God. The emphasis is on praise and thanksgiving, and on bringing ourselves back into right relationship with God. I want to affirm the relational character of worship, but shift the emphasis toward relationship that is more mutual and more empowering. Sometimes such worship is about celebrating relationship; at other times it is about restoring relationship. It is always about the power of relationship to sustain and to be life-giving, about the power of relationship for transformation. It is always remembering for the sake of re-membering. Relationships exist and are effective only to the extent that they are practiced and enacted. So too with worship—

the church only exists to the extent that it practices redemptive relationships of healing and transformation.

For the witness of the church to make a difference for those who have been victimized, it must incorporate multiple memorative practices into its prayer and rituals. It must be a community of remembrance for redemption. Such practices are necessary both for the life and faith of survivors and for the community as a whole. The church can enable the healing of individual survivors or groups of survivors by providing rites of mourning, healing, and integration. It can also fulfill its redemptive mission more adequately by expanding its corporate memory to include witness to the suffering, survival, and transformation of others. By so doing, it enters into its own process of transformation, toward a community dedicated to being with those who suffer for the sake of life. It enacts its faithfulness to God as the one whose witness is always to life, even in the midst of death.

The article "Spirit Song: The Use of Christian Healing Rites in Trauma Recovery" offers an example of the use of ritual for personal healing in relation. The authors—Rebecca, a survivor of sexual, sadistic abuse (only her first name is given and it is a pseudonym), Lea Nicoll Kramer, her therapist, and Susan Lukey, a minister—describe the healing journey of Rebecca and the role that rituals play in it. These rituals are planned and conducted by Lukey, but Rebecca has control over what happens in these "healing rites." They are based on traditional Christian rituals, but altered to fit the need. The first takes the form of a renouncing of evil, a turning toward freedom, a cleansing, and an embracing of life and hope. Through this rite, Rebecca is able to reclaim her body and soul by renouncing evil and turning toward God. She is able to feel new strength and begin integrating her abuse into a larger narrative of self. A second rite involves confession and reconciliation. Initially, Lukey is hesitant to perform such a ritual because she does not want to suggest that Rebecca is guilty of what was done to her. Yet it becomes clear that Rebecca feels guilt and needs to experience reconciliation. Lukey is able to embrace this ambiguity. The third ritual is one of baptism, the enactment and celebration of new life. It contains parts similar to the other healing rites. This repetition is reported as allowing Rebecca to take in the meanings more fully. The baptismal ritual is followed by a service of communion, which is described as "a meal of celebration and hope." Traditional rituals are adapted to fit the particular needs of this survivor, but all the participants are transformed through their sharing in these experiences. The church present in these personal and private rites is a witness not only to Rebecca's victimization, but to her agency, healing, and transformation. Although any one of the rites used might be viewed as problematic to an abuse survivor, they work in this case. That effectiveness is due in no small part to the fact that Rebecca is the one who chooses them and is able to control what happens in them. The emphasis in the rites is not simply on reconciling Rebecca to God, but on restoring relationship—between Rebecca and God and others, and especially between Rebecca and herself. In that way the rites acknowledge that something was taken from Rebecca that has to be redeemed. Such redemption involves remembering and re-membering in and through relationship.[18]

The witness of remembering and re-membering in the corporate worship of the church necessarily follows a different process. The healing rites for Rebecca were specifically designed for her. Their purpose was to enable her healing. Corporate worship has by nature a broader focus and purpose. Such worship affects the whole body of participants. Indeed, worship is a setting in which the church is formed and re-formed.

In the summer of 1998, as they do every ten years, Anglican bishops from around the world gathered at Lambeth, in England. Their meetings were characterized by great tension and even contentiousness, particularly on the issues of women's ordination and homosexuality. Underlying such tensions were concerns of identity and power. During these meetings, on August 6 (the feast of the Transfiguration, and also the anniversary of the bombing of Hiroshima) the bishops of Nippon Sei Ko Kai (Japan) were responsible for the liturgy of the day. These bishops faced choices about what in particular to remember and how. They could have used that occasion to call attention to their own victimization as a result of the bombing. Instead, the bishops focused on taking responsibility and asking forgiveness for the complicity of the Japanese churches in going along with Japanese atrocities during the war. A statement to that effect was handed to each person as she or he arrived for the service. The daughter of the bishop of Singapore, who had been tortured by the Japanese army, preached. The congregational responses to the prayers of the people were in Korean, the language of another group systematically persecuted by the Japanese. The liturgy was intended to remember the history of that time in a way that acknowledged the misuses of power. It sought to move toward reconciliation by acknowledging, giving voice to, and empowering those who had been persecuted.[19]

✳ ✳ ✳

The central ritual of the Christian church is the Eucharist, the memorial meal of Christ's body and blood. At the heart of Christian worship is an action of remembering Jesus' life, death, and resurrection. This remembering is an action in response to a specific command. The words of the Eucharist prayer in many churches recall Jesus' words: "This is my body given for you. Do this in remembrance of me. This is my blood poured out for you. Do this in remembrance of me." The *anamnesis* of the liturgy not only recalls the words and actions of Jesus Christ, but makes them present, in and through the Body of Christ gathered and shared. Remembering Christ re-members the community. And reciprocally, the community makes remembrance possible. In other words, re-membering also leads to remembering.

At the core of the Eucharistic liturgy is the recalling of a traumatic event of suffering, degradation, and death. What does it mean to repeat this action again and again and reenact the trauma, so to speak? On the one hand, it means that God in Christ is present in suffering. God is victim and witness. Therefore, the sufferings of all those who have been victimized can be brought to the table and remembered through the action of the Eucharist. On the other hand, it means that if the Eucharist only remembers the suffering, our redemptive memories are incomplete and indeed stigmatized. The repetition of suffering without an experience of resurrection and a reclaiming of life is not redemptively anamnetic. The Eucharist must be reenacted as the memory of Jesus' life and resurrection, as well as his crucifixion. The celebration of the Body of Christ is most properly one of incarnation and not of death. As these fuller purposes are recalled and enacted, the Eucharist might become a rite that both witnesses and transforms.

Further, in a theology of redeeming memories, recognition of the power of the sacramental rites will read them not only as vehicles of God's grace, but as political acts. Hence, Elisabeth Schüssler Fiorenza's question: "How can we point to the eucharistic bread and say 'this is my body' as long as women's bodies are battered, raped, sterilized, mutilated, prostituted, and used to male ends?"[20] The Eucharist is not an innocent act; its theology is not innocent knowledge. All the rituals and worship life of the church are political actions. The witness of remembrance in the prayers and actions of the church needs to be inclusive if it is to empower the victimized for resistance and for life. In this way, the people might be made and remade, membered and re-membered, as the Body of Christ. In this way, remembering may give way to hope. The worship and rituals of the church would then be not only commemorations, but anticipations of future life, in fullness and abundance and hope.

There are many specific rituals or forms of prayer that lend themselves to the memorative practices being advocated in this work. Some of these have already been mentioned. Lament is one obvious form of prayer that attends to suffering. We can lament for ourselves or on behalf of others. Intercession and confession also afford opportunities for the community to bear witness, lend support, acknowledge, and take responsibility for complicity. Prayers of thanksgiving and praise can be occasions for celebrating healing and transformation. Rites of healing are powerful occasions of remembrance and transformation. Certain elements of the Christian story may also be expanded to include the remembrance of victims. The symbol of Christ's descent to the dead before his resurrection and ascension is a powerful reminder that no one is forgotten by God. It may also symbolize that hidden parts can be retrieved and are accessible to God. Rituals of cleansing and renewal, often associated with baptism, are another way to symbolize and enact remembrance and transformation. Indeed, there are rich resources in the liturgical life of the church to enhance its memorative witness and offer support to those who struggle for life. Through these liturgies the church might be brought into a relationship of authentic witness with those who have been victimized. God will then emerge and be affirmed as the one present in the healing and transforming power of remembrance and witness.

If the church's witness through worship is to be effective for healing and transformation, then the church must be careful to make sure its liturgies do not harm those who have already suffered so much, often with Christian complicity in the abuse and oppression. There has been growing sensitivity in some churches to the ways in which churches continue to promote anti-Semitism. Efforts have been made to eliminate anti-Semitic references, especially in the liturgies of Holy Week, particularly Good Friday. As noted, many women indict the liturgies of the churches for their sexist language and hierarchical forms and peoples from around the world are raising questions about the specificity of the cultural forms of worship and the exclusion of local customs and rites. The language, structure, and forms used in worship need to be evaluated and changed to respond to these challenges and to become sites of healing, rather than of further injury.

Preaching and Teaching

The church not only remembers and bears witness through its worship and prayer, but through its teaching and preaching. Indeed, preaching is the act of witnessing to the life-giving and redeeming presence of God. If the teaching and preaching of the church are to be authentic and effective as redeeming memories, then its practices of teaching and preaching need to include and be attentive to those who have and continue to suffer.

The church as a community of remembrance would be a place where people learn about forms of abuse, genocides, and the cultural histories of particular groups. These stories of suffering and oppression would be told in such a way that the church would take responsibility for its complicity in the social dynamics and political structures that perpetrated violence. Many church bodies began such a process of remembering differently during the sequicentennial of Columbus's voyage several years ago. Churches sought to tell the story of what happened in 1492 and the years after as one of conquest and not discovery. In so doing, they also acknowledged some of their complicity in the conquest and colonizing of the Americas. Along with such repentance and retelling, the churches invited the witness of indigenous peoples to their own experiences and spiritualities. In these ways, a very different story got told and a new memory began to be fashioned.

Taking such responsibility would then lead to reformation of the church's teachings. Not only the liturgies, but the scriptures and theologies of the church are rife with sexism, racism, anti-Semitism, and other forms of discriminatory teachings. The church cannot be a community of redemptive remembrance if it continues with such teachings. For example, passages of scripture that tell women or slaves to be submissive or that are accusatory of Jews cannot be proclaimed as God's word and therefore authentic memory. If they are going to be continued to be read and/or preached, they must be approached critically and put into a clear historical context.[21] Some churches are taking further action to eliminate sexism, racism, anti-Semitism, and other oppressive behaviors from their teachings and proclamations. For example, there are now inclusive language translations of the Bible available.[22]

At the same time, the church needs to provide occasions for specific testimony by those who have been victimized and by their heirs and witnesses. Those who have been victimized might then have a place to testify to their histories and to find witnesses. Especially, because these memories are so often contested and challenged, if not denied, it is important for the church as a body to align in a witness that is clear and public.

The witness needs to be not only to the suffering, but to survival and life affirmation. Too often the church's witness to the victimized is only to their suffering and not to their resistance and agency. Yet, as we have seen, that is an inadequate and even harmful form of witness. It serves the interests of charity, but not of healing and transformation for those who live with victimization.

The church's witness in teaching and preaching might well include judgment and denunciation of those who continue to perpetrate harm and abuse. The church is then using its power not only to offer support, but to work toward justice and right relationship. The church should set the example by being honest about its own complicity and failings.

In order for the church's witness in preaching and teaching to be attentive to the practice of redeeming memories, the church needs to do more than teach the history of those who suffer and struggle, and even more than change its own teachings. It is important for the church to cultivate in itself and in society a critical consciousness about the dynamics of power and the nature of truth. Therefore, the church needs to embody and nurture an epistemology of ambiguity. Too often the church's insistence on the certainty and absoluteness of truth has created the kind of social and political space for the forces of domination to enter and establish themselves. Too often the church has opposed criticism of any sort and has asked for a kind of innocence of knowledge in its members that leaves people vulnerable to the dominating powers in the world.

Remembering for redemption requires a critical consciousness able to discern and stand for truth that is always ambiguous, always contested, always a matter of power. There is no room for naïveté or innocence in the struggle for truth on behalf of those who suffer injustice and cruelty. The church needs to teach not only the values of right rela-

tionship, but the skills necessary to practice the making of right relationship in the midst of a conflictual, violence-threatened world.

One place to begin such teaching is in relation to the church's own
history. The history of the church is full of conflict. If the church
approaches its own historical memory as a story of conflicts and clashes,
as a story of power dynamics played out in the name of and for the sake
of truth, then it will be educating its members toward a different
process of remembering. Idyllic images of the early church will be
replaced by the pluralistic, conflicted reality that it was. Tributes to the
courage and faith of reformers will be coupled with stories of the blood-
iness of the reformation and other campaigns for the "true faith."

As the history of the church is remembered differently, the sharply
drawn lines between church and world, that often obscure and obfus-
cate the workings of power in the church, will be blurred. The church
will be viewed as an institution fully in and of the world, whose ethical
and spiritual mission does not exempt it from accountability for its uses
and misuses of power. Such a critical and political consciousness of the
church will help cultivate in its members transformed ethical and theological understandings of power and truth.

Social and Political Witness

As an institution in and of the world, the church is accountable for
its actions. The witness of remembering is present also in its pastoral
practices and in its programs of social and political action. Its witnessing ought to be toward a multiple memorative practice of redemption
that is manifest as right relation. Such remembering is not only an
action directed toward the past, but also toward the present, with a
future intent. The church's remembering ought to result in re-membering, not only of itself but of the world. Such re-membering involves the
righting of relationships, the work of justice.

These principles apply to the pastoral presence and care offered by the
church. Such care is a form and expression of the church's witness. The
church as a community of remembrance would practice remembering by
creating and nurturing settings of healing and empowerment for those who
suffer victimization of all kinds. Group settings would be places for testimony and witness, as church members listen to and support one another.
Because it is difficult to remember the pain of the past and because it is difficult to remember anything *but* the pain of the past, ecclesial and pastoral
support of the remembering process cannot be underestimated.

Such concrete invitations to remember help counter the internal and external challenges that are forever present. Individual pastoral counseling might coordinate with the work of such groups. The intent of both group and personal support would be to help those who have been victimized remember and mourn the suffering and loss, claim resistance and agency, reclaim wholeness of life, and practice new life commitments and patterns. Such processes would honor both the fragility and the resiliency of memory. The church can be a place that holds the memories even when the victimized cannot recall or utter them.

The church would also hold accountable those who perpetuate violence and victimization. This would mean that the church would admit responsibility for its own complicity in a variety of forms of victimization. Again, this is no easy task. Most of us would rather not, most of the time, remember and face into the harm that has been done to others in which we are in some sense complicit. Remembering may make us uncomfortable, indict our behavior, force us to rethink cherished values and beliefs, and/or reconsider an unreflected stance. Remembering would lead to accountability that, in turn, would entail confession, amendment of life, and offers of restitution. Restitution can never make up for the losses endured by those who have been victimized, but it is an important element of accountability. It is a gesture toward right relationship.

Acts of restitution, if they are to be authentic, would effect change in relations of privilege that adhere to positions of dominance. For example, it is not enough for white Christians to apologize for slavery and racism, and to offer monetary or programmatic "amends." Whites in churches need also examine and share their privilege, personal and institutional. Such sharing is neither easy to commit to nor to accomplish. But its practice will produce a very different kind of memory about race relations in this country. It will be a profound re-membering. Men who work to combat violence against women must examine their own privilege and the subtle ways such privilege contributes to attitudes of dominance and ownership of women. Beyond examining privilege, men need to be willing to learn to move toward truer partnerships with women.

The church's theological approach to divestiture has been to proffer self-sacrifice, sacrificial giving, and love as virtues. The forgoing of privilege is then viewed through lenses of suffering and loss; for example, putting another's interests ahead of one's own. The standard is one of agapic love, which is symbolized in Jesus' laying down his life for his friends. In this way of thinking, virtue and true love require sacrifice and a "giving up" of oneself. In a relational and political theology of witness, however, the emphasis shifts to the righting of relation, which is in everyone's interests. To change patterns of privilege is an expansion of relationship, with a recognition that there is power and love enough for all. Sharon Welch writes of such witness as solidarity: "Solidarity does not require self-sacrifice but an enlargement of the self to include community with others."[23] Such a self is enhanced, not diminished, through relationship with others. It is in everyone's best interest to share privilege. It is in all of our interests to live in a just and caring world, as it is to remember the past truly and fully.

The witness of remembering for the sake of accountability and present action extends to the church's mission in the world. For example, if a church or a community marks the Jewish Holocaust or the Armenian genocide with an event of remembrance, but does not make connections with the genocides being perpetrated in the world today, then it is not practicing redeeming memories. Remembering past suffering is not fully authentic if it does not respond to present need.

The work of justice is a re-membering in and through remembering the past in order to pay due honor for all the losses sustained and in order to work for transformation in the present and the future. Justice is witness and action toward change that is rooted in right relationship. It is a never-ending challenge and task that is both ground and fruit of remembering. It is central to the mission of the church.

The goal of the church's social and political witness is integrity, wholeness, and fullness of life. Integrity is of spirit and body. The church's witness is concrete, addressing material conditions, as well as spiritual needs. Indeed, unless people have fundamental safety in their lives and their basic physical needs are met, they are often unable to focus on questions of identity, meaning, or even justice. One of the characteristics of trauma is that it is not known in the event itself. The suffering is only acknowledged and even experienced after the event of trauma. In that way, any knowledge of trauma is a memorative witness.[24] The church as a community of remembrance can make the trauma real by naming it and holding it in memory with and for survivors and their heirs, as well as by providing the safety and care needed to allow the traumatic memories to emerge and be told. It is here that the church's social and political witness must begin.

230

In the End, the Beginning

I have written much in these pages of what the church, as a community of remembrance, ought to be and do. The church's witness, first and foremost, is one of listening—listening to the sometimes barely audible and emerging voices of those who have been victimized. The church's witness is about providing sanctuary, a place of safety, for these voices to be heard, honored, and responded to. It means standing with and holding in its heart the pain and the suffering in order to begin to create spaces for new life to emerge. This witness requires humility—a willingness to be open and vulnerable on the part of the church and its members. It also requires the use of power with all its ambiguity and danger.

Such a witness is to holiness. If the church attends truly, it will hear the call of the Holy Spirit in and through voices of the victimized. It will enter into the depth of the mystery of God in Jesus Christ: that life, which is ever-precious, seeks itself, even in the midst of degradation and suffering and death. The testimony to suffering is at heart a witness to life, the power of life to endure and to continue to love and be effective. The Holy Spirit, the bearer of life, will be revealed as transforming power, able to manifest itself when life seems no longer possible. This Spirit, whose name is hope, arises out of remembering for the sake of re-membering. In this way, the church as a community of remembrance carries on the process of redeeming memories for the sake of a hope that can make real the promise of salvation contained in Jesus' command to remember in his name.

Conclusion

Witnessing to the Hope
That Is in Us

I have often been asked how I can study and write about so much evil and so much suffering. "Oh," I reply, "but I am offered so much hope." I am moved continually by the thirst for life that I encounter again and again. I am in awe of the courage and insight displayed by those who have been victimized; I marvel at their clinging to faith in the midst of despair. Nor do I point to these things with any hint of naive optimism. The courage of survivors is accompanied by profound doubt that throws them into convulsive shaking. Their faith is often but a faint echo in a chasm of solitary confinement. Their humanity and goodness that survived the assaults of degradation and torture remain invisible to them. Yet, they go on, most of them, most of the time, and they choose life, most of them, most of the time. And if and when they are willing to share their experiences and their remembering, they honor and grace us all.

They also invite us into relationships of witnessing. Such relationships enable the remembering and indeed, give life to memories hidden and unrealized. Witnessing is an ongoing process, shared by testifiers and listeners, that weaves from all the threads of memories—memories of terrible suffering and irretrievable loss, of survival through resistance and creative agency, of nurturing life connections and affirmation. The fullness of memory is manifest through working all these threads together, not into one strand, but into a multiform, multitextured weaving. It is only through witnessing that the multiple process of remembering is enacted in such a way that both the dead and the living are honored.[1] We remember not only to preserve the past, but to claim the present for the living, and create and transform the future toward a vision of how things might be. Such a vision is developed in relation to the past and present, and in relation to our remembering.

In the process of witnessing, we encounter the divine as source of ambiguous power and unsettling love. God as witness becomes known and manifest through the process of bearing testimony, at the same time that God is the ground of the possibility of witness. God as witness-in-relationship remains constant, ready to hear and honor the testimony as it is offered and enable the testimony in all its complexities. Such testimony also witnesses to divine energy present in the unceasing yearning for hope. There is no possibility of witness without hope. God as witness-to-hope testifies to that.

Hope is an attitude of openness to the future and a commitment to change. It grounds action for change in one's own life and in the world.

Faith and hope together engender solidarity and enable ongoing struggle. To speak of God's power as mighty is to proclaim that the divine is on the side of life, but not to talk of victories or final triumphs, or of goodness being realized fully. The dynamics of power are played out continually and conflictually in the world, in history, and in nature. Divine presence is in and through the process and practice of power that makes life possible.

For Christians, that presence is interpreted through the incarnation, life, death, and resurrection of Jesus Christ. The authenticity and effectiveness of the Christian witness is to be measured by the capacity of the Christian story to be faithful to those victimized. In other words, the truth of the Christian story is manifest in whether and how it makes a difference to those who have suffered. Adequate witness is tested by the ability to hold together the experiences of suffering, survival, and life connection. Together these make up the tapestry of life. The type of remembrance that reveals redemption is a faithful witness to the complexities of suffering and survival, life connection and wholeness, shown to us in Jesus Christ. Such remembrance is being revealed today through the struggle for life of all those who suffer from violence and oppression. Christ *is* present in, with, and among them.

In this theology of redemptive memory, revelation is to be understood as a changing narrative. What was read as revelatory in the past has a particular claim upon us because it has shaped us and is our memory. But is is not true *a priori;* its present status as revelation is to be determined by its effectiveness. What is deemed as true must be continually tested and made true by what it makes possible. Revelation is that which re-members us toward resistance and hope, liberation and justice.

Such an understanding of revelation is partnered with an epistemology of ambiguity in which knowing is ambiguous and relational. It is apprehended in and through struggle and solidarity. Truth emerges from this process as a delicate, precious, and shared joining of lives in witness. It is not a possession, but a commitment, attitude, and practice. We do not know something to be the truth, so much as we know it as true. Such knowledge is guided by love and faith. It knows by heart. Our hearts seek remembrance for the sake of redemption. Redemption is the going on, the continuing to embrace living with commitment and faith. Just as the Spirit of God called Mary into a partnership of redemption, the Spirit calls us all into such partnership. For those who have been victimized, the partnership is realized through their struggle for life, their witness of remembering and re-membering. For others of us, it is manifest in faithful and effective witness that begins in listening and ends in transformation of ourselves and the world.

Witnessing is a shared and universal task that does not end in time or space. There is no resolution, no realized redemption. In the place of resolution, this theology offers remembrance and witness. Indeed, remembering replaces resolution in the story of redemption.[2] Remembering bears witness to life, ever-threatened, ever-renewed.

✳ ✳ ✳

Toward the end of the Gospel of John, the author states directly his purpose: "Now Jesus did many other signs in the presence of the disciples, which are not written in this book. But these are written so that you may come to believe that Jesus is the Messiah, the Child of God, and that through believing you may have life in Jesus' name."[3] The author wants to invite belief for the sake of life and points to Jesus' actions as sign witnesses to the presence and power of God in and through Jesus. The final "sign" is Jesus' own death and resurrection. The offer of life is thereby made possible for all.

Though the author of the Gospel of John and I may mean different things by the life we seek, we share an interest that our theologies be life-giving. Toward that end, I too have recorded signs, in the promise that truth for life is known by attentive witness.

>Excerpt from "The Last Witness"
>"I would not want to be the last witness." —Elie Wiesel

>Close your eyes in peace
>if you have borne witness aloud
>in peace
>if you have sworn the truth
>in peace
>if you have shared the horror
>and the vision
>if you have defied those who deny
>if you have added your testimony
>to the roll call of truth
>in peace

if you have raised your voice
against all who would silence you
if you have written the story
if you have named the names
if you have listed the places
if you have called down from heaven
the witnesses who have gone

Close your eyes in peace
if you have taken one step
on the path that heals.

Diana Der-Hovanessian[4]

Notes

Preface

1. The genocide is often portrayed as a result of the refusal by Armenians to convert to Islam. In other words, if Armenians converted from Christianity to Islam, their lives would have been spared. Although there is some evidence that Turks tried to convert Armenians in the name of Muhammad or that occasionally "conversion" was a survival strategy Armenians deployed or were forced into, most Armenians were given no choice or opportunity to save themselves through conversion.

2. The liturgy of the Armenian Church is chanted in three parts by priest, deacon, and choir. Therefore, there is a substantial liturgical role for deacons. The Armenian Church also practices "ordination" of all liturgical assistants: acolytes, deacons, and so on. Women are not ordained. They may only serve as choir members and are simply tonsured for that purpose. The Armenian Church is an independent ethnic denomination which, while sharing much in common with Eastern Orthodoxy, is separate and distinctive. The Armenian Church did not accept the formulation of Christ's person as determined by the Council of Chalcedon. Because of this doctrinal difference and because of Armenia's history of occupation, it was often cut off from the rest of Christendom.

3. In the Armenian Church, deacons most often wear a stole draped over one shoulder and hanging straight down.

4. For example, Donald Miller and Lorna Touryan Miller point out in *Survivors: An Oral History of the Armenian Genocide* (Berkeley: University of California Press, 1993) that a number of the survivors they interviewed had previously told no one their stories (30).

Introduction

1. These quotations from the Gospel of John are taken from *The New Testament and Psalms: An Inclusive Version* (New York: Oxford University Press, 1995).

2. Dorothee Soelle, *Suffering,* trans. Everett R. Kalin (Philadelphia: Fortress Press, 1975), 68.

3. See Paolo Freire, *Pedagogy of the Oppressed,* trans. Myra Bergman Ramos (New York: Herder & Herder, 1972). The authors Mary Field Belenky, Blythe McVicker Clinchy, Nancy Rule Goldberger, and Jill Mattuck Tarule of *Women's Ways of Knowing: The Development of Self, Voice, and Mind* also suggest silence as the first and least developed form of knowing, which reflects the powerlessness and subjugation of the knower (New York: BasicBooks, 1986).

4. Nelle Morton, *The Journey Is Home* (Boston: Beacon Press, 1985). The woman's story is on pages 204-5.

5. Elizabeth Johnson, *She Who Is: The Mystery of God in Feminist Theological Discourse* (New York: Crossroad, 1992), 87.

6. Ibid., 99, 100.

7. Michael Arlen uses this phrase to describe the pain Armenians carry because of the genocide. See his memoir/historical essay, *Passage to Ararat* (New York: Farrar, Straus & Giroux, 1975), 189.

8. See Elisabeth Schüssler Fiorenza, *But She Said: Feminist Practices of Biblical Inter-pretation* (Boston: Beacon Press, 1992), 117 and *Jesus: Miriam's Child, Sophia's Prophet: Critical Issues in Feminist Christology* (New York: Continuum, 1994), 14. Schüssler Fiorenza developed the term "kyriarchy" as a more adequate signifier than patriarchy. Derived from the Greek word for Lord, *kyrios,* it is meant to incorporate not only gender, but race, class, and religious and cultural dominations. Kyriarchy is rule of the lords or masters, who are elite, propertied, educated, freeborn men.

9. See Charles Elliot, *Memory and Salvation* (London: Darton, Longman & Todd, 1995) for a seemingly similar, yet markedly different, treatment of the relationship of memory and salvation. Although Elliot and I share concerns and even goals, our methods are quite different.

10. George W. Stroup, *The Promise of Narrative Theology* (Atlanta: John Knox Press, 1981), 167. Other works on narrative theology include Terrence W. Tilley, *Story Theology* (Wilmington, Del.: Michael Glazier, 1985) and Stephen Crites, "The Narrative Quality of Experience," *Journal of the American Academy of Religion,* 39/3 (September 1971): 291-311. I draw primarily on the work of Johann Baptist Metz, who advocates a form of narrative theology. See chapter 4 below.

11. Ibid., 170.

12. Ibid., 168.

13. Judith L. Herman uses the concept of captivity to describe the situation of those who are "prisoners" of abuse and violence (that is, they have no means of escape). Captivity may be the result of physical constraint, psychological control, or social circumstance, for example, being too young or dependent to leave. See her *Trauma and Recovery* (New York: BasicBooks, 1992), chapter 4, for a fuller description of the state of captivity.

14. As Judith L. Herman points out: "The conflict between the will to deny horrible events and the will to proclaim them aloud is the central dialectic of psychological trauma" (*Trauma and Recovery,* 1). I would add "and of social trauma."

15. I draw especially upon Herman, *Trauma and Recovery.* Other works of note are Paul Antze and Michael Lambek, eds., *Tense Past: Cultural Essays in Trauma and Memory* (New York: Routledge, 1996); Cathy Caruth, *Unclaimed Experience: Trauma, Narrative, and History* (Baltimore: Johns Hopkins University Press, 1996); Cathy Caruth, ed., *Trauma: Explorations in Memory* (Baltimore: Johns Hopkins University Press, 1995); Shoshana Felman and Dori Laub, eds., *Testimony: Crises of Witnessing Literature, Psychoanalysis, and History* (New York: Routledge, 1992); Maurice Halbwachs, *On Collective Memory,* trans. Lewis A. Coser (Chicago: University of Chicago Press, 1992); Michael S. Roth, *The Ironist's Cage: Memory, Trauma, and the Construction of History* (New York: Columbia University Press, 1995); and James C. Scott, *Domination and the Arts of Resistance* (New Haven: Yale University Press, 1990).

1. "And Then I Remembered": Childhood Sexual Abuse

1. See Phyllis Trible, *God and the Rhetoric of Sexuality* (Philadelphia: Fortress Press, 1978), chapter 6, entitled "A Human Comedy."

2. In recent years, more men have been coming forward with memories of abuse. This is a relatively new phenomenon and it is difficult to tell yet how widespread it is or how it will influence our understanding of child sexual abuse.

3. In my work, I have had the experience, as have many practitioners, of listening to survivors say things such as: "I never knew what happened to me was rape or abuse." As little children, these survivors knew they did not like what was happening to them, or felt very uncomfortable and hurt, but they did not have a conceptual grasp of the behavior or activity or the implications of it.

4. Denise J. Gelinas reports that: "Most researchers have found that approximately 97-98% of incest offenders are male." See "The Persisting Negative Effects of Incest," *Psychiatry* 46 (November 1983): 313. Shirley J. Asher, in her chapter entitled "The Effects of Childhood Sexual Abuse: A Review of the Issues and Evidence," in *Handbook on Sexual Abuse of Children,* states that 94 to 97 percent of perpetrators are male. See *Handbook on Sexual Abuse of Children,* ed. Lenore E. A. Walker (New York: Springer Publishing, 1988), 4. In the last several years, there have been more reports of abuse by women. It is not clear yet how such reports might change statistics and ratios.

5. Judith L. Herman, *Trauma and Recovery* (New York: BasicBooks, 1992), 33.

6. Jennifer Freyd argues that it is precisely the betrayal of trust that is traumatic and especially harmful. See her *Betrayal Trauma: The Logic of Forgetting Childhood Abuse* (Cambridge, Mass.: Harvard University Press, 1996). Because those victimized by child sexual abuse are more often female, I will use the female pronoun when referring to the victimized.

7. Herman, *Trauma and Recovery,* 42.

8. Ibid., 74.

9. Ibid., 75.

10. Ibid., 96.

11. Ibid., 101.

12. Ibid., 103.

13. There is considerable discussion among psychologists about the differences between denial, repression, and dissociation. Elizabeth A. Waites argues that it is more accurate to describe what happens with memories of abuse as dissociation rather then repression. Dissociation connotes disconnection and attends to the social dimension of remembering. When memories are denied by self or others, they become socially disconnected. See her *Memory Quest: Trauma and the Search for Personal History* (New York: W. W. Norton, 1997).

14. Flashbacks may be triggered by almost anything. Sensory experiences often trigger flashbacks because the body retains the memory and may respond even when the mind is in active denial. New situations that trigger remembering vary widely as well. Often going off to school and being away from home for the first time elicits memories.

15. Herman, *Trauma and Recovery,* 175.

16. Ellen Bass and Laura Davis, *The Courage to Heal* (New York: Harper & Row, 1988), 58. Revised 3rd edition HarperCollins, 1994.

17. Herman, *Trauma and Recovery,* 188.

18. Ibid.

19. Ibid., 178.

20. Waites, *Memory Quest,* 271.

21. Herman, *Trauma and Recovery,* 196.

22. See Brenda J. Vander Mey and Ronald L. Neff, eds., *Incest as Child Abuse: Research and Applications* (New York: Praeger, 1986), 128, for such an assessment. "The Battered Child Syndrome" was also authored by Frederic N. Silverman, F. Brant, William Droegemuller, and Henry K. Silver and appeared in the *Journal of the American Medical Association,* 181 (1962): 17-24.

23. Adopted by the American Psychiatric Association in 1980. See Herman, *Trauma and Recovery,* 33.

24. A major goal of Herman's book, *Trauma and Recovery,* is to propose a new diagnostic category for those with histories of abuse: complex post-traumatic stress disorder. She argues that the diagnostic criteria for post-traumatic stress disorder "are derived mainly from survivors of circumscribed traumatic events" (119). A different set of criteria are necessary for survivors of prolonged and repeated trauma and abuse. She concludes: "The current formulation of post-traumatic stress disorder fails to capture either the protean symptomatic manifestations of prolonged, repeated trauma or the profound deformations of personality that occur in captivity" (119). The outline of conditions and symptomology of complex post-traumatic stress disorder are to be found on page 121.

25. See, for example, Joanne Carlson Brown and Carole R. Bohn, eds., *Christianity, Patriarchy, and Abuse: A Feminist Critique* (New York: Pilgrim Press, 1989) and Annie Imbens and Ineke Jonker, *Christianity and Incest* (Minneapolis: Fortress Press, 1992). Churches and other religious bodies are slowly beginning to change pastoral practices. Theological change is still more possibility than actuality.

26. See Freud's "Heredity and the Aetiology of the Neuroses," especially pages 151-52. This essay was first published in 1896 and is printed in *The Standard Edition of the Complete Psychological Works of Sigmund Freud,* vol. 3, trans. and ed. James Strachey (London: Hogarth Press, 1962). See also "The Aetiology of Hysteria," a paper Freud delivered on April 21, 1896, to the Society for Psychiatry and Neurology meeting in Vienna. James Strachey's translation is included as an appendix in Jeffrey M. Mason, *The Assault on Truth: Freud's Suppression of the Seduction Theory* (New York: Farrar, Strauss & Giroux, 1984).

27. Masson, *The Assault on Truth,* appendix B, 272.

28. To be fair to Freud, the correspondence with Fliess reveals that Freud does not change his mind all at once. Even after the letter of September 21, he writes to Fliess about abuse by the father. Freud seems to go back and forth between believing that fathers and others abuse their daughters, and suggesting that such reports are fantasy. I do think that it is appropriate to say that "eventually" Freud changed his mind.

29. Both essays are included in volume 7 of *The Standard Edition of the Complete Psychological Works of Sigmund Freud,* trans. and ed. James Strachey (London: Hogarth Press, 1953). The second essay was published in 1906 in a volume edited by Ludwig Loewenfeld.

30. See Elaine Westerlund, "Freud on Sexual Trauma: An Historical Review of Seduction and Betrayal," *Psychology of Women Quarterly* 10 (1986): 307.

31. Florence Rush, *The Best Kept Secret: Sexual Abuse of Children* (Englewood Cliffs, N.J.: Prentice-Hall, 1980), 82.

32. Judith L. Herman, *Father-Daughter Incest* (Cambridge, Mass.: Harvard University Press, 1981), 10.

33. Alice Miller, *Thou Shalt Not Be Aware: Society's Betrayal of the Child* (New York: Meridian Books, 1986).

34. This "syndrome" is not recognized as an offical diagnostic category. It is being promoted as a condition by the False Memory Syndrome Foundation.

35. Loftus's study consisted of having an older brother tell his younger sibling a fabricated story about the younger sibling having been lost in a shopping mall when he was five years old, some nine years previously. In a couple of days, the younger sibling began to recall this experience and over the course of some more days elaborated on the event. When he was informed that this memory was false, he was surprised. See Elizabeth F. Loftus, "The Reality of Repressed Memories," *American Psychologist* 48 (May 1993): 532.

36. Ibid., 524.

37. Elizabeth Loftus and Katherine Ketcham, *The Myth of Repressed Memory* (New York: St. Martin's Press, 1994), 4.

38. Ibid., 141.

39. Michael D. Yapko, *True and False Memories of Childhood Sexual Trauma* (New York: Simon & Schuster, 1994), 31.

40. See Lawrence Wright, *Remembering Satan* (New York: Alfred A. Knopf, 1994) for a sympathetic portrayal of Ingram, a deputy sheriff and fundamentalist Protestant, who was accused of abuse by his daughters. After his arrest, he "confessed" to these crimes. He has since recanted his confession, but a clemency hearing reaffirmed his conviction.

41. Other texts that criticize repression and retrieval of memories include: Richard Ofshe and Ethan Watters, *Making Monsters: False Memories, Psychotherapy, and Sexual Hysteria* (New York: Charles Scribner's Sons, 1994); Claudette Wassil-Grimm, *Diagnosis for Disaster: The Devastating Truth About False Memory Syndrome and Its Impact on Accusers and Families* (Woodstock, N.Y.: Overlook Press, 1995); and Mark Pendergast, *Victims of Memory: Incest Accusations and Shattered Lives* (Hinesburg, Vt.: Upper Access Books, 1995). Pendergast is a father accused by his two daughters who refuse to have contact with him.

42. Charles Whitfield, *Memory and Abuse: Remembering and Healing the Effects of Trauma* (Deerfield Beach, Fla.: Health Communications, 1995), 12.

43. Ibid., 236.

44. See Elizabeth Waites, *Memory Quest* and Jennifer Freyd, *Betrayal Trauma*. Though not written strictly to "answer" the false memory accusations, both of these books, the former by a psychologist and the latter by a cognitive scientist, are composed against the backdrop of that debate. There is an ever-growing body of literature either taking sides about memory or trying to offer balanced investigation or new evidence. One investigative volume, purporting balance, is *Child Sexual Abuse and False Memory Syndrome*, ed. Robert A. Baker (Amherst, New York: Prometheus Books, 1998). Another volume is *Recovered Memories and False Memories*, ed. Martin A. Conway (Oxford: Oxford University Press, 1997). Conway tries to offer a "middle line." Although there does need to be further scientific investigation of the process of remembering and forgetting, one could argue that a middle ground is not possible when "one side" is accusing the other of being "false."

45. Whitfield, *Memory and Abuse*, 234.

46. Herman and Harvey, "The False Memory Debate: Social Science or Social Backlash?" *Working Together* 14 (fall 1993): 9.

47. See Wright, *Remembering Satan.* Referring to the 1980s, Wright notes: "No longer ruled by psychiatry, the counseling profession itself was undergoing an informal deregulation" (161). Ellen Bass and Laura Davis are not therapists, but they have worked with survivors in a number of settings over a number of years. Davis is herself a survivor of incestuous abuse and the book includes many testimonies and quotations from survivors, in their own words. The third edition of *The Courage to Heal,* published in 1994 by Harper-Collins, includes a section of response to the backlash represented by the false memory movement (477-534).

48. Bass and Davis themselves observe in the preface to the third edition of *The Courage to Heal* that they are revising certain statements made in the original manuscript so they might not be "misread" (14-15).

49. Whitfield, *Memory and Abuse,* 174.

50. These dynamics are further complicated by the legal system. If cases are bound for court, then questions of evidence and verifiablity take on a different importance. The issue of impressionability and how much memories can be formed or shaped by suggestion also assume a different status. Most survivors do not, however, pursue legal redress.

51. See article in the *Providence Sunday Journal,* 5 December 1993, sec. 1, pp. 11 and 16.

2. "Never Forget": The Armenian Genocide and the Jewish Holocaust

1. Genocide is defined as action "with intent to destroy, in whole or in part, a national, ethnical, racial, or religious group." See Leo Kuper, *Genocide: Its Political Use in the Twentieth Century* (New Haven: Yale University Press, 1981), 210. Kuper's book includes a complete text of the United Nations Genocide Convention, as well as an exploration of the concept of genocide and its history. The United States did not ratify this convention until 1986. See Herbert Hirsch, *Genocide and the Politics of Memory* (Chapel Hill: University of North Carolina Press, 1995), 197-99, for a review of this history.

2. Hitler is reported to have made this statement in 1939 at the Wannasee Conference. This quotation can be found on a wall in the United States Holocaust Museum.

3. I do realize that my choice of these genocides is somewhat arbitrary and that alternative arguments can be made, especially regarding American complicity in the genocide of Native Americans, as well as the role of America in slavery and the destruction of African tribes. These histories will be considered in chapter 3.

4. Leonardo P. Alishan, "An Exercise on a Genre for Genocide and Exorcism," in *The Armenian Genocide: History, Politics, Ethics,* ed. Richard G. Hovannisian (New York: St. Martin's Press, 1992), 352. See also Saul Friedlander, *Memory, History, and the Extermination of the Jews of Europe* (Bloomington: Indiana University Press, 1993), especially chapters 3, 5, and 7 on the dilemmas of remembrance and the incomprehensibility and irreducibility of the Holocaust.

5. See Joseph L. Grabill, *Protestant Diplomacy and the Near East: Missionary Influence*

on American Policy, 1810–1927 (Minneapolis: University of Minnesota Press, 1971) for a treatment of the history of missionary and relief efforts, and their political agendas.

6. Donald E. Miller and Lorna Touryan Miller, *Survivors: An Oral History of the Armenian Genocide* (Berkeley: University of California Press, 1993). This major work on oral histories is the most comprehensive study published to date and is based on one hundred interviews that the Millers conducted. According to the Millers' investigation and report, the first oral history project was initiated in 1967, some fifty years after the genocide. The first large-scale project, involving over one hundred interviews, followed in 1973. Subsequent major projects were conducted by UCLA under the auspices of Professor Richard Hovannisian and by the Zoryan Institute, an independent research center located in Cambridge, Massachusetts. The Millers estimate that, to their knowledge, approximately 1,700 audiotaped interviews and 934 videotaped interviews have been conducted. These numbers include interviews done not only in the United States, but in Canada, Syria, Greece, France, Armenia, and Argentina as well (notes 41-45, 212-13).

7. "An Oral History Perspective," in *The Armenian Genocide in Perspective*, ed. Richard G. Hovannisian, 2nd printing (New Brunswick, N.J.: Transaction Books, 1987), 188, 189.

8. Hovannisian makes this point in the foreword to *The Armenian Genocide in Perspective*, 2.

9. Ibid., 122.

10. See Donald E. Miller and Lorna Touryan Miller, "A Case Study of Armenian Surviors and Their Progeny," *Qualitative Sociology* 14:1 (1991): 13-38. The Millers indicate that between 1973 and 1985 there were over two hundred terrorist incidents claiming over sixty lives, Turkish and non-Turkish. Two groups seem to be behind these attacks: the Justice Commandos of the Armenian Genocide and the Armenian Secret Army for the Liberation of Armenia (14). The Millers' article draws on interviews with convicted terrorists.

11. Edward T. Linenthal, *Preserving Memory: The Struggle to Create America's Holocaust Museum* (New York: Viking Penguin, 1995), 230, 233. See pages 228-40 for a full discussion of the question of whether or not to include the Armenian genocide in the museum.

12. Ibid., 233. Another earlier example of pressure by the Turkish government against any attempts at recognition of the Armenian genocide is presented in Peter Sourian's introduction to a recent edition of *The Forty Days of Musa Dagh*, a novel about the genocide and resistance to it, by Franz Werfel, 2nd ed. (New York: Carroll & Graff, 1990). Sourian chronicles the pressure the American Department of State put on Metro-Goldwyn-Mayer studio to not produce the film version. In 1935, the Turkish ambassador to the United States pressured the State Department, which in turn asked the studio to withdraw the project. The studio concurred (introduction, p. ix). See also Richard Hovannisian, "The Armenian Genocide and Patterns of Denial," in *Armenian Genocide in Perspective*, 120.

13. Van was an urban center toward the eastern border of the Armenian lands under Turkish rule. The people of Van engaged in armed resistance to Turkish troops. They held out for some time and then were assisted by a Russian army. However, when the Russians withdrew before a larger Turkish army, the city fell, and many of its

Armenians fled. This instance of military resistance is one of the few chronicled. A short account appears in *Martyrdom and Rebirth: Fateful Events in the Recent History of the Armenian People* (New York: Diocese of the Armenian Church of America, 1965) in a chapter entitled "Unsung Heroes" by Behdros Norehad. See pages 49-50.

14. Marjorie Housepian, "What Genocide? What Holocaust? News from Turkey, 1915–1923: A Case Study," in *Armenian Genocide in Perspective*, 106.

15. Hovannisian, "The Armenian Genocide and Patterns of Denials," 119.

16. Linenthal, *Preserving Memory*, 238. See also Vigen Guroian, "The Politics and Morality of Genocide" in *The Armenian Genocide: History, Politics, Ethics*, 311-39 for a discussion of these congressional proceedings and votes.

17. Ishkhan Jinbashian, "Memory of the Skin: Gérard Chaliand on the Geopolitics of Cultures," *Armenian International Magazine* 4:7 (August 1993): 15.

18. Ibid.

19. The establishment of the Republic of Armenia, following the fall of the Soviet Union, has affected these dynamics. For the first time in over seventy years, there is an independent Armenian homeland and a locus for an Armenian future. There is a place for Armenian Americans to focus energy and activity. The government of Armenia has even been working toward establishing a relationship with Turkey, despite protests that Turkey has yet to recognize the genocide. Such attempts seem motivated by pragmatic concerns for economic and political development. The continuing existence of Armenia will no doubt have a long-ranging impact on the genocide in Armenian consciousness and history, but for now, although the independent Armenian Republic is an important reality and symbol, its status remains precarious. Additionally, the "homeland" from which many Armenian Americans emigrated, including all those who emigrated as a result of the genocide, is still part of Turkey.

20. See note 13 of this chapter.

21. Although there are occasional stories of Armenian Christians being offered the option of converting to Islam and having their lives spared, such instances are rare. More often Armenian children were "adopted" or abducted by Turkish and/or Arab families and raised as Muslims. This, however, was not a widespread phenomenon. Sometimes it was a "strategic" move by Armenians to save their children by placing them with Turkish neighbors, other times it amounted to a form of slavery. There are many stories of these "adoptees" running away to find family members after the war.

22. The church may have taken such a step by the time this book is published.

23. Alishan, "An Exercise on a Genre for Genocide and Exorcism," 346.

24. Ibid.

25. Miller and Touryan Miller, *Survivors*, 158-60.

26. Ibid., 162.

27. Ibid., 193.

28. Ibid., 182-90.

29. Rubina Peroomian, *Literary Responses to Catastrophe: A Comparison of the Armenian and the Jewish Experience* (Atlanta: Scholars Press, 1993), 223.

30. See Vigen Guroian, "Armenian Genocide and Christian Existence," *Cross Currents* 41 (1991): 322-42.

31. Vigen Guroian, "The Suffering God of Armenian Christology," *Dialog* 32 (1993): 98.

32. Vigen Guroian, "How Shall We Remember?" *Window* 1 (1990): 5.

33. Arlene Voski Avakian, *Lion Woman's Legacy: An Armenian-American Memoir* (New York: Feminist Press, 1992).

34. Ibid., 34.

35. Ibid., 265.

36. Ibid., 266.

37. Ibid., 281.

38. Ibid., 281-82.

39. Ibid., 275.

40. Ibid., 282.

41. The quotation is frequently invoked. It is inscribed on a plaque before the entrance to *Yad Vashem*, the Holocaust memorial in Israel, and was used on a commemorative stamp, issued on November 9, 1988, by the West German postal service, to mark the anniversary of *Kristallnacht*. I have also seen this line translated as "remembrance is the secret of redemption" and "redemption lies in remembering."

42. The claim to the uniqueness of the Holocaust is a complicated and charged issue, politically and emotionally. I cannot go into all the questions and dynamics involved, but my sense is that for those who argue strongly for the uniqueness of the Holocaust, as a historical event without compare, there is a connection between that claim and the need to underscore the horror, the immense suffering, and the loss endured. In other words, emphasis on uniqueness is a way to try to remember all who suffered and died. I want to honor this need to claim a special status for the Holocaust, but not at the risk—or cost—of dismissing other genocides. I do not want to create a hierarchy of genocide or suffering. See Peter Haidu, "The Dialetics of Unspeakability: Language, Silence, and the Narratives of Desubjectification," in *Probing the Limits of Representation: Nazism and the "Final Solution,"* ed. Saul Friedlander (Cambridge, Mass.: Harvard University Press, 1992) for an exploration of the limits of the uniqueness argument. Haidu suggests a distinction between "uniqueness" and "specificity" (295).

43. Discussions about uniqueness and incommensurability extend also to the name given to Hitler's campaign to eliminate Jews. Arguments abound about whether the term "genocide" can be applied to other instances of systematic killing aimed at certain ethnic or racial groups. I side with those who see this as a general and descriptive term that can be used to name campaigns aimed at annihilating a people. More heated debate attends the term "Holocaust," which has been applied to other instances of mass death, including the Armenian genocide and the treatment of Native Americans by the United States. "Holocaust" is a term that carries a religious and bibical connotation of immolation and sacrifice. I understand this term to refer singularly to the Jewish genocide. Such uniqueness ought to be honored. Other common terms used, such as *Shoah* and *Final Solution*, are also to be reserved for use in reference to the Jewish genocide. Because "Holocaust" is the most commonly used term, especially in American culture, I use it most frequently in this text.

44. Other groups were also targeted, especially gypsies and homosexuals. My focus here, however, will be on the Jewish victims.

45. See John K. Roth and Michael Berenbaum, eds., *Holocaust: Religious and Philosophical Implications* (New York: Paragon House, 1989), 367.

46. From "The Awakening" in *Holocaust Remembrance: The Shapes of Memory*, ed.

Geoffrey H. Hartman (Cambridge: Mass.: Blackwell Publishers, 1994), 150.

47. Judith Miller, *One, by One, by One* (New York: Simon & Schuster, 1990), 221.

48. Ibid.

49. Ibid., 222.

50. Aaron Hass, *The Aftermath: Living with the Holocaust* (New York: Cambridge University Press, 1995), 20-21. Hass indicates that it was not until 1979 that the Holocaust was made a compulsory subject in Israeli school curricula (20).

51. Ibid., 22.

52. For example, see Linenthal, *Preserving Memory*, for an exploration and chronicling of such questions regarding one museum, the United States Holocaust Museum. Other works dealing with the nature of remembrance include James Young, *Writing and Rewriting the Holocaust: Narrative and the Consequences of Interpretation* (Bloomington: Indiana University Press, 1988); James Young, *The Texture of Memory: Holocaust Memorials and Meaning* (New Haven: Yale University Press, 1994); Friedlander, ed., *Probing the Limits*; and Miller, *One, by One, by One.*

53. Their books include Elie Wiesel, *Night* (New York: Bantam Books, 1960); *The Testament* (New York: Summit Books, 1981); and *The Fifth Son,* trans. Marion Wiesel (New York: Summit Books, 1985); and Primo Levi, *Survival in Auschwitz: The Nazi Assault on Humanity,* trans. Stuart Wolf (New York: Collier Books, 1958); and *The Drowned and the Saved* (New York: Summit Books, 1988).

54. Lawrence L. Langer, *Holocaust Testimonies: The Ruins of Memory* (New Haven: Yale University Press, 1991).

55. Such mechanisms seem similar to the "splitting" practiced by sexual assault survivors, as well as others dealing with trauma.

56. Langer, *Holocaust Testimonies,* xi.

57. Ibid., 6.

58. Ibid., 52.

59. Ibid., 75.

60. Ibid., 92, 109.

61. Ibid., 95.

62. Ibid., 126.

63. Ibid., 140.

64. Ibid., 144.

65. Ibid., 186.

66. Ibid., 193.

67. Ibid., 204-5.

68. Ibid., 157.

69. Lawrence L. Langer, *Admitting the Holocaust: Collected Essays* (New York: Oxford University Press, 1995), 15.

70. Langer, *Holocaust Testimonies,* 82.

71. Ibid., 161.

72. Lawrence L. Langer, "The Dilemma of Choice in the Deathcamps," in Roth and Berenbaum, eds., *Holocaust: Religious and Philosophical Implications,* 224, 231.

73. I recognize that survivor testimonies contained in written memoirs are different from those in oral histories. Most writers of written testimonies adopt a point of view and impose a narrative structure which in itself seeks to order and thus give some

sort of meaning to the past. Oral testimony, which is primarily what Langer studied, is more spontaneous and does not call for such ordering.

74. Judith Magyar Isaacson, *Seed of Sarah: Memoirs of a Survivor,* 2nd ed. (Urbana: University of Illinois Press, 1991), 85-86.

75. Frieda W. Aaron, "A Handful of Memories: Two Levels of Recollection," in *Burning Memory: Times of Testing & Reckoning,* ed. Alice Eckhardt (New York: Pergamon Press, 1993), 169-70. Aaron explores the complexities of memory, including the pain of remembering at all. Her emphasis, however, is on the importance of recalling how she maintained her humanity and human bonds, especially with her mother and sister.

76. Harold Kaplan, *Conscience and Memory: Meditations in a Museum of the Holocaust* (Chicago: University of Chicago Press, 1994), 43.

77. In Alan L. Berger, ed., *Bearing Witness to the Holocaust, 1939–1989,* Symposium Series, vol. 31 (Lewiston/Queenston/Lampeter: Edwin Mellen Press, 1991), 30.

78. See also the essays in Joel E. Dimsdale, ed., *Survivors, Victims, and Perpetrators: Essays on the Nazi Holocaust* (New York: Hemisphere Publishing, 1980) for an overview of some varying approaches to these questions of victimization and resistance.

79. Saul Friedlander, *Memory, History, and the Extermination of the Jews of Europe,* 43-47.

80. Herbert Hirsch, *Genocide and the Politics of Memory: Studying Death to Preserve Life* (Chapel Hill: University of North Carolina Press, 1995), 57. Hirsch's discussion is based on Bruno Bettelheim's *Surviving and Other Essays* (New York: Vintage Books, 1980) and Terrence Des Pres's *The Survivor: An Anatomy of Life in the Death Camps* (New York: Pocket Books, 1976).

81. Ibid., 62.

82. Ibid., 63.

83. Ibid., 64.

84. Ibid., 66-67.

85. Ibid., 70.

86. For example, a "survivor syndrome" rooted in psychoanalytic categories tended to focus on psychopathology, rather than adaptive mechanisms.

87. See, for example, Richard Rubenstein, *After Auschwitz* (Indianapolis: Bobbs-Merrill, 1966).

88. Friedlander, *Memory, History, and the Extermination of the Jews of Europe,* 119.

89. Ibid., 130.

90. See Saul Friedlander, *When Memory Comes,* trans. Helen R. Lane (New York: Noonday Press, 1991). The text was first published in French in 1978 and then in English in 1979 by Farrar, Strauss & Giroux.

91. Deborah Lipstadt, *Denying the Holocaust: The Growing Assault on Truth and Memory* (New York: Penguin Books, 1994), 1-2. See also Pierre Vidal-Naquet, *Assassins of Memory: Essays on the Denial of the Holocaust,* trans. Jeffrey Mehlman (New York: Columbia University Press, 1992).

92. Lipstadt, *Denying the Holocaust,* 20.

93. Ibid., 23.

94. Ibid., 137. According to Lipstadt, the Institute was created in 1978 and held its first Revisionist Convention in 1979. The Institute also publishes the *Journal of Historical Review.*

95. Ibid., 209.

96. Ibid., 216.

97. Ibid.

98. Young, *Writing and Rewriting the Holocaust,* 189.

99. See Kaplan, *Conscience and Memory.*

100. Ibid., vii.

101. Ibid., 192.

102. See Paul M. Van Buren, *The Burden of Freedom: Americans and the God of Israel* (New York: Seabury Press, 1976); *A Theology of the Jewish-Christian Reality. Part 1: Discerning the Way* (New York: Seabury Press, 1980); *Part 2: A Christian Theology of the People Israel* (New York: Seabury Press, 1983); *Part 3: Christ in Context* (New York: Harper & Row, 1988).

103. See, for example, Franklin Littell, *The Crucifixion of the Jews: The Failure of Christians to Understand the Jewish Experience* (New York: Harper & Row, 1975; Macon, Ga.: Mercer University Press, 1986); Alice L. Eckhardt and A. Roy Eckhardt, *Long Day's Journey into Day: A Revised Retrospective on the Holocaust* (Detroit: Wayne State University Press, 1988); John T. Pawlikowski, *Christ in the Light of the Christian-Jewish Dialogue* (New York: Paulist Press, 1982); Clark M. Williamson, *A Guest in the House of Israel* (Louisville: Westminster John Knox Press, 1993); Johann Baptist Metz, *The Emergent Church,* trans. Peter Mann (New York: Crossroad, 1981).

104. Karl A. Plank, *Mother of the Wire Fence: Inside and Outside the Holocaust* (Louisville: Westminster John Knox, 1994), 42.

105. Kaplan, *Conscience and Memory,* xii.

106. Ibid., 16, 17.

107. Anne Roiphe, *A Season for Healing* (New York: Summit Books, 1988), 214.

3. "I Remember; It Happened": Retrieving Voices, Reconstructing Histories

1. Elisabeth Schüssler Fiorenza, *In Memory of Her* (New York: Crossroad, 1983).

2. Alice Walker, *In Search of Our Mothers' Gardens* (New York: Harcourt Brace Jovanovich, 1983), 382.

3. From Monique Wittig, *Les Guerilleres,* trans. David LeVay (New York: Avon Books, 1971) as quoted in Carol Christ, *Laughter of Aphrodite* (San Francisco: Harper San Francisco, 1987), 121.

4. Judith Plaskow, *Standing Again at Sinai* (San Francisco: Harper & Row, 1990).

5. Simone de Beauvoir, *The Second Sex,* trans. H. M. Parshley (New York: Alfred A. Knopf, 1952), xxii.

6. Rosemary Ruether and Eleanor McLaughlin, eds., *Women of Spirit* (New York: Simon & Schuster, 1979). See also Mary Beard, *Woman as Force in History* (1946; reprint, New York: Octagon Books, 1985).

7. Phyllis Trible, *Texts of Terror* (Philadelphia: Fortress Press, 1984).

8. Mary Daly, *Gyn/Ecology,* Second Passage (Boston: Beacon Press, 1978).

9. Merlin Stone, *When God Was a Woman* (New York: Dial Press, 1976).

10. Christ, *Laughter of Aphrodite,* chapter ten.

11. The concept of separate spheres began as a resource for historians trying to study women's lives. The approach was based on the argument that since men dominated the "public" sphere and women were to be found in the "private" sphere, the

study of women's domestic lives and the work of women "behind the scenes" might add a great deal to our understanding of the history of women. This approach did allow women's historians to discover whole new realities of women's lives and uncover the amazing histories of the way in which women extended the "private" sphere to include all sorts of philanthropic and political activities. However, the concept is also problematic. Since the definitions of public and private spheres were delineated by traditional approaches to history, they tend to reflect men's definitions of women's experience. Historians such as Carroll Smith-Rosenberg and Linda K. Kerber point to the need to be careful about such categories. See Smith-Rosenberg, "Healing Women's Words: A Feminist Reconstruction of History" in *Disorderly Conduct* (New York: Oxford University Press, 1985) and Kerber, "Separate Spheres, Female Worlds, Woman's Place: The Rhetoric of Women's History," *Journal of American History* 75 (June 1988).

12. These four are outlined in Schüssler Fiorenza, *In Memory of Her* and in *Bread Not Stone: The Challenge of Biblical Interpretation* (Boston: Beacon Press, 1985). In "The Will to Choose or to Reject: Continuing Our Critical Work," in *Feminist Interpretation of the Bible,* ed. Letty Russell (Philadelphia: Westminster Press, 1985), 125-36, Schüssler Fiorenza adds a fifth, a hermeneutics of critical evaluation, which she uses elsewhere to refer to the overall hermeneutical process. A hermeneutics of critical evaluation is to be contrasted with a method of correlation.

13. Schüssler Fiorenza, *Bread Not Stone,* 19.

14. Denise Riley, *"Am I That Name?" Feminism and the Category of "Women" in History* (Minneapolis: University of Minnesota Press, 1988), 1.

15. Ibid., 98.

16. Joan Wallach Scott, *Only Paradoxes to Offer: French Feminists and the Rights of Man* (Cambridge, Mass.: Harvard University Press, 1996), 3-4.

17. Ibid., 16.

18. Ibid.

19. Scott, introduction to *Feminism and History,* ed. Joan Wallach Scott (New York: Oxford University Press, 1996), 12.

20. Scott, *Only Paradoxes to Offer,* 18.

21. Linda Gordon, "What's New in Women's History," in *Feminist Studies/Critical Studies,* ed. Teresa de Lauretis (Bloomington: Indiana University Press, 1986), 21. In the same article, Gordon points out that there was a women's history movement in the nineteenth century that was suppressed and forgotten until twentieth century feminist historians began to uncover it.

22. Anson Rabinbach, "Rationalism and Utopia as Language of Nature: A Note," *International Labor and Working-Class History* (spring 1987): 31.

23. Judith Butler, "Contingent Foundations: Feminism and the Question of 'Postmodernism,'" in *Feminists Theorize the Political,* eds. Joan W. Scott and Judith Butler (New York: Routledge, 1992), 7.

24. See Victor Anderson, *Beyond Ontological Blackness* (New York: Continuum, 1995).

25. Toni Morrison, *Beloved* (London: Picador, 1987), 274-75.

26. Ibid., 273.

27. The generally recognized founder of contemporary Afrocentrism is Molefi Kete Asante. His book, *Afrocentricity,* 4th printing (Trenton, N.J.: Africa World Press, 1991)

defines the key aspects of Afrocentric thought and culture.

28. There is a range of thinking that can be put under the general umbrella of Afrocentrism. I see the range as including an extreme Afrocentricism that argues that "all good things" come out of Africa. See, for example, Martin Bernal, *Black Athena: The Afroasiatic Roots of Classical Civilization* (New Brunswick, N.J.: Rutgers University, vol.1, 1987; vol. 2, 1991) and Yosef A. A. ben-Jochannan, *Africa, Mother of Western Civilization* (Baltimore: Black Classic Press, 1971) for arguments that Greek philosophy originated in Africa. Mary Lefkowitz, a classicist, refutes such arguments in *Not Out of Africa: How Afrocentrism Became an Excuse to Teach Myth as History* (New York: BasicBooks, 1996). More "mild" forms argue that there is much to uncover from African origins that will both help to explain and support distinctive African American cultural patterns.

29. For example, Marcus Garvey, earlier this century, led such a movement.

30. Lawrence W. Levine, "Slave Songs and Slave Consciousness: Explorations in Neglected Sources," in his collection, *The Unpredictable Past: Explorations in American Cultural History* (New York: Oxford University Press, 1993), 52.

31. Albert J. Raboteau, *Slave Religion: The "Invisible Institution" in the Antebellum South* (New York: Oxford University Press, 1978.)

32. M. Shawn Copeland, "Wading Through Many Sorrows," in *A Troubling in My Soul,* ed. Emilie Townes (Maryknoll: Orbis, 1993), 118.

33. Ibid., 119-22.

34. Dwight N. Hopkins and George Cummings, eds. *Cut Loose Your Stammering Tongue: Black Theology in the Slave Narratives* (Maryknoll: Orbis, 1991). See Hopkins, "Slave Theology in the 'Invisible Institution,'" 37-42.

35. Cummings, "Slave Narratives, Black Theology of Liberation (USA), and the Future," in *Cut Loose Your Stammering Tongue,* 138.

36. Sanders's essay is entitled "Liberation Ethics in the Ex-Slave Interviews."

37. David Emmanuel Goatley, *Were You There? Godforsakenness in Slave Religion* (Maryknoll: Orbis, 1996), 3. See also Lawrence W. Levine, " 'Some Go Up and Some Go Down': The Meaning of the Slave Trickster," in *The Unpredictable Past,* 59-77 and Dwight Hopkins, *Shoes That Fit Our Feet* (Maryknoll: Orbis, 1993), chapter 3.

38. Levine, "African Culture and U.S. Slavery," in *The Unpredictable Past,* 84-85. Dwight Hopkins surveys a range of attitudes and behaviors, and categorizes them as religious, political, and/or cultural resistance. See *Shoes That Fit Our Feet,* chapter one.

39. Cornel West, *Prophecy Deliverance! An Afro-American Revolutionary Christianity* (Philadelphia: Westminster Press, 1982), 121.

40. Anthony Pinn, *Why Lord? Suffering and Evil in Black Theology* (New York: Continuum, 1995), 140.

41. Ibid., 157.

42. Anderson, *Beyond Ontological Blackness,* 13.

43. Ibid., 87.

44. Ibid., 161.

45. See Donald H. Matthews, *Honoring the Ancestors: An African Cultural Interpretation of Black Religion* (New York: Oxford University Press, 1998) and Hopkins, *Shoes That Fit Our Feet.*

46. Cheryl J. Sanders, *Empowerment Ethics for a Liberated People* (Minneapolis: Fortress Press, 1995), 114.

47. See, for example, Dinesh D'Souza, *The End of Racism* (New York: Free Press, 1995).

48. Matthews, *Honoring the Ancestors*, 130-31.

49. Ibid., 131. Matthews suggests that reparations are needed if whites are serious about taking responsibility for the history of slavery and racism.

50. Morrison, *Beloved*, 293.

51. Ibid., 275.

52. Ibid., 88.

53. Although there is much literature on this question, a particularly relevant volume is *History and Memory in African-American Culture*, ed. Genevieve Fabre and Robert O'Meally (New York: Oxford University Press, 1994). In the final essay, "Between Memory and History: Les Lieux de Mémoire," Pierre Nora articulates that the quest for memory and the search for history have become the same.

54. Albert J. Raboteau, *A Fire in the Bones: Reflections on African-American Religious History* (Boston: Beacon Press, 1995), 185.

55. Ibid., 195.

56. Ibid., 185.

Section 2. Introduction

1. Alice Walker, *Horses Make a Landscape Look More Beautiful* (New York: Harcourt Brace Jovanovich, 1984), 1-2.

2. Luke 24, *The New Testament and Psalms: An Inclusive Version* (New York: Oxford University Press, 1995).

4. The Call to Remembrance and Witness in Contemporary Theology

1. Johann Baptist Metz, *The Emergent Church*, trans. Peter Mann (New York: Crossroad, 1981), 27.

2. Johann Baptist Metz, *A Passion for God: The Mystical-Political Dimension of Christianity*, trans. J. Matthew Ashley (New York: Paulist Press, 1998), 5.

3. Metz makes frequent reference to this idea. A brief description can be found in *The Emergent Church*, 61.

4. Johann Baptist Metz in *How I Have Changed: Reflecting on Thirty Years of Theology*, ed. Jürgen Moltmann, trans. John Bowden (Harrisburg: Trinty Press International, 1997), 33.

5. Johann Baptist Metz, *Faith in History and Society*, trans. David Smith (New York: Seabury Press, 1980), 185.

6. Metz presupposes such an anthropological desire for freedom and liberation. He adopts and develops the idea of the human being as possibility, from his teacher, Karl Rahner.

7. Metz writes cryptically: "The shortest definition of religion: interruption." See *Faith in History and Society*, 171.

8. See Walter Benjamin, "Theses on the Philosophy of History" in *Illuminations* (New York: Harcourt, Brace & World, 1968) and Herbert Marcuse, *One-Dimensional Man* (Boston: Beacon Press, 1964) and *Eros and Civilization* (Boston: Beacon Press, 1955).

9. See Metz, *Faith in History and Society*, 113.

10. Such eternalizing of suffering in the Godhead is Metz's criticism of Jürgen Moltmann. See *Faith in History and Society,* 132.

11. See Metz, *A Passion for God* for a discussion of the phrase, *"Leiden an Gott."* J. Matthew Ashley, the translator, argues for translating *"an"* as "unto." He points out that *"an"* is most often translated "from." He writes: "I have chosen a more unusual rendering in order to avoid the passive connotation of suffering 'from' something. It is helpful in this regard to keep in mind that *Leiden an Gott* is . . . both a passive *and* an active spiritual disposition. To 'suffer unto God' denotes a spiritual disposition in which suffering, either that suffering that I experience, or others' suffering that I perceive in the present, or *remember and keep in mind* from the past, drives me toward God, crying out, protesting, questioning. Its Old Testament exemplar is Job, and the New Testament exemplar is Jesus, particularly as presented in the Gospel of Mark" (Introduction: Reading Metz, note 19, 177-78).

12. Metz, *Faith in History and Society,* 129.

13. Ibid., 133.

14. See Metz, *The Emergent Church* and *Followers of Christ,* trans. Thomas Linton (New York: Paulist Press, 1978) for fuller explications of Metz's ecclesiology.

15. See Cynthia L. Rigby, "Is There Joy Before Mourning? 'Dangerous Memory,' in the Work of Sharon Welch and Johann Baptist Metz," *Koinonia* 5 (spring 1993): 1-30, for a related discussion of these questions and concerns.

16. Metz in Moltmann, *How I Have Changed,* 35. Emphasis added.

17. Metz, *A Passion for God,* 143.

18. Metz, "The Future in the Memory of Suffering" in Johann Baptist Metz and Jürgen Moltmann, *Faith and the Future: Essays on Theology, Solidarity, and Modernity* (Maryknoll: Orbis, 1995), 11. This version of the essay, translated by John Griffiths, is revised and expanded from the one found in *Faith in History and Society.* This particular quotation is not found in the earlier version.

19. See Metz, *Faith in History and Society,* 113.

20. Metz, "The Future in the Memory of Suffering," 10.

21. For a similar criticism, see Charles Davis, *Theology and Political Society* (Cambridge: Cambridge University Press, 1978), 46.

22. For a challenge to this claim and critical discussion of feminist theology as academic "certifying discourses," see Mary McClintock Fulkerson, *Changing the Subject: Women's Discourses and Feminist Theology* (Minneapolis: Fortress Press, 1994), chapter 6.

23. Elizabeth A. Johnson, *Friends of God and Prophets* (New York: Continuum, 1999), 142. Chapter 8 surveys and explores these practices.

24. Ibid., 155.

25. Ibid., 156.

26. Ibid., 155-56.

27. Ibid., 163.

28. Ibid., 167.

29. Ibid.

30. Ibid., 168.

31. Ibid.

32. Elisabeth Schüssler Fiorenza, *In Memory of Her: A Feminist Theological Reconstruction of Christian Origins* (New York: Crossroad, 1983), 19.

33. Sharon Welch, *Communities of Resistance and Solidarity* (Maryknoll: Orbis, 1985), 19.

34. Ibid., 39.

35. Ibid.

36. Ibid., 87.

37. Sharon Welch, *A Feminist Ethic of Risk* (Minneapolis: Fortress Press, 1990), 155.

38. Ibid., 137.

39. Ibid., 151. Welch's understanding of difference is not to be confused with Metz's understanding of binary otherness. For Welch, knowing is rooted in connection and mutuality, not otherness.

40. Rita Nakashima Brock, "And a Little Child Will Lead Us," in *Christianity, Patriarchy, and Abuse*, eds. Joanne Carlson Brown and Carole R. Bohn (New York: Pilgrim Press, 1989), 54.

41. Rita Nakashima Brock, *Journeys By Heart : A Christology of Erotic Power* (New York: Crossroad, 1988), 17.

42. Ibid., 23.

43. Ibid., 46.

44. Ibid., 106.

45. Ibid., 107.

46. Metz, *Faith in History and Society*, 234.

47. Many contemporary theologians, such as Karl Rahner, Johann Baptist Metz, and Rebecca Chopp, adhere to theological anthropologies in which the desire for freedom is constitutive of the human subject. Chopp refers to this anthropological affirmation as the "anticipatory structure of freedom in the subject" who is an "active agent in history." She writes: "Transcendence is located through the anticipatory structure of the human subject as an active agent in history." In other words, freedom and agency make possible transcendence and the possibility for change. See Chopp, "The Interruption of the Forgotten," in *The Holocaust as Interruption*, eds. Elisabeth Schüssler Fiorenza and David Tracy, *Concilium* 175 (Edinburgh: T. & T. Clark, 1984), 21.

48. Margaret R. Somers, "The Narrative Constitution of Identity: A Relational and Network Approach," *Theory and Society* 23 (October 1994): 618. Somer's article includes an extensive bibliography.

49. Ibid.

50. Ibid., 626.

51. Ibid., 629.

52. See Christine Gudorf, *Victimization: Examining Christian Complicity* (Philadelphia: Trinity Press International, 1992). Chapter 3 is entitled "Ending the Romanticization of Victims."

53. See Mary Potter Engel, "Evil, Sin, and Violation of the Vulnerable," in *Lift Every Voice: Constructing Christian Theologies from the Underside*, eds. Susan Brooks Thistlethwaite and Mary Potter Engel (San Francisco: Harper & Row, 1990), 152-64. See also Susan L. Nelson, *Healing the Broken Heart* (St. Louis: Chalice Press, 1997).

54. Copeland, "Wading Through Many Sorrows," in *A Troubling in My Soul*, ed. Emilie Townes (Maryknoll: Orbis, 1993), 121.

55. Ibid., 124.

56. Michael S. Roth, *The Ironist's Cage: Memory, Trauma, and the Construction of History* (New York: Columbia University Press, 1995), 225.

57. Ibid., 211.

5. Remembering Jesus Christ, Remembering Redemption

1. Judith Perkins, *The Suffering Self: Pain and Narrative Representation in the Early Christian Era* (New York: Routledge, 1995), 24. This book argues the thesis that Christianity formed and established itself around the "suffering self" and deployed a range of discursive practices to construct that self in changing circumstances.

2. Jane Strohl, "Suffering as Redemptive: A Comparison of Christian Experience in the Sixteenth and Twentieth Centuries," in *Revisioning the Past: Prospects in Historical Theology*, eds. Mary Potter Engel and Walter E. Wyman, Jr. (Minneapolis: Fortress Press, 1992), 95.

3. I intend this noninclusive language because it is part of this way of thinking theologically.

4. For a variety of such perspectives see Yacob Tesfai, ed. *The Scandal of a Crucified World: Perspectives on the Cross and Suffering* (Maryknoll: Orbis, 1994). This volume includes authors from around the world.

5. Chung Hyun Kyung, *Struggle to Be the Sun Again* (Maryknoll: Orbis, 1990), 54.

6. Ibid.

7. Elizabeth Johnson, *She Who Is: The Mystery of God in Feminist Theological Discourse* (New York: Crossroad, 1992), 254.

8. Feminist theologian Mary Grey also offers a strong, but mitigated, critique of atonement theories. While indicting the tendency of such theories to condone and even sacralize suffering, she reinterprets the idea of atonement as about relationality: "at-one-ment" and "redemptive mutuality." As does Elizabeth Johnson, Grey also turns to women's experience and the image of the birthing of God to express "the creative energy for wholeness and transformation ceaselessly at work in creation" and for alternative images of at-one-ment as incarnational. See Grey, *Feminism, Redemption and the Christian Tradition* (Mystic, Conn.: Twenty-Third Publications, 1990), 157, 174.

9. Joanne Carlson Brown, "For God So Loved the World?" in *Christianity, Patriarchy, and Abuse*, eds. Joanne Carlson Brown and Carole R. Bohn (New York: Pilgrim Press, 1989), 27.

10. Rita Nakashima Brock, *Journeys by Heart* (New York: Crossroad, 1988), especially chapter 3, and "And a Little Child Will Lead Us," in *Christianity, Patriarchy, and Abuse*, 42-61.

11. See Delores Williams, *Sisters in the Wilderness: The Challenge of Womanist God-Talk* (Maryknoll: Orbis, 1993), especially chapter 6, and "Black Women's Surrogacy Experience and the Christian Notion of Redemption," in *After Patriarchy: Feminist Transformations of the World Religions*, ed. Paula M. Cooey, William R. Eakin, and Jay B. McDaniel (Maryknoll: Orbis, 1991), chapter 1. African American male theologian Anthony Pinn goes even further in denying any redemptive value to suffering. Arguing that for Williams, suffering is still the locus of God's revelation, albeit through commitment to the survival of the oppressed, he wants to indict any move to justify God through seeing suffering as necessary or good. See Anthony Pinn, *Why, Lord? Suffering and Evil in Black Theology* (New York: Continuum, 1995), chapter 4.

12. Elisabeth Schüssler Fiorenza, *Jesus: Miriam's Child, Sophia's Prophet: Critical Issues in Feminist Christology* (New York: Continuum, 1994), 125-27.

13. There are many who would argue the opposite, that the cross stands as judgment against the misuses of power and so can be used to indict those who abuse and

oppress. Such approaches tend not to analyze sufficiently social and political dynamics, and exempt Christian theology from ideological bias.

14. See JoAnne Marie Terrell, *Power in the Blood? The Cross in the African American Experience* (Maryknoll: Orbis, 1998) and Jon Sobrino "The Crucified Peoples: Yahweh's Suffering Servant Today," in *1492–1992: The Voice of the Victims*, ed. Leonardo Boff and Virgil Elizondo, *Concilium* 1990/6 (Philadelphia: Trinity Press International, 1990), 120-29. Sobrino takes the term, "the crucified peoples" from the work of Ignacio Ellacuria. Sobrino argues that the crucified peoples are the bearers of salvation, that they offer something positive to the work of salvation.

15. In that sense, Jesus' cry of abandonment from the cross is not a final word.

16. Williams, *Sisters in the Wilderness*, especially chapter 1.

17. Christine Gudorf, *Victimization: Examining Christian Complicity* (Philadelphia: Trinty Press International, 1992), chapter 3.

18. See Isabel Carter Heyward, *The Redemption of God* (Lanham, Md.: University Press of America, 1982) for a similar argument.

19. Lou Ann Trost adds another slant on such arguments by suggesting: "The glorification of suffering turns theology of the cross into a strange sort of theology of glory." See her "On Suffering, Violence, and Power," *Currents in Theology and Mission* 21 (February 1994): 37.

20. Schüssler Fiorenza, *Jesus: Miriam's Child, Sophia's Prophet*, 123.

21. Ibid., 126.

22. Gustav Aulén, *Christus Victor*, trans. A. G. Hebert (New York: Macmillan, 1969).

23. Brock, *Journeys by Heart*, 58.

24. Ibid., 66.

25. Mark Kline Taylor, *Remembering Esperanza* (Maryknoll: Orbis, 1990), 169.

26. Brock, *Journeys by Heart*, 70, 100.

27. Mark Kline Taylor also wants to emphasize the importance of community, but he uses the idea of "Christ dynamic," which issues in reconciliatory emancipation: "The sign of the christic interpersonal presence in communal praxis that is of Christ is the presence of the reconciliatory emancipation" (*Remembering Esperanza*, 175). His emphasis, then, is on the character and effect of the Christ dynamic in community. A community that practices reconciliatory emancipation is of Christ.

28. Rubem A. Alves, *A Theology of Human Hope* (New York: Corpus Publications, 1969), 127.

29. Schüssler Fiorenza, *Jesus: Miriam's Child, Sophia's Prophet*, 125-26.

30. Jon Sobrino's theology is illustrative of this approach. See Sobrino, *Christology at the Crossroads*, trans. John Drury (Maryknoll: Orbis, 1978), 201-2.

31. Williams, *Sisters in the Wilderness*, 164-65.

32. Ibid., 166.

33. See, for example, Virginia Fabella and Mercy Amba Oduyoye, eds., *With Passion and Compassion* (Maryknoll: Orbis, 1988) and Chung Hyun Kyung *Struggle to Be the Sun Again*.

34. Kwok Pui Lan, "God Weeps with Our Pain," in *New Eyes for Reading*, ed. John S. Pobee and Barbel von Wartenberg-Potter (Bloomington: Meyer Stone Books, 1987), 90-95.

35. See Wendy Farley, *Tragic Vision and Divine Compassion* (Louisville: Westminster John Knox Press, 1990) and Johnson, *She Who Is*.

36. The concept of erotic power is drawn primarily from Audre Lorde. See Lorde's essay "Uses of The Erotic: The Erotic as Power" in *Sister Outsider* (Freedom, Calif.: The Crossing Press, 1984).

37. See also Mary Grey, *Feminism, Redemption, and the Christian Tradition*. Grey draws on both Heyward and Brock for her own theology of redeeming relation.

38. See Heyward, *Redemption of God; Touching Our Strength* (New York: HarperCollins, 1989); and *Staying Power* (Cleveland: The Pilgrim Press, 1995) for fuller expositions of these ideas.

39. Brock, *Journeys by Heart*, 37, 39.

40. Ibid., 45-46.

41. Ibid., 49.

42. Ibid., 69.

43. Kathleen Sands has, from a different vantage point, offered a critique of dualism in relation to erotic power, particularly in the works of Heyward, Brock, and other feminists. If erotic power is always good power, she argues, then there is insufficient accounting for its "bad" uses. See her *Escape from Paradise* (Minneapolis: Augsburg Fortress, 1994), 45. See also Kathleen Sands, "Uses of the Thea(o)logian: Sex and Theodicy in Religious Feminism," *Journal of Feminist Studies in Religion* 8:1 (spring 1992): 7-33.

44. Chung Nyun Kyung, *Struggle to Be the Sun Again*, chapter 4.

45. Fabella and Oduyoye, *With Passion and Compassion*, 44.

46. Ibid., 45.

47. Ibid., 42.

48. See, for example, James Cone, *God of the Oppressed* (New York: Seabury Press, 1975) and Albert Cleage, *The Black Messiah* (New York: Sheed & Ward, 1969).

49. Jacquelyn Grant, *White Woman's Christ and Black Women's Jesus: Feminist Christology and Womanist Response* (Atlanta: Scholars Press, 1989), 215. See also, Grant, "Subjectification as a Requirement for Christological Construction," in *Lift Every Voice*, ed. Susan Brooks Thistlethwaite and Mary Potter Engel (San Francisco: Harper & Row, 1990), 210 and Kelly Brown Douglas, *The Black Christ* (Maryknoll: Orbis, 1994), 108.

50. Grant, "Subjectification as a Requirement for Christological Construction," 213.

51. See Margaret Miles, *Carnal Knowing* (Boston: Beacon Press, 1989), 177-78 for a discussion of such issues in relation to the sculpture of Christa, a female figure on a cross, by Edwina Sandys.

52. Paul Lehmann, *Ethics in a Christian Context* (New York: Harper and Bros., 1963), 85.

53. Pamela Dickey Young, "Beyond Moral Influence to an Atoning Life," *Theology Today* 52 (1995): 351.

54. Writing from a "process-relational view of reality," James Poling comes to a similar view of power: "power in its ideal form is virtually synonymous with life itself. To live is to desire power to relate to others." See James Poling, *The Abuse of Power: A Theological Problem* (Nashville: Abingdon Press, 1991), 24. Such power "is enhanced when the web of relationships is benevolent and encourages the most creativity" (25). Such power oper-

ates both personally and socially. I agree with Poling that the self, life, even God are ambiguous realities. Though I do not frame my work within a process perspective and would not speak of "ideal forms," we share a similar goal: to affirm the power of life and to understand God as present in resilience and hope and the desire for life itself.

55. In "Losing Your Innocence But Not Your Hope," Rita Nakashima Brock offers a criticism of innocence and obedience as virtues. She proposes rejecting both and replacing innocence with "an active sense of agency" (41). She argues: "An emphasis on the innocence of victims can lead both to the tendency to blame victims, if anything can be found wrong with them or if they disobey their oppressors, and to dichotomies that paint oppressors as one-dimensionally evil and victims as helpless" (43). In place of such thinking, Brock suggests "life in the messy middle." See "Losing Your Innocence But Not Your Hope," in *Reconstructing the Christ Symbol,* ed. Maryanne Stevens (New York: Paulist Press, 1993), 30-53.

56. Cf. Susan L. Nelson on healing as re-membering: "a process of *re*-membering ourselves—a bringing together, a reconciliation, of all the pieces of ourselves that we have bound to shame and apart from 'us.' This is not a linear process; each part folds back into the others until the healing is complete." Nelson sees this process as also including remembering and relationship. See Susan L. Nelson, *Healing the Broken Heart* (St. Louis: Chalice Press, 1997), 66.

57. See Dickey Young, "Beyond Moral Influence to an Atoning Life," especially page 354, for a similar perspective on the problems of asking those more powerless to offer reconciliation.

6. The Church as a Community of Remembrance and Witness

1. Often the church is only seen in two dimensions: visible and invisible or historical institution and spirit-filled community. Cf. Rosemary Ruether, *Women-Church* (New York: Harper & Row, 1986), chapter 1. I think two-dimensional thinking reinforces the dualistic thinking about God and world or divine and human. I want to avoid such binaries and also allow for a more complex and adequate understanding of power and how it is deployed.

2. See Paolo Freire, *Pedagogy of the Oppressed,* trans. Myra Bergman Ramos (New York: Continuum, 1987).

3. This experience of connection is recounted time and again in feminist writings. See, for example, Nelle Morton, *The Journey Is Home* (Boston: Beacon Press, 1985) and Judith Plaskow, "The Coming of Lilith: Toward a Feminist Theology," in *Womanspirit Rising: A Feminist Reader in Religion,* ed. Judith Plaskow and Carol Christ (San Francisco: Harper & Row, 1979), 198-209.

4. See, for example, Ruether, *Women-Church* and Miriam Therese Winters, Adair Lummis, and Allison Stokes, eds., *Defecting in Place: Women Claiming Responsibility for Their Own Spiritual Lives* (New York: Crossroad, 1994) for descriptions of such communities. For fuller theological considerations, see Elisabeth Schüssler Fiorenza, *The Discipleship of Equals: A Critical Feminist Ekklesia-logy of Liberation* (New York: Crossroad, 1993) and Letty Russell, *Church in the Round* (Louisville: Westminster John Knox Press, 1993). Schüssler Fiorenza uses the term *ekklesia of women* to describe such communities, which she argues, model a discipleship of equals.

5. Johann Baptist Metz, *The Emergent Church,* trans. Peter Mann (New York:

Crossroad, 1981), 83. Metz actually offers three competing images or forms of the church: "a prebourgeois paternalistic church, a bourgeois supply—or services—church, and a postbourgeois initiative-taking church" (86).

6. Ibid., 76.

7. Schüssler Fiorenza, *In Memory of Her* (New York: Crossroad, 1983), 350.

8. Delores Williams, *Sisters in the Wilderness* (Maryknoll: Orbis, 1993), chapter 8.

9. Sharon Welch, *A Feminist Ethic of Risk* (Minneapolis: Fortress Press, 1990), 151.

10. Ibid., 160.

11. For example, see the volume, *Women of Spirit: Female Leadership in the Jewish and Christian Traditions*, ed. Rosemary Ruether and Eleanor McLaughlin (New York: Simon & Schuster, 1979) and Schüssler Fiorenza, *In Memory of Her.*

12. See Elizabeth A. Johnson, *Friends of God and Prophets* (New York: Continuum, 1999).

13. Gustavo Gutierrez, *Las Casas: In Search of the Poor of Jesus Christ*, trans. Robert R. Barr (Maryknoll: Orbis, 1993).

14. Paul Connerton, *How Societies Remember* (Cambridge: Cambridge University Press, 1989), 104.

15. Johann Baptist Metz's response to those who question the possibility of prayer after the Holocaust is that we can pray *after* Auschwitz because people prayed *in* Auschwitz. I find his response too facile. See Metz, *The Emergent Church*, 18-19.

16. Marjorie Proctor-Smith, *In Her Own Rite: Constructing Feminist Liturgical Tradition* (Nashville: Abingdon Press, 1990), 36.

17. Delores Williams, "Rituals of Resistance in Womanist Worship," in *Women at Worship*, ed. Marjorie Proctor-Smith and Janet R. Walton (Louisville: Westminster John Knox Press, 1993), 221.

18. Rebecca, Lea Nicoll Kramer, and Susan A. Lukey, "Spirit Song: The Use of Christian Healing Rites in Trauma Recovery," *Treating Abuse Today* 5 and 6 (November/December 1995 and January/February 1996): 39-47.

19. See Nan Cobbey, "In worship, the Anglican spirit shows forth," *Episcopal Life* 9 (September 1998): 5.

20. Schüssler Fiorenza, *In Memory of Her,* 350.

21. See, for example, Schüssler Fiorenza, *In Memory of Her* and *Bread Not Stone* (Boston: Beacon Press, 1985) for a discussion of a complex hermeneutic.

22. See, for example, *The New Testament and Psalms: An Inclusive Version* (New York: Oxford University Press, 1995).

23. Welch, *A Feminist Ethic of Risk,* 162.

24. See the essays in Cathy Caruth, ed., *Trauma: Explorations in Memory* for a discussion of the experience and knowledge of trauma. Caruth points out in the introduction that traumatic events are not really experienced as they occur and are only experienced in a way that is accessible later (7-8). These essays address both the necessity and difficulties of remembering and bearing witness. See also Dori Laub, "Bearing Witness, or the Vicissitudes of Listening" and "An Event Without a Witness: Truth, Testimony, and Survival," in *Testimony: Crises of Witnessing in Literature, Psychoanalysis, and History*, ed. Shoshana Felman and Dori Laub (New York: Routledge Press, 1992), 57-92. Laub, a psychiatrist and cofounder of the Fortunoff Video Archive for Holocaust Testimonies at Yale University, looks particularly at the difficulties and dynamics

of testifying to the Holocaust. He also examines the psychological dynamics of listening as witness.

Conclusion. Witnessing to the Hope That Is in Us

1. For fuller consideration of the dynamics and difficulties of bearing witness to suffering and trauma, see Judith L. Herman, *Trauma and Recovery* (New York: Basic-Books, 1992); Dori Laub, "Bearing Witness, or the Vicissitudes of Listening" and "An Event Without a Witness: Truth, Testimony, and Survival," in *Testimony: Crises of Witnessing in Literature, Psychoanalysis, and History* ed. Shoshana Felman and Dori Lamb (New York: Routledge Press, 1992); and Cathy Caruth, ed. *Trauma: Explorations in Memory* (Baltimore: Johns Hopkins University Press, 1995).

2. I thank Yon Walls for the formulation of this insight. Her own work examines how memory stands in for resolution in Toni Morrison's *Beloved* (London: Picador, 1987). See "Lily of the Valley: Denver's Liminality in Toni Morrison's *Beloved*," unpublished essay, 3.

3. John 20:30-31, *The New Testament and Psalms: An Inclusive Version* (New York: Oxford University Press, 1995).

4. See Diana Der-Hovanessian, *Any Day Now* (Riverdale-on-Hudson: Sheep Meadow Press, 1999) for the full text of the poem.

Bibliography

Social Context and Theory

Antze, Paul, and Michael Lambek, eds. *Tense Past: Cultural Essays in Trauma and Memory.* New York: Routledge, 1996.

Arlen, Michael. *Passage to Ararat.* New York: Farrar, Straus & Giroux, 1975.

Belenky, Mary Field, Blythe McVicker Clinchy, Nancy Rule Goldberger, and Jill Mattuck Tarule. *Women's Ways of Knowing: The Development of Self, Voice, and Mind.* New York: BasicBooks, 1986.

Blumenthal, David. *Facing the Abusing God.* Louisville: Westminster John Knox Press, 1993.

Caruth, Cathy. *Unclaimed Experience: Trauma, Narrative, and History.* Baltimore: Johns Hopkins University Press, 1996.

_____. ed. *Trauma: Explorations in Memory.* Baltimore: Johns Hopkins University Press, 1995.

Childs, Brevard. *Memory and Tradition in Israel.* Naperville: Alec R. Allenson, 1962.

Connerton, Paul. *How Societies Remember.* Cambridge: Cambridge University Press, 1989.

Crites, Stephen. "The Narrative Quality of Experience." *Journal of the American Academy of Religion* 39/3 (September 1971): 291-311.

DeConcini, Barbara. *Narrative Remembering.* Lanham, Md.: University Press of America, 1990.

Elliott, Charles. *Memory and Salvation.* London: Darton, Longman & Todd, 1995.

Felman, Shoshana, and Dori Laub, eds. *Testimony: Crises of Witnessing Literature, Psychoanalysis, and History.* New York: Routledge, 1992.

Foucault, Michel. *Power/Knowledge.* Edited by Colin Gordon. Translated by Colin Gordon et al. New York: Pantheon Books, 1980.

Freire, Paolo. *Pedagogy of the Oppressed.* Translated by Myra Bergman Ramos. New York: Herder & Herder, 1972.

Halbwachs, Maurice. *On Collective Memory.* Translated by Lewis A. Coser. Chicago: University of Chicago Press, 1992.

Herman, Judith L. *Trauma and Recovery.* New York: BasicBooks, 1992.

Middleton, David, and Derek Edwards, eds. *Collective Remembering.* London: Sage Publications, 1990.

Morton, Nelle. *The Journey Is Home.* Boston: Beacon Press, 1985.

Rankka, Kristine M. *Women and the Value of Suffering: An Aw(e)ful Rowing Toward God.* Collegeville, Minn.: Liturgical Press, 1998.

Richard, Lucien. *What Are They Saying About the Theology of Suffering?* New York: Paulist Press, 1992.

Roth, Michael S. *The Ironist's Cage: Memory, Trauma, and the Construction of History.* New York: Columbia University Press, 1995.

Scott, James C. *Domination and the Arts of Resistance.* New Haven: Yale University Press, 1990.

Scott, Joan Wallach. *Gender and the Politics of History.* New York: Columbia University Press, 1988.

Soelle, Dorothee. *Suffering.* Translated by Everett R. Kalin. Philadelphia: Fortress Press, 1975.

Stroup, George W. *The Promise of Narrative Theology.* Atlanta: John Knox Press, 1981.

Tal, Kali. *Worlds of Hurt: Reading the Literature of Trauma.* Cambridge: Cambridge University Press, 1996.

Tilley, Terrence W. *Story Theology.* Wilmington, Del.: Michael Glazier, 1985.

Trible, Phyllis. *God and the Rhetoric of Sexuality.* Philadelphia: Fortress Press, 1978.

Theological Context and Construction

Alves, Rubem A. *A Theology of Human Hope.* New York: Corpus Publications, 1969.

Aulen, Gustav. *Christus Victor.* Translated by A. G. Hebert. New York: Macmillan, 1969.

Benjamin, Walter. "Theses on the Philosophy of History." In *Illuminations.* New York: Harcourt, Brace & World, 1968.

Brock, Rita Nakashima. *Journeys by Heart: A Christology of Erotic Power.* New York: Crossroad, 1988.

————. "Losing Your Innocence But Not Your Hope." In *Reconstructing the Christ Symbol.* Edited by Maryanne Stevens. New York: Paulist Press, 1993.

Chung Hyun Kyung. *Struggle to Be the Sun Again.* Maryknoll: Orbis, 1990.

Cleage, Albert. *The Black Messiah.* New York: Sheed & Ward, 1969.

Cone, James. *God of the Oppressed.* New York: Seabury Press, 1975.

Davis, Charles. *Theology and Political Society.* Cambridge: Cambridge University Press, 1978.

Douglas, Kelly Brown. *The Black Christ.* Maryknoll: Orbis, 1994.

Downey, Michael. "Worship Between the Holocausts." *Theology Today* 43 (April 1986): 75-87.

Engel, Mary Potter. "Evil, Sin, and Violation of the Vunerable." In *Lift Every Voice: Constructing Christian Theologies from the Underside.* Edited by Susan Brooks Thistlethwaite and Mary Potter Engel. San Francisco: Harper & Row, 1990.

Fabella, Virginia, and Mercy Amba Oduyoye, eds. *With Passion and Compassion.* Maryknoll: Orbis, 1988.

Farley, Wendy. *Tragic Vision and Divine Compassion.* Louisville: Westminster John Knox Press, 1990.

Fulkerson, Mary McClintock. *Changing the Subject: Women's Discourses and Feminist Theology.* Minneapolis: Fortress Press, 1994.

Grant, Jaquelyn. "Subjectification as a Requirement for Christological Construction." In *Lift Every Voice: Constructing Christian Theologies from the Underside.* Edited by Susan Brooks Thistlethwaite and Mary Potter Engel. San Francisco: Harper & Row, 1990.

————. *White Woman's Christ and Black Women's Jesus: Feminist Christology and Womanist Response.* Atlanta: Scholars Press, 1989.

Grey, Mary. *Feminism, Redemption and the Christian Tradition.* Mystic, Conn.: Twenty-Third Publications, 1990.

Gudorf, Christine. *Victimization: Examining Christian Complicity.* Philadelphia: Trinity Press International, 1992.

Gutierrez, Gustavo. *Las Casas: In Search of the Poor of Jesus Christ.* Translated by Robert R. Barr. Maryknoll: Orbis, 1993.

Heyward, Isabel Carter. *The Redemption of God.* Lanham, Md.: University Press of America, 1982.

————. *Staying Power.* Cleveland: Pilgrim Press, 1995.

————. *Touching Our Strength.* New York: HarperCollins, 1989.

Johnson, Elizabeth A. *Friends of God and Prophets.* New York: Continuum, 1999.

————. *She Who Is: The Mystery of God in Feminist Theological Discourse.* New York: Crossroad, 1992.

Kwok, Pui Lan. "God Weeps with Our Pain." In *New Eyes for Reading.* Edited by John S. Pobee and Barbel von Wartenberg-Potter. Bloomington: Meyer Stone Books, 1987.

Lehmann, Paul. *Ethics in a Christian Context.* New York: Harper & Row, 1963.

Littell, Marcia Sachs, and Sharon Weissman Gutman, eds. *Liturgies of the Holocaust: An Interfaith Anthology.* Revised edition. Valley Forge: Trinty Press International, 1996.

Marcuse, Herbert. *Eros and Civilization.* Boston: Beacon Press, 1955.

_____. *One-Dimensional Man.* Boston: Beacon Press, 1964.

Metz, Johann Baptist. *The Emergent Church.* Translated by Peter Mann. New York: Crossroad, 1981.

_____. *Faith in History and Society.* Translated by David Smith. New York: Seabury Press, 1978.

_____. *How I Have Changed: Reflecting on Thirty Years of Theology.* Edited by Jürgen Moltmann. Translated by John Bowden. Harrisburg: Trinty Press International, 1997.

_____. *A Passion for God: The Mystical-Political Dimension of Christianity.* Translated and with an introduction by J. Matthew Ashley. New York: Paulist Press, 1998.

Metz, Johann Baptist, and Jürgen Moltmann, eds. *Faith and the Future: Essays on Theology, Solidarity, and Modernity.* Maryknoll: Orbis, 1995.

Miles, Margaret. *Carnal Knowing.* Boston: Beacon Press, 1989.

Nelson, Susan L. *Healing the Broken Heart.* St. Louis: Chalice Press, 1997.

Park, Andrew Sung. *The Wounded Heart of God: The Asian Concept of Han and the Christian Doctrine of Sin.* Nashville: Abingdon Press, 1993.

Perkins, Judith. *The Suffering Self: Pain and Narrative Representation in the Early Christian Era.* New York: Routledge, 1995.

Plaskow, Judith. "The Coming of Lilith: Toward a Feminist Theology." In *Womanspirit Rising: A Feminist Reader in Religion.* Edited by Judith Plaskow and Carol Christ. San Francisco: Harper & Row, 1979.

Poling, James N. *The Abuse of Power: A Theological Problem.* Nashville: Abingdon Press, 1991.

Proctor-Smith, Marjorie. "Liturgical Anamnesis and Women's Memory: 'Something Missing.' " *Worship* 61 (September 1987): 405-24.

_____. *In Her Own Rite: Constructing Feminist Liturgical Tradition.* Nashville: Abingdon Press, 1990.

Proctor-Smith, Marjorie, and Janet R. Walton, eds. *Women at Worship.* Louisville: Westminster John Knox Press, 1993.

Rebecca, Lea Nicoll Kramer, and Susan A. Lukey. "Spirit Song: The Use of Christian Healing Rites in Trauma Recovery." *Treating Abuse Today* 5 and 6 (November/December 1995 and January/February 1996): 39-47.

Rigby, Cynthia L. "Is There Joy Before Mourning? 'Dangerous Memory' in the Work of Sharon Welch and Johann Baptist Metz." *Koinonia* 5 (spring 1993): 1-30.

Ruether, Rosemary. *Women-Church*. New York: Harper & Row, 1986.

Russell, Letty. *Church in the Round*. Louisville: Westminster John Knox Press, 1993.

Sands, Kathleen. "Uses of the Thea(o)logian: Sex and Theodicy in Religious Feminism." *Journal of Feminist Studies in Religion* 8:1 (spring 1992): 7-33.

_____. *Escape From Paradise*. Minneapolis: Augsburg Fortress, 1994.

Schüssler Fiorenza, Elisabeth. *But She Said: Feminist Practices of Biblical Interpretation*. Boston: Beacon Press, 1992.

_____. *The Discipleship of Equals: A Critical Feminist Ekklesia-logy of Liberation*. New York: Crossroad, 1993.

_____. *Jesus: Miriam's Child, Sophia's Prophet: Critical Issues in Feminist Christology*. New York: Continuum, 1994.

Schüssler Fiorenza, Elisabeth and David Tracy, eds. *The Holocaust as Interruption*. *Concilium* 175. Edinburgh: T. & T. Clark, 1984.

Sobrino, Jon. *Christology at the Crossroads*. Translated by John Drury. Maryknoll: Orbis, 1978.

_____. "The Crucified Peoples: Yahweh's Suffering Servant Today." In *1492-1992: The Voice of the Victims*. Edited by Leonardo Boff and Virgil Elizondo. *Concilium* 1990/6. 120-29. Philadelphia: Trinity Press International, 1990.

Somers, Margaret R. "The Narrative Constitution of Identity: A Relational and Network Approach." *Theory and Society* 23 (October 1994): 605-49.

Strohl, Jane. "Suffering as Redemptive: A Comparison of Christian Experience in the Sixteenth and Twentieth Centuries." In *Revisioning the Past: Prospects in Historical Theology*. Edited by Mary Potter Engel and Walter E. Wyman, Jr. Minneapolis: Fortress Press, 1992.

Taylor, Mark Kline. *Remembering Esperanza*. Maryknoll: Orbis, 1990.

Terrell, JoAnne Marie. *Power in the Blood? The Cross in the African American Experience*. Maryknoll: Orbis, 1998.

Tesfai, Yacob, ed. *The Scandal of a Crucified World: Perspectives on the Cross and Suffering*. Maryknoll: Orbis, 1994.

Trost, Lou Ann. "On Suffering, Violence, and Power." *Currents in Theology and Mission* 21 (February 1994): 35-40.

Welch, Sharon. *Communities of Resistance and Solidarity*. Maryknoll: Orbis, 1985.

_____. *A Feminist Ethic of Risk*. Minneapolis: Fortress Press, 1990.

Williams, Delores. "Black Women's Surrogacy Experience and the Christian Notion of Redemption." In *After Patriarchy: Feminist Transformations of the World Religions*. Edited by Paula M. Cooey, William R. Eakin, and Jay B. McDaniel. Maryknoll: Orbis, 1991.

_____. *Sisters in the Wilderness: The Challenge of Womanist God-Talk*. Maryknoll: Orbis, 1993.

Winters, Miriam Therese, Adair Lummis, and Allison Stokes, eds. *Defecting in Place: Women Claiming Responsibility for Their Own Spiritual Lives*. New York: Crossroad, 1994.

Young, Pamela Dickey. "Beyond Moral Influence to an Atoning Life." *Theology Today* 52 (1995): 344-55.

Remembering Childhood Sexual Abuse

Asher, Shirley J. "The Effects of Childhood Sexual Abuse: A Review of the Issues and Evidence." In *Handbook on Sexual Abuse of Children*. Edited by Lenore E. A. Walker. New York: Springer Publishing, 1988.

Baker, Robert A., ed. *Child Sexual Abuse and False Memory Syndrome*. Amherst, N.Y.: Prometheus Books, 1998.

Bass, Ellen, and Laura Davis. *The Courage to Heal*. New York: Harper & Row, 1988. Revised 3rd edition HarperCollins, 1994.

Brown, Joanne Carlson, and Carole R. Bohn, eds. *Christianity, Patriarchy, and Abuse: A Feminist Critique*. New York: Pilgrim Press, 1989.

Conway, Martin A., ed. *Recovered Memories and False Memories*. Oxford: Oxford University Press, 1997.

Freud, Sigmund. *The Standard Edition of the Complete Psychological Works of Sigmund Freud*. Vol. 3. Translated and edited by James Strachey. London: Hogarth Press, 1962.

_____. *The Standard Edition of the Complete Psychological Works of Sigmund Freud*. Vol. 7. Translated and edited by James Strachey. London: Hogarth Press, 1953.

Freyd, Jennifer. *Betrayal Trauma: The Logic of Forgetting Childhood Abuse*. Cambridge, Mass.: Harvard University Press, 1996.

Gelinas, Denise J. "The Persisting Negative Effects of Incest." *Psychiatry* 46 (November 1983): 312-32.

Herman, Judith. *Father-Daughter Incest*. Cambridge, Mass.: Harvard University Press, 1981.

Herman, Judith, and Mary Harvey. "The False Memory Debate:

Social Science or Social Backlash?" *Working Together* 14 (fall 1993): 7-9. Reprinted from the *Harvard Mental Health Letter* (April 1993).

Imbens, Annie, and Ineke Jonker. *Christianity and Incest.* Minneapolis: Fortress Press, 1992.

Kempe, C. Henry, Frederic N. Silverman, F. Brant, William Droegemuller, and Henry K. Silver. "The Battered Child Syndrome." *Journal of the American Medical Association* 181 (1962): 17-24.

Loftus, Elizabeth, and Katherine Ketcham. *The Myth of Repressed Memory.* New York: St. Martin's Press, 1994.

Masson, Jeffrey M. *The Assault on Truth: Freud's Suppression of the Seduction Theory.* New York: Strauss & Giroux, 1984.

Ofshe, Richard, and Ethan Watters. *Making Monsters: False Memories, Psychotherapy, and Sexual Hysteria.* New York: Charles Scribner's Sons, 1994.

Pendergast, Mark. *Victims of Memory: Incest Accusations and Shattered Lives.* Hinesburg, Vt.: Upper Access Books, 1995.

Rush, Florence. *The Best Kept Secret: Sexual Abuse of Children.* Englewood Cliffs, N.J.: Prentice-Hall, 1980.

Vander Mey, Brenda J. and Ronald L. Neff, eds. *Incest as Child Abuse: Research and Applications.* New York: Praeger, 1986.

Waites, Elizabeth A. *Memory Quest: Trauma and the Search for Personal History.* New York: W. W. Norton, 1997.

Wassil-Grimm, Claudette. *Diagnosis for Disaster: The Devastating Truth About False Memory Syndrome and Its Impact on Accusers and Families.* Woodstock, N.Y.: Overlook Press, 1995.

Westerlund, Elaine. "Freud on Sexual Trauma: An Historical Review of Seduction and Betrayal." *Psychology of Women Quarterly* 10 (1986): 297-309.

Whitfield, Charles. *Memory and Abuse: Remembering and Healing the Effects of Trauma.* Deerfield Beach, Fla.: Health Communications, 1995.

Wright, Lawrence. *Remembering Satan.* New York: Alfred A. Knopf, 1994.

Yapko, Michael D. *True and False Memories of Childhood Sexual Trauma.* New York: Simon & Schuster, 1994.

Remembering Genocides

Avakian, Arlene Voski. *Lion Woman's Legacy: An Armenian-American Memoir.* New York: Feminist Press, 1992.

Berger, Alan L., ed. *Bearing Witness to the Holocaust, 1939–1989.* Symposium Series, Vol. 31. Lewiston/Queenston/Lampeter: Edwin Mellen Press, 1991.

Bettelheim, Bruno. *Surviving and Other Essays*. New York: Vintage Books, 1980.

Des Pres, Terrence. *The Survivor: An Anatomy of Life in the Death Camps*. New York: Pocket Books, 1976.

Dimsdale, Joel E., ed. *Survivors, Victims, and Perpetrators: Essays on the Nazi Holocaust*. New York: Hemisphere Publishing, 1980.

Diocese of the Armenian Church in America. *Martyrdom and Rebirth: Fateful Events in the Recent History of the Armenian People*. New York: Diocese of the Armenian Church in America, 1965.

Eckhardt, Alice L., ed. *Burning Memory: Times of Testing and Reckoning*. New York: Pergamon Press, 1993.

Eckhardt, Alice L., and A. Roy Eckhardt. *Long Day's Journey into Day: A Revised Retrospective on the Holocaust*. Detroit: Wayne State University Press, 1988.

Friedlander, Saul. *Memory, History, and the Extermination of the Jews of Europe*. Bloomington: Indiana University Press, 1993.

_____. *When Memory Comes*. Translated by Helen R. Lane. New York: Noonday Press, 1991.

_____. ed. *Probing the Limits of Representation: Nazism and the "Final Solution."* Cambridge, Mass.: Harvard University Press, 1992.

Grabill, Joseph L. *Protestant Diplomacy and the Near East: Missionary Influence on American Policy, 1810–1927*. Minneapolis: University of Minnesota Press, 1971.

Guroian, Vigen. "Armenian Genocide and Christian Existence." *Cross Currents* 41 (1991): 322-43.

_____. "How Shall We Remember?" *Window* 1 (1990): 4-7, 19-20.

_____. "The Suffering God of Armenian Christology." *Dialog* 32 (1993): 97-101.

Hartman, Geoffrey H., ed. *Holocaust Remembrance: The Shapes of Memory*. Cambridge, Mass.: Blackwell Publishers, 1994.

Hass, Aaron. *The Aftermath: Living with the Holocaust*. New York: Cambridge University Press, 1995.

Hirsch, Herbert. *Genocide and the Politics of Memory: Studying Death to Preserve Life*. Chapel Hill: University of North Carolina Press, 1995.

Hovannisian, Richard G., ed. *The Armenian Genocide: History, Politics, Ethics*. New York: St. Martin's Press, 1992.

_____. ed. *The Armenian Genocide in Perspective*. New Brunswick, N.J.: Transaction Books, 1987.

Isaacson, Judith Magyar. *Seed of Sarah: Memoirs of a Survivor*. 2nd ed.

Urbana: University of Illinois Press, 1991.

Jinbashian, Ishkhan. "Memory of the Skin: Gérard Chaliand on the Geopolitics of Cultures." *Armenian International Magazine* 4:7 (August 1993): 11-15.

Kaplan, Harold. *Conscience and Memory: Meditations in a Museum of the Holocaust.* Chicago: University of Chicago Press, 1994.

Kuper, Leo. *Genocide: Its Political Use in the Twentieth Century.* New Haven: Yale University Press, 1994.

Langer, Lawrence L. *Admitting the Holocaust: Collected Essays.* New York: Oxford University Press, 1995.

_____. *Holocaust Testimonies: The Ruins of Memory.* New Haven: Yale University Press, 1991.

_____. *Versions of Survival.* Albany: State University of New York Press, 1982.

Levi, Primo. *The Drowned and the Saved.* New York: Summit Books, 1988.

_____. *Survival in Auschwitz: The Nazi Assault on Humanity.* Translated by Stuart Wolf. New York: Collier Books, 1958.

Linenthal, Edward T. *Preserving Memory: The Struggle to Create America's Holocaust Museum.* New York: Viking Penguin, 1995.

Lipstadt, Deborah. *Denying the Holocaust: The Growing Assault on Truth and Memory.* New York: Penguin Books, 1994.

Littell, Franklin. *The Crucifixion of the Jews: The Failure of Christians to Understand the Jewish Experience.* New York: Harper & Row, 1975.

Miller, Donald E., and Lorna Touryan Miller. "A Case Study of Armenian Survivors and Their Progeny." *Qualitative Sociology* 14:1 (1991): 13-38.

_____. *Survivors: An Oral History of the Armenian Genocide.* Berkeley: University of California Press, 1993.

Miller, Judith. *One, by One, by One.* New York: Simon & Schuster, 1990.

Pawlikowski, John T. *Christ in the Light of the Christian-Jewish Dialogue.* New York: Paulist Press, 1982.

Peroomian, Rubina. *Literary Responses to Catastrophe: A Comparison of the Armenian and the Jewish Experience.* Atlanta: Scholars Press, 1993.

Plank, Karl A. *Mother of the Wire Fence: Inside and Outside the Holocaust.* Louisvillle: Westminster John Knox Press, 1994.

Roiphe, Anne. *A Season for Healing.* New York: Summit Books, 1988.

Roth, John K., and Michael Berenbaum, eds. *Holocaust: Religious and Philosophical Implications.* New York: Paragon House, 1989.

Rubenstein, Richard. *After Auschwitz.* Indianapolis: Bobbs-Merrill, 1966.

Van Buren, Paul. *The Burden of Freedom: Americans and the God of Israel.* New York: Seabury Press, 1976.

_____. *A Theology of the Jewish-Christian Reality. Part 1: Discerning the Way.* New York: Seabury Press, 1980.

_____. *A Theology of the Jewish-Christian Reality. Part 2: A Christian Theology of the People Israel.* New York: Seabury Press, 1983.

_____. *A Theology of the Jewish-Christian Reality. Part 3: Christ in Context.* New York: Harper & Row, 1988.

Vidal-Naquet, Pierre. *Assassins of Memory: Essays on the Denial of the Holocaust.* Translated by Jeffrey Mehlman. New York: Columbia University Press, 1992.

Werfel, Franz. *The Forty Days of Musa Dagh.* 2nd ed. New York: Carroll & Graf, 1990.

Wiesel, Elie. *The Fifth Son.* Translated by Marion Wiesel. New York: Summit Books, 1985.

_____. *Night.* New York: Bantam Books, 1960.

_____. *The Testament.* New York: Summit Books, 1981.

Williamson, Clark M. *A Guest in the House of Israel.* Louisville: Westminster John Knox Press, 1993.

Young, James. *Writing and Rewriting the Holocaust: Narrative and the Consequences of Interpretation.* Bloomington: Indiana University Press, 1988.

Remembering Histories

Anderson, Victor. *Beyond Ontological Blackness.* New York: Continuum, 1995.

Asante, Molefi Kete. *Afrocentricity.* Trenton, N.J.: Africa World Press, 1991.

ben-Jochannan, Yosef A. A. *Africa, Mother of Western Civilization.* Baltimore: Black Classic Press, 1971.

Bernal, Martin. *Black Athena: The Afroasiatic Roots of Classical Civilization.* 2 vols. New Brunswick: Rutgers University, 1987 and 1991.

Christ, Carol. *Laughter of Aphrodite.* San Francisco: Harper San Francisco, 1987.

Copeland, M. Shawn. "Wading Through Many Sorrows." In *A Troubling in My Soul.* Edited by Emilie Townes. Maryknoll: Orbis, 1993.

Daly, Mary. *Gyn/Ecology.* Boston: Beacon Press, 1978.

de Beauvoir, Simone. *The Second Sex.* Translated by H .M. Parshley. New York: Alfred A. Knopf, 1952.

D'Souza, Dinesh. *The End of Racism.* New York: Free Press, 1995.

Fabre, Genevieve, and Robert O'Meally, eds. *History and Memory in African-American Culture.* New York: Oxford University Press, 1994.

Goatley, David Emmanuel. *Were You There? Godforsakenness in Slave Religion.* Maryknoll: Orbis, 1996.

Gordon, Linda. "What's New in Women's History." In *Feminist Studies/Critical Studies.* Edited by Teresa de Lauretis. Bloomington: Indiana University Press, 1986.

Hopkins, Dwight N. *Shoes That Fit Our Feet.* Maryknoll: Orbis, 1993.

Hopkins, Dwight N., and George Cummings, eds. *Cut Loose Your Stammering Tongue: Black Theology in the Slave Narratives.* Maryknoll: Orbis, 1991.

Kerber, Linda K. "Separate Spheres, Female Worlds, Woman's Place: The Rhetoric of Women's History." *Journal of American History* 75 (June 1988): 9-39.

Lefkowitz, Mary. *Not Out of Africa: How Afrocentrism Became an Excuse to Teach Myth as History.* New York: BasicBooks, 1996.

Lerner, Gerda. *The Creation of Patriarchy.* New York: Oxford University Press, 1986.

Levine, Lawrence W. *The Unpredictable Past: Explorations in American Cultural History.* New York: Oxford University Press, 1993.

Matthews, Donald H. *Honoring the Ancestors: An African Cultural Interpretation of Black Religion.* New York: Oxford University Press, 1998.

Morrison, Toni. *Beloved.* London: Picador, 1987.

Pinn, Anthony. *Why Lord? Suffering and Evil in Black Theology.* New York: Continuum, 1995.

Plaskow, Judith. *Standing Again at Sinai.* San Francisco: Harper & Row, 1990.

Rabinbach, Anson. "Rationalism and Utopia as Languages of Nature: A Note." *International Labor and Working-Class History* (spring 1987): 30-36.

Raboteau, Albert J. *A Fire in the Bones: Reflections on African-American Religious History.* Boston: Beacon Press, 1995.

————. *Slave Religion: The "Invisible Institution" in the Antebellum South.* New York: Oxford University Press, 1978.

Riley, Denise. *"Am I That Name?" Feminism and the Category of "Women" in History.* Minneapolis: University of Minnesota Press, 1988.

Ruether, Rosemary, and Eleanor McLaughlin, eds. *Women of Spirit: Female Leadership in the Jewish and Christian Traditions.* New York: Simon & Schuster, 1979.

Russell, Letty, ed. *Feminist Interpretation of the Bible.* Philadelphia: Westminster Press, 1985.

Sanders, Cheryl J. *Empowerment Ethics for a Liberated People.* Minneapolis: Fortress Press, 1995.

Schüssler Fiorenza, Elisabeth. *Bread Not Stone: The Challenge of Biblical Interpretation.* Boston: Beacon Press, 1985.

_____. *In Memory of Her: A Feminist Theological Reconstruction of Christian Origins.* New York: Crossroad, 1983.

Scott, Joan Wallach. *Only Paradoxes to Offer: French Feminists and the Rights of Man.* Cambridge, Mass.: Harvard University Press, 1996.

Scott, Joan W., and Judith Butler, eds. *Feminists Theorize the Political.* New York: Routledge, 1992.

Smith-Rosenberg, Carroll. *Disorderly Conduct.* New York: Oxford University Press, 1985.

Stone, Merlin. *When God Was a Woman.* New York: Dial Press, 1976.

Trible, Phyllis. *Texts of Terror.* Philadelphia: Fortress Press, 1984.

West, Cornel. *Prophecy Deliverance! An Afro-American Revolutionary Christianity.* Philadelphia: Westminster Press, 1982.

Index